DOING BUSINESS
IN EMERGING
MARKETS

DOING BUSINESS IN EMERGING MARKETS

Entry and Negotiation Strategies

S. Tamer Cavusgil
Michigan State University, USA

Pervez N. Ghauri
Manchester School of Management, UMIST, UK

Milind R. Agarwal
Logistics Corporation of India, Ltd.

SAGE Publications
International Educational and Professional Publisher
Thousand Oaks ▪ London ▪ New Delhi

For information:

Sage Publications, Inc.
2455 Teller Road
Thousand Oaks, California 91320
E-mail: order@sagepub.com

Sage Publications Ltd.
6 Bonhill Street
London EC2A 4PU
United Kingdom

Sage Publications India Pvt. Ltd.
M-32 Market
Greater Kailash I
New Delhi 110 048 India

Printed in the United States of America

Library of Congress Cataloging-in-Publication Data

Cavusgil, S. Tamer.
  Doing business in emerging markets: Entry and negotiation strategies/
S. Tamer Cavusgil, Pervez N. Ghauri, Milind R. Agarwal.
    p. cm.
Includes bibliographical references and index.
  ISBN 0-7619-1374-2 (c) — ISBN 0-7619-1375-0 (p)
  1. International business enterprises. 2. Export marketing.
3. Negotiation in business. I. Ghauri, Pervez N., 1948- II. Agarwal, Milind R. III. Title.
  HD62.4 .C387 2002
  658.8′48—dc21   2002005207

This book is printed on acid-free paper.

02 03 04 05 10 9 8 7 6 5 4 3 2 1

Acquisitions Editor:	Marquita Flemming
Editorial Assistant:	MaryAnn Vail
Copy Editor:	Carla Freeman
Production Editor:	Diane S. Foster
Typesetter:	C&M Digitals (P) Ltd., Chennai, India
Proofreader:	Scott Oney
Indexer:	Cristina Haley
Cover Designer:	Michelle Lee

Contents

Preface

*D*oing Business in Emerging Markets: Entry and Negotiation Strategies is aimed at Western business executives who are actively contemplating business in emerging markets. These countries represent more than half of the world population and are growing at more than double the rate of Western economies. Much of the recent expansion in cross-border trade and investment can be attributed to rapid industrialization and modernization taking place in these countries. The middle class is rapidly gaining ground in the emerging markets, creating abundant business opportunities for Western business enterprises. Although the importance of these markets is now well established, they are not well understood in terms of their market potential, business customs, political and social environment, and negotiating styles.

Despite recent setbacks, such as the Asian financial crisis and the tragic events of September 11, 2001, these countries remain of critical interest to companies seeking growth opportunities in world markets. Indeed, the emerging-market economies in East Asia, Latin America, and elsewhere are following a long-term growth and expansion trajectory. The income levels in these markets are escalating, and consumers are striving to reach the standards of living they learn about in industrialized societies. The middle class in India and China, both markets with more than 1 billion people, now make up target market segments that are larger than many individual Western economies. China's accession to the World Trade Organization (WTO) and inclusion of developing countries in G-7 and WTO meetings would accelerate this process even more.

This book thus serves an important purpose by enhancing our understanding of the emerging-market economies and cultures, which are often misunderstood in Western societies. It fills a gap in the business literature by positioning itself as an authoritative and timely guide for thoughtful business executives and students. The book is designed to equip them with the necessary knowledge and skills required for successful business ventures in the emerging markets.

The orientation of the book is to expose the commercial realities, national cultures, and business negotiation styles of emerging markets. It aims to provide a systematic approach to analyze and evaluate these markets for potential entry and to manage the negotiation process efficiently, without any hurdles. The book includes extensive exhibits and examples and relates well to situations faced by managers of global companies.

We suggest that the reader first quickly read through the book and then use respective chapters as the basis for developing specific ideas for issues, such as evaluating a market, understanding market potential, or negotiating.

List of Exhibits

1

Why Look at
Emerging Economies?

A s we begin our adventure into the next millennium, human innovation and accomplishment are occurring at a breakneck pace. From the theoretical sciences to the emerging biotechnologies, advances are happening faster than our society can assimilate them. Communication and information technologies continue to shrink geographical distances and put more of the world's knowledge at our fingertips. Economic and political developments are rapidly transforming our world and prompting us to consider more global perspectives. Social and cultural changes are helping us renegotiate our identities as well as our values, shaping our vision of the future. Undoubtedly, the challenges ahead of us will be formidable. But the opportunities are simply too great to ignore. Our potential to succeed in this exciting environment will depend on our ability to recognize and act on these opportunities. As always, the future will belong to the ambitious.

For businesses and corporations of the 21st century, this will mean establishing an international presence now. International business activities have exploded in the last several decades and will continue to change our lives. And as we become increasingly intertwined with the lives of our neighbors, all future business people will stake their fortunes in the growing world economy. Over the next two decades, most of the world's growth is expected to occur in today's emerging markets. Once thought of as backward and low tech, these regions are now rapidly transforming their economies. By adopting new technologies and production techniques, countries such as China, South Korea, and India have become important places for production. And because purchasing power continues to increase with development in these countries, their populations are becoming important consumer markets as well.

The ability to learn from Western experience has had a huge effect on these emerging markets. Importing technologies and knowledge from industrial leaders as well as sending their students to top American and European universities has allowed many developing countries to catch up with the Western world. As social and political problems come under control, a wide variety of resources and talents are also being revealed. Barriers previously barring direct investment are melting away, and many of these regions are becoming attractive areas for investment.

For Western managers struggling to sustain growth, cut costs, and launch new products and industries, emerging markets could be an ideal answer. With literacy and education levels rising, skilled labor in these countries is relatively inexpensive. In the next several years, millions of new consumers in the emerging markets will desire and be able to afford Western goods. Western organizations may even have to enhance their capabilities if new markets can be discovered for their products. The old notion that developing countries are inherently risky for foreign businesses is no longer true. Conditions are continuing to stabilize, and our ability to predict and manage these risks has gotten better. The advantages of being a first-mover in these markets are overwhelmingly enticing.

The Paradigm Shift in International Business in the 21st Century

Increased globalization of our economies has allowed technology and capital to become very mobile. Now, in an era of intense global competition, Western firms are seeking every opportunity to gain a competitive advantage. Emerging economies have provided numerous avenues for exploration. (See Exhibit 1.1 and Exhibit 1.2.) The following sociopolitical events have helped to shape these possibilities:

- The end of the Cold War, with the breakdown of the Eastern and Central European economies. Eastern and Central Europe have opened up as a large emerging market.
- The reunification of Germany
- Increasing cooperation in the European community by moving toward a larger and more closely knit European Union, eventually creating the European Economic Space
- Increasing cooperation in North America, through NAFTA (North American Free Trade Area), incorporating the United States, Canada, and Mexico
- The General Agreement on Tariffs and Trade (GATT), accepted by various developed and developing nations, transformed into the World Trade Organization (WTO)

Exhibit 1.1   The Paradigm Shift of International Business

During the early 1990s, a number of perceptional changes occurred within the realm of international business.

Developing Countries
(prior to 2000)

- High risk for foreign business
- Economically and technologically backward
- Consumers had poor purchasing power
- Few opportunities for business

Emerging Markets
(2000 and beyond)

- Risks are increasingly manageable
- Higher income growth than developed nations
- Technologically competitive
- Increasing purchasing power among consumers
- Offer many opportunities as large untapped markets and low-cost, high-quality sources

Exhibit 1.2   Doing Business in Developing Countries: The Old Paradigm

Under the old paradigm, doing business with developing countries required a unique selling approach and thus was not an ordinary process. This was mainly due to the fact that these countries had different expectations from an international business deal. During an interview, Altaf Gauhar, editor-in-chief of *South*, a publication oriented toward developing countries, commented,

We are interdependent—you need our raw materials and we need your manufactured goods and services in order to develop. But the costs of manufactured goods keep going up because of wage increases and inflation, while our prices keep falling because our economies are depressed. So we are being fleeced. (p. 34)

This remark reflected a major complaint of developing countries. Gauhar outlined the key global issues:

The first issue is a negotiated arrangement that will reflect the needs of an interdependent world and give the producers of goods and commodities the feeling that the system is fair. Second, the reordering of priorities so that the social needs are the first consideration in allocating national and international resources. Third, the tremendous need for those who believe in democratic values to pursue them universally rather than pursue democracy only at home. (p. 36)

Under the new paradigm, emerging economies are increasingly looking at Western firms for mutually beneficial partnerships.

SOURCE: Moskin (1998).

- Rapid developments in telecommunications and transportation technologies, making the marketplace "global"
- Adoption of quality and continuous improvement goals by Western firms, putting them back in global competition
- Adoption of quality and continuous improvement goals by various Asian firms, making them high-quality sources and competitors
- Economic liberalization of countries such as China, India, Mexico, Turkey, and others, inviting foreign investment, reducing import barriers, and offering large markets
- Rapid growth of economies such as China, Indonesia, Malaysia, and Thailand

Two important changes are under way in the global economy. First, the governments of many developing countries (including Eastern Europe and the former Soviet Union) have embarked on revolutionizing their economic policies. Second, after a dip during the 1996/1997 Asian crisis, the influx of private capital into the new world market has revived to higher than precrisis levels. Together, economic reform and adequate supplies of capital should lead the developing countries to a rapid pace of economic development and modernization. It is thus important that we revise our understanding about the Third World, as illustrated in Exhibit 1.3.

It is clear to Western managers that today, it is no longer wise to alienate or ignore businesses in developing countries, and to succeed there, it is important to have a clear understanding of the process of doing business in these emerging markets. Moreover, it is important that there is no competition between the Third World and the First World and that prosperity in the Third World does not threaten the prosperity of the Western nations (see Exhibit 1.4).

The Emerging Economies

The concept of emerging economies is relatively new, and most Western managers look at these economies only as large, untapped markets. The reality is that countries with emerging economies are also becoming competitors and sourcing locations for Western nations. But it is important to realize that all developing countries cannot be characterized as emerging economies. Only those that have (a) started an economic reform process aimed at alleviating problems, for example, of poverty, poor infrastructure, and overpopulation, and (b) achieved a steady growth in gross national product (GNP) per capita may truly be called emerging economies. These economies will play an increasing role in international business over the next decades, which in turn will also foster regional and global political changes.

Exhibit 1.3   What Are the First, Second, and Third Worlds?

The World Bank had defined Third World countries as those with less than $7,300 annual GNP per capita. These included most of the countries of Asia (excluding Japan), Africa, the Middle East, the Caribbean, Central America, and South America. These countries had been further divided into low-income economies with less than $400, lower-middle-income economies, $400 to $1,700, and upper-middle-income economies, $1,700 to $7,300 (annual GNP per capita).

Industrialized countries, including North America and Western Europe, were often referred to as *First World Countries*, while the Eastern Bloc was referred to as the *Second World.*

With the breakdown of the communist economies (except China and North Korea), the term Second World has become redundant, and now the terms *developed* and *developing* or *emerging nations* are popularly used.

The more recent classification of country groups by the World Bank (2001b) is that low-income economies are those with a GNP per capita of $755 or less in 1999; middle-income economies are those with a GNP per capita of more than $755 but less than $9,266 in 1999 (a further division, at GNP per capita of $2,995 in 1999, is made between lower-middle-income and upper-middle-income economies); and high-income economies are those with a GNP per capita of $9,266 or more in 1999.

Low-income and middle-income economies are sometimes referred to as *developing economies.* The use of the term is convenient; it is not intended to imply that all economies in the group are experiencing similar development or that other economies have reached a preferred or final stage of development.

The Economist ("Emerging Market Indicators," 2001) has identified 25 emerging-market economies on the basis of both the size of their gross domestic product (GDP) and the capitalization of their stock markets (see Exhibit 1.5).

The Economist ("Emerging Market Indicators," 2001) also reported that rich industrial countries dominate the world economy rather less than they used to. Five of the world's 12 largest economies are those of developing countries. China, India, Russia, Brazil, and Mexico have GDPs bigger than Canada's, currently the G-7's seventh member. On a PPP (purchasing-power parities) basis, China has the world's third-largest economy, behind America and Japan.

Exhibit 1.4   Will Third World Prosperity Threaten Western Nations?

According to Stanford economist Paul Krugman, Western fears of Third World competition are questionable in theory and flatly rejected by data. Illustrating his argument by examining patterns of wages and productivity in a series of increasingly realistic model economies, he concludes that Third World labor productivity means an increase in world output. The increase in world output shows up in higher wages for Third World workers, not in decreased living standards for the developed nations. Krugman warns that if the Western nations respond to fears of Third World competition by erecting import barriers to protect their own living standards, the effects would be disastrous—ruining any hope of a decent living standard for hundreds of millions of people throughout the developing world.

Additionally, *The Economist* ("He Wants Your Job," June 12, 1993) said this about Western fears about Third World prosperity:

> Instead of fearing success in other countries, as they seem to, Western Europe and America should concentrate on becoming even more successful themselves. And the only lasting way to do so is to raise their productivity. With that as a starting point, the prescriptions for policy alter. In practice, trade protection has nothing to do with spurring productivity at home. Industries seek import barriers (or export assistance) precisely to avoid the need for higher productivity. Instead of trade policy, the need for higher productivity calls for measures such as these: better education and training, lower taxes on saving and investment, greater subsidies for some forms of research and development, more investment in infrastructure, more help for workers from shrinking industries to move to expanding ones, and so on. (p. 15)

SOURCE: Krugman, P. (July-August 1994). Does Third World Growth Hurt First World Prosperity? *Harvard Business Review* (p. 153).

The U.S. Department of Commerce (2000) has identified the "10 Biggest Emerging Markets" (BEMs): China Economic Area (People's Republic of China, Taiwan, and Hong Kong), India, Indonesia, South Korea, Turkey, Poland, Mexico, Brazil, Argentina, and South Africa. The department is also developing a country-by-country strategy to use when doing business with these BEMs. The great interest among U.S. investors and industrialists in these countries has led the department to state that of all the world trade growth in the next two decades, almost three fourths is expected to come from less-developed countries (LDCs) but a small core of those LDCs (just 10 of them) will account for more than half of that growth, as explained in Exhibit 1.6 ("Big Emerging Markets," 1994).

Exhibit 1.5 The Emerging Economies

	Population 2000 Est. (Million)**	Literacy Rate (%)**	Average Annual GDP Growth Rate, 1990-1999 (%)*	Inflation Rate—1999 Est. (%)**	Gross Domestic Savings, 1999 (% of GDP)*	GDP—1999 (U.S. $ Billions)*	Per Nominal Capita GNP, 1999 (U.S. $)*	GDP-PPP, 1999 Est. (U.S. $ Billions)**	Per Capita GNP-PPP, 1999 U.S. = 100*
China	1,261.8	81	10.7	-1.3	42	991.2	780	4,800.0	10.8
Hong Kong	7.1	92	3.9	-4.0	30	158.6	23,520	158.2	68.5
India	1,014.0	52	6.1	6.7	20	459.7	450	1,805.0	7.0
Indonesia	224.7	83	4.7	2.0	24	140.9	580	610.0	8.0
Malaysia	21.7	83	6.3	2.8	45	74.6	3,400	229.1	26.0
Philippines	81.1	94	3.2	6.8	16	75.3	1,020	282.0	12.5
Singapore	4.1	91	8.0	0.4	52	84.9	29,610	98.0	88.3
South Korea	47.4	98	5.7	0.8	34	406.9	8,490	625.7	47.8
Thailand	61.2	93	4.7	2.4	32	123.8	1,960	388.7	18.3
Argentina	36.9	96	4.9	-2.0	16	281.9	7,600	367.0	37.0
Brazil	172.8	83	2.9	5.0	20	760.3	4,420	1,057.0	20.6
Chile	15.1	95	7.2	3.4	23	71.0	4,740	185.1	27.4
Colombia	39.6	91.3	3.3	9.2	19	46.9	2,250	245.1	18.6
Mexico	100.3	89	2.7	15.0	23	474.9	4,400	865.5	25.2
Peru	27.0	88.7	5.4	5.5	20	57.3	2,390	116.0	14.3
Venezuela	23.5	91	1.7	20.0	17	103.9	3,670	182.8	17.2
Israel	5.8	95	5.1	1.3	10	99.0	N/A	105.4	N/A
Portugal	10.0	87	2.5	2.4	17	107.7	10,600	151.4	49.5
South Africa	43.4	81	1.9	5.5	18	131.1	3,160	296.1	27.2
Turkey	65.6	82	4.1	65.0	21	188.3	2,900	409.4	20.0
Czech Republic	10.2	99	0.9	2.5	29	56.3	5,060	120.8	40.2
Hungary	10.1	99	1.0	10.0	28	48.3	4,650	79.4	34.2
Poland	38.6	99	4.7	8.4	18	154.1	3,960	276.5	25.8
Russia	146.0	98	-6.1	86.0	29	375.3	2,270	620.3	20.7

* World Bank (2001b).
**Central Intelligence Agency (2000).

Exhibit 1.6   How Are *Emerging* and *Developing* Used in
                   This Book?

We are using the list of 25 countries identified by *The Economist* (2001,
January 13, p. 110) to interchangeably refer to as *emerging markets* or *emerging economies*. We have had to be careful in using the terms *emerging* and
developing—all emerging economies are developing, but the reverse is not
true (i.e., not all developing economies are emerging). Wherever we have
examples or references applicable to most developing countries, we have used
the word *developing*. Wherever we have examples relating to emerging
economies or markets, we have used the word *emerging*.

Recent developments in the global marketplace are unprecedented, and
economists have failed to provide an answer to the important question
about the direction in which these changes will lead us. Experts say that
these changes will stimulate economic efficiency, growth, and equitable
income distribution—both within and across regions—while at the same
time maximizing democratic representation and local autonomy. We predict that it will be a positive change for both developed and developing
nations and that relationships and trade linkages between the two will
become more balanced. Exhibit 1.7 shows the important drivers of foreign
trade policies of developed and emerging nations, as well as the common
interests and conflicts of interest between the two groups.

As seen in Exhibit 1.7, Western nations are forced to look at emerging
markets due to more or less stagnant economic growth in their own
economies. Emerging economies, however, will grow very rapidly in the
next two decades. High unemployment rates in Western nations are leading
to increasing public pressure on governments to generate new jobs—many
of which will be export based. In June 1994, President Clinton, of the
United States, granted China a most favored nation status (MFN) again,
despite some political differences about human rights issues. The underlying
reason was that in the following months, the United States expected to export
various products to China (including Boeing Aircraft) worth $5 billion, on
which approximately 100,000 American jobs were based.

Emerging economies have also realized the worth of replacing a policy of
import substitution with export promotion. Western nations will have to
understand ways of doing business in emerging economies, because they
will simultaneously act as markets, sources, and competitors. Rapid
advances in transportation and information technologies are bringing
developed and emerging economies closer to each other. However, some

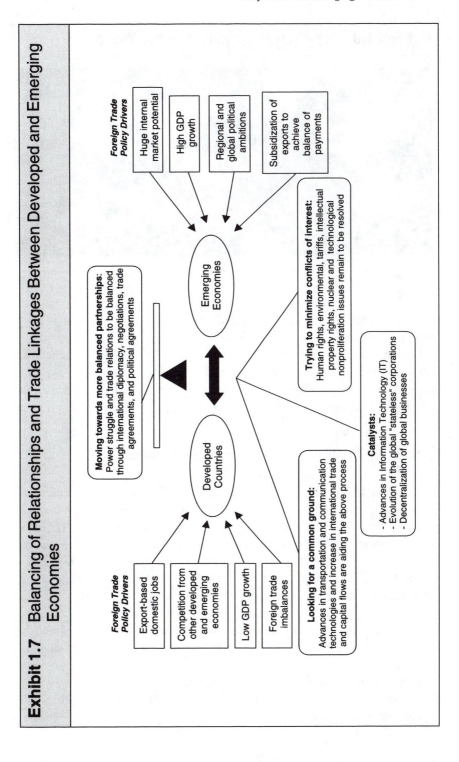

Exhibit 1.7   Balancing of Relationships and Trade Linkages Between Developed and Emerging Economies

Foreign Trade Policy Drivers

- Huge internal market potential
- High GDP growth
- Regional and global political ambitions
- Subsidization of exports to achieve balance of payments

Emerging Economies

Moving towards more balanced partnerships: Power struggle and trade relations to be balanced through international diplomacy, negotiations, trade agreements, and political agreements

Trying to minimize conflicts of interest: Human rights, environmental, tariffs, intellectual property rights, nuclear and technological nonproliferation issues remain to be resolved

Foreign Trade Policy Drivers

- Export-based domestic jobs
- Competition from other developed and emerging economies
- Low GDP growth
- Foreign trade imbalances

Developed Countries

Looking for a common ground: Advances in transportation and communication technologies and increase in international trade and capital flows are aiding the above process

Catalysts:
- Advances in Information Technology (IT)
- Evolution of the global "stateless" corporations
- Decentralization of global businesses

Exhibit 1.8   Emerging Economies of the World

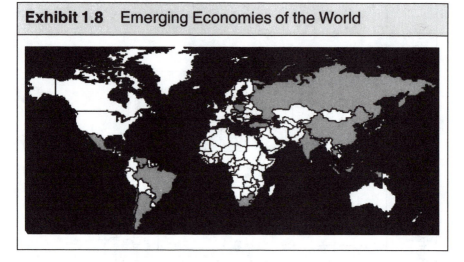

issues of conflict between developed and developing nations—such as human rights violations, tariffs, intellectual property rights, and nuclear and technological proliferation—still remain to be resolved. Business and political leaders of both developed and emerging nations will use international diplomacy, politics, and trade agreements to achieve and maintain industrial and technological leadership of their respective nations.

Emerging Economies as Growing Markets

Approximately 75% of the world's population lives in emerging economies (see Exhibit 1.8). The population growth rates of emerging economies are the highest of all countries. The populations of China and India, 1.2 billion and more than 1 billion respectively, easily outnumber those of many developed countries put together. Africa's population is also growing rapidly.

The Open Door policies of the Peoples' Republic of China and India have enhanced the importance of these markets even more. One may imagine the effects of doing business in China on firms such as Coca-Cola, Caterpillar, Carrefour, and Ericsson, which have successfully established themselves in this market. Exhibit 1.9 provides an example of one such industry.

Industrialized countries are relying on expanding their markets in the developing countries to increase their exports. The WTO reported that developing countries accounted for 27.5% of world merchandise exports in

Exhibit 1.9   The Telecommunications Industry: An Example

An example of the size of growing markets is the telecommunications equipment and services industry. Independent researchers expect the telecommunications market to top $195 billion by 1997 for two reasons:

1. The emerging economies of Latin America, Asia-Pacific, and Eastern Europe require massive infrastructure investment.
2. The industrialized countries of Western Europe and Asia are fast privatizing their telecom monopolies and dismantling restrictive regulations.

Just the digital-switching market alone, which is a small portion of the entire telecommunications market, topped $4.6 billion in 1992 in emerging economies and is expected to rise over $7 billion by the year 2000. A lack of telecommunications facilities in developing countries is also driving investment in private satellite networks, which again offers many opportunities to Western companies. Increasingly, developing countries are realizing that telecommunications can spur economic development. More than 20 countries around the world, many of which are emerging, have plans to privatize their public telecommunications companies over the coming years. Both governments and investors tend to favor telecommunications issues because of the generally high yield of stocks.

The key point to note in the above example is that many small and medium-sized companies are thriving on the "trickle-down" effect of the foreign business of large companies.

SOURCE: Gross, Hester, & Rajshekhar (1995, pp. 55-60); Dana (1997, pp. 99-104).

1999 (WTO, 2000). In most technology-transfer projects, Western machinery and equipment are being bought by developing countries. Moreover, most of the production of manufactured goods still takes place in advanced industrialized countries, and emerging economies have become important customers for these goods. Even other developing economies that cannot be considered as emerging are striving hard to build up their infrastructures and basic industry sectors, for which they are importing Western technologies and components. In other words, although industrialized countries have most of the production of manufactured goods, developing countries represent a substantial and growing market for capital goods and for industrial components. Exhibit 1.10 and Exhibit 1.11 illustrate the flow of

Exhibit 1.10 Sources of Foreign Direct Investment in Emerging Economics

Emerging Market:	Largest Investor*		Second-Largest Investor*		Third-Largest Investor*		Fourth-Largest Investor*		Corresponding Year	TOTAL** FDI-1999
	Country	(U.S. $ Millions)	Country	(U.S. $ Millions)	Country	(U.S. $ Millions)	Country	(U.S. $ Millions)		(U.S. $ Billions)
China	Hong Kong	20,630	Japan	4,330	Taiwan	3,290	U.S.	3,240	1997	40.4
Hong Kong	Japan	3,620	U.K.	2,420	China	2,230	U.S.	1,610	1996	23.1
India	U.S.	3,418	Mauritius	2,638	U.K.	1,140	Germany	548	1997	2.1
Indonesia	Japan	13,176	U.S.	4,426	Hong Kong	4,179	Singapore	4,018	1967-1996	(3.2)
Malaysia	U.S.	853	Japan	770	Germany	644	Taiwan	479	1997	3.5
Philippines	Japan	331	Brit. Vir. Isl.	176	U.S.	116			1997	0.7
Singapore	U.S.	1,593	Japan	1,369	U.K.	299			1997	7.0
South Korea	U.S.	3,189	Japan	265					1997	10.3
Thailand	Japan	1,032	U.S.	543	Singapore	294	Hong Kong	284	1997	6.1
Taiwan	Japan	854	U.S.	491	Hong Kong	237			1997	2.9
Argentina	U.S.	8,060							1996	23.2
Brazil	U.S.	17,210	Germany	6,210	Cayman Isl.	4,560	France	4,341	1997	31.3
Chile	Spain	1,498	U.S.	913	Canada	679			1997	9.2
Mexico	U.S.	4,673	U.K.	1,741	Japan	306			1997	11.2
Venezuela	U.S.	3,306	Netherlands	662	Switzerland	424			1995	2.6
Greece										0.9
Israel										2.3
Portugal	Spain	451	Germany	223	U.S.	461			1997	0.6
South Africa	U.K.	3,342	Germany	1,338	U.S.	1,346			1994	1.4
Turkey	U.S.	1,500							1997	0.7
Czech Rep.	Germany	391	U.K.	196	Netherlands	133			1997	5.1
Hungary	U.S.	6,000	Germany	5,400	Australia	2,500	France	1,500	1997	1.9
Poland	U.S.	3,981	Germany	2,104	Italy	1,636			1997	7.5
Russia	U.S.	2,806	U.K.	2,299	Switzerland	1,719	Germany	1,543	1997	2.8

*U.S. Department of Commerce, National Trade Data Bank (1999).
**United Nations Conference on Trade and Development (2000).

Exhibit 1.11 World Trade Between Developed and Emerging Economies

1998 Trade Balance With Three Leading Trade Partners (U.S. $ Millions)

EMERGING MARKET	Country	Trade Balance	Country	Trade Balance	Country	Trade Balance
China	Japan	1,385.0	Hong Kong	32,083.8	U.S.	21,100.1
Hong Kong	China	(15,116.0)	Japan	(14,229.9)	U.S.	26,845.5
India	U.S.	3,028.6	Hong Kong	1,613.5	Germany	603.3
Indonesia	Japan	4,823.6	Germany	(961.4)	U.S.	3,522.7
Malaysia	Japan	(3,729.8)	Singapore	4,542.8	U.S.	4,435.3
Philippines	U.S.	3,258.0	Japan	(2,136.7)	U.K.	1,409.4
Singapore	U.S.	3,036.9	Japan	(9,708.8)	Hong Kong	6,371.1
South Korea						
Thailand	Japan	(7,240.5)	U.S.	2,763.4	Singapore	3,287.0
Taiwan						
Argentina	Chile	979.1	U.S.	(4,036.7)	Germany	(1,321.5)
Brazil	Netherlands	1,999.8	Germany	(2,457.2)	U.S.	(4,429.8)
Chile	U.S.	(1,665.8)	Japan	1,079.1	Argentina	(1,166.0)
Mexico	U.S.	8,689.9	Japan	(3,997.2)	Germany	(3,440.1)
Venezuela	U.S.	7,059.3	Colombia	477.2	Germany	(290.8)
Greece	Germany	(2,428.2)	Italy	(3,412.0)	France	(2,004.0)
Israel	Belgium	(1,768.0)	Germany	(1,306.9)	U.S.	2,867.9
Portugal	Spain	(5,154.3)	Italy	(1,959.4)	U.K.	467.0
South Africa	Germany	(2,245.2)	U.S.	(1,646.4)	Netherlands	449.0
Turkey	Germany	(1,861.7)	U.S.	(1,814.9)	Italy	(2,679.7)
Czech Rep.	Poland	549.5	Slovakia	747.6	Russia	(911.8)
Hungary	Germany	1,123.2	Russia	(890.0)	Italy	(672.4)
Poland	Italy	(2,740.0)	Germany	(2,207.8)	France	(1,702.7)
Russia	Netherlands	3,077.0	Switzerland	2,813.9	Ukraine	2,281.2

SOURCE: United Nations (1999).

foreign direct investment and trade in developing countries and the countries that provide them. One can see that Western countries are the major sources for inflow of direct investment and partners for trade.

Emerging Economies as Global Sources

Western and American firms must look at developing countries not merely as emerging markets but also as potential sources (with sourcing niches) that may provide competitive advantages to the buying firms. Whenever a foreign market is explored, the risks involved in doing business must be evaluated; the same process can be used to make a decision about developing a long-term supplier in that country. Intercultural differences must be taken into account when deciding to develop a supplier in a foreign country and, if possible, the buying company must use a cross-functional and cross-cultural buying team for negotiations. Companies that have reaped the most benefits from global sourcing have the following characteristics: (a) a high percentage of costs in purchased materials, (b) complex bills of materials and a large volume of individual parts, and (c) a sudden opportunity to expand the market base (Kohn, 1993, pp. 17-20). Examples are Nike and IKEA.

After an exhaustive data analysis from various national and international sources, experts have identified six countries best suited for building new plants, making acquisitions, or forming joint ventures: the United Kingdom, France, Canada, China, Mexico, and Malaysia. It should be noted that three out of these six countries are emerging economies. Nearly half of the 2,000 Japanese companies surveyed in a study indicated that they were planning to move their manufacturing production overseas, as shown in Exhibit 1.12 (Japan External Trade Organization [JETRO], 2000). However, the Japanese did not aim to move their manufacturing to the traditional marketplaces of Europe and America, but rather to emerging economies in Asia. It is clear from such evidence that it will become increasingly difficult for Western firms looking for market share and profits to ignore emerging economies as ideal offshore production and sourcing sites.

Organization of This Book

The authors hope the brief introduction provided in this chapter has convinced the Western business executive that emerging country markets deserve special attention because of the promise they hold and unique aspects of doing business in such countries. The remainder of this book will provide specific guidelines to Western managers on how to internationalize and how to approach and to negotiate with their counterparts in emerging markets.

Chapter 2 details the specifics of the promise emerging markets hold and how to determine the costs of embarking on relationships with these developing countries. The critical issues of risk factors, infrastructure, and sustainability are addressed in this chapter, as well as the process of negotiation.

Chapter 3 explains the process of making internationalization a corporate strategy. This chapter stresses the need to align resources and technology for internationalization and highlights the importance of using information technology for integration of business operations.

Exhibit 1.12 Regions Cited by Japanese Manufacturers as Best Places for Production

Production Items	First	Second	Third
Textile	Asia	North America	Europe
Chemical	Europe	North America	Asia
Ferrous and nonferrous metal	Asia	North America	Europe
Machinery	North America	Asia	Europe
Electronic machinery	North America	Europe	Asia
Transport equipment	Asia	North America	Europe
Wood and pulp	North America	Asia	Europe

SOURCE: Japan External Trade Organization (2000).

Chapter 4 provides specific guidelines on exporting to and sourcing from emerging economies. A recommended approach to the marketing process is also offered.

Chapter 5 details alternative ways of tapping emerging country market potentials. The businessperson needs to recognize that there are different options and trade-offs in becoming involved in overseas business. A recommended approach to the marketing process is also offered.

Chapter 6 discusses the importance of relationships in international business and strategies to manage relationships with foreign governments, expatriates, foreign partners, foreign communities, and foreign customers. The latter half of this chapter describes the properties and characteristics of different types of business alliances and gives detailed guidelines on the selection of foreign partners, foreign distributors, and freight forwarders.

Chapter 7 provides a structure for approaching cross-cultural negotiations. This discussion elaborates on the key components of negotiations and provides the executive with international business negotiation strategies.

Chapters 8, 9, and 10 explain entry and negotiation strategies for the emerging economies of Asia, Eastern and Central Europe, Central and Latin America, and Africa. A word of caution is provided at the end of every chapter to provide managers/students with a more realistic appreciation of what goes into doing business in these emerging economies.

Finally, Chapter 11 provides guidelines for successful execution of international business agreements. It also discusses arbitration and international business dispute settlement issues.

2

Emerging-Market Potential

Despite political instability in some of these countries, which introduces a major risk factor for doing business, emerging economies have become increasingly attractive to businesses in recent years. According to the International Monetary Fund (IMF), developing countries will achieve a growth rate of more than 6% per year in the next couple of decades, whereas industrialized countries are likely to average only 2.5% (Dunham, 1993, pp. 54-55). Due to the economic reforms introduced by emerging economies in the late 1980s, the markets of Asia, Europe, and Latin America have returned to the international equity and bond markets with force. Experts say that the following changes in the policies of the emerging economies have been responsible for the shift in financial markets (Davis, 1993, pp. 2-6):

- Legal obstacles to foreign ownership have been removed, and punitive taxation on portfolio investment has been reduced or eliminated.
- Economic policy has created a more attractive climate for foreign investment.
- Monetary policy has been overhauled, with a new focus on controlling inflation.

Thailand, for example, has experienced a return to steady economic growth despite political infighting, the Asian crisis, and some bureaucratic delays resulting from tough economic problems. The growth of the Thai economy is due to the expansion of exports, which has led to significant and sustained improvements in the nation's trade balance. Thailand is attempting to achieve the status of a "Thai-style NIC" (newly industrialized country), relying mostly on resource-based and agro-industrial development to take advantage of the country's natural resources. Thailand has become a very attractive location for Japanese offshore production due to its close links to the dollar. Some outstanding Japanese companies, such as Sony, Sharp, and Mitsubishi, have made strategic investments there. A careful analysis of the investment climate in emerging economies may reveal some very profitable opportunities (Dohrs, 1987). There are several reasons why scholars and marketers overlooked trade with the developing countries in the past:

1. Market potential in individual countries was considered too small for targeted marketing efforts.

2. Selling costs as a proportion of sales were considerably higher in developing countries.

3. Developing countries tended to have unstable market structures, making demand estimation difficult. This discouraged export managers who needed to make long-term plans for production and sales.

4. Most noncommodity-type imports of developing countries were job orders requiring special planning and customized production. This required careful planning and manufacturing by exporters—a requirement that many believed was not worth the effort.

5. The process of reaching agreements with customers in developing countries was cumbersome and lengthy, increasing not only the cost of sales but also the commercial risks. Often, a business deal failed because of a change in administration, import policies, or personnel.

6. There was a lack of information about market potential and appropriate strategies to be followed in developing countries.

Many factors have helped to overcome most of the above problems. The key factors are as follows:

1. Market potential is no longer too small for marketing efforts. Maximum population growth and infrastructure development rates are predicted for emerging economies. The size of the market is huge and cannot be ignored.

2. Many emerging economies are investing in infrastructure development, especially in transportation, power, and communication. This, coupled with modern management techniques and close working relationships with foreign distributors and agents, has helped bring down costs of selling in emerging markets.

3. Though some emerging markets have highly differentiated structures, demand estimation has become easier with professional consulting and advertising organizations established in most of these markets.

4. Many emerging economies have developed or accessed technologies that have made them competitive on a global basis. More and more managers in emerging economies are training themselves with modern management tools and skills, and this has made production planning much simpler.

5. With governments in emerging economies providing full support to foreign investment, reaching business agreements is no longer a cumbersome process. Though intercultural differences remain in some countries, more and more managers have realized the value of creating global "win-win" relationships and alliances. Many Western managers have started learning foreign languages and have a better understanding of foreign cultures. These changes have helped to develop a common ground during business negotiations. Also, many local managers are educated in the West and have vast experience in dealing with Western firms and cultures.

6. The information revolution has made more and more information available about emerging economies, and business strategy formulation has become a lot easier.

The Significance of Emerging Markets

Although the individual markets for some emerging economies may seem too small for concentrated marketing efforts, all the emerging markets collectively constitute a large proportion of world market potential. Approximately 75% of the world population lives in these markets, with the share of emerging economies in world trade constantly increasing (see Exhibit 2.1).

Export-oriented growth strategies of some countries, such as Brazil, China, Taiwan, Malaysia, and Turkey, have enabled them to play more active roles in world trade. Liberalization of many emerging economies has led to an increased flow of imported finished and semifinished goods from Western countries. One of the reasons for these increased imports is that manufacturing industries in these countries are largely dependent on imports. Exports to emerging markets account for one third of total merchandise exports from the United States. As shown by Exhibit 2.2, the biggest emerging markets are expected to more than double their share of world imports, reaching about 27% by 2010 (U.S. Department of Commerce, 1999).

Manufacturing has grown at an impressive pace in many emerging and developing economies. Once primarily agricultural, these nations are taking on the look of developed economies in terms of the proportion of their gross domestic product (GDP) devoted to industry and services. The countries classified by the World Bank as "lower-middle income," such as Kenya, Senegal, Bolivia, and Jordan, now average 35% of their GDP from industry and 43% from service, whereas the share of agriculture has fallen

Exhibit 2.1   World Population by Region 1998 – 2050
                   Life Expectancy at Birth 1995 – 2000
                   (Millions)

Region	Population 1998	Population 2025	Population 2050	Life Expectancy at Birth 1995-2000
World	5,901	7,823	8,909	65
More-developed regions*	1,182	1,214	1,155	75
Less-developed regions**	4,718	6,608	7,753	63
Least-developed regions***	614	1,092	1,494	51
Africa	748	1,298	1,766	51
Asia	3,585	4,723	5,268	66
Europe	728	702	627	73
Latin America	503	696	808	69
Northern America	304	363	391	77
Oceania	29	39	46	74

SOURCE: United Nations Population Division Department of Economics and Social Information and Policy Analysis (1998).
*More-developed regions comprise all regions of Europe and Northern America, Australia-New Zealand, and Japan.
**Less-developed regions comprise all regions of Africa, Asia (excluding Japan), Latin America and the Caribbean, and the regions of Melanesia, Micronesia, and Polynesia.
***Least-developed countries, as defined by the United Nations General Assembly as of 1998, include 48 countries: 33 in Africa, 9 in Asia, 1 in Latin America and the Caribbean, and 5 in Oceania.

to an average of 22%. Even in the poorest economies, such as Bangladesh, Sudan, and Mozambique, manufacturing and services account for 55% of GDP, whereas the share of agriculture has fallen from 48% to 35% (U.S. Department of Commerce, 1999).

These changes, plus a large and increasing GDP, provide opportunities for products tailored to the needs of developing countries. Western firms

Exhibit 2.2   World Trade Share of Emerging Markets

Country	Exports 1998—Est. ($ Billions)	Imports 1998—Est. ($ Billions)
China	192.0	146.0
Hong Kong	192.7	211.6
India	30.0	36.3
Indonesia	12.5	7.2
Malaysia	74.7	73.2
Philippines	29.7	36.3
Singapore	125.0*	131.3*
South Korea	145.0	117.0
Thailand	56.4**	61.3**
Taiwan	118.8	114.1
Argentina	29.0	36.0
Brazil	63.0	72.0
Chile	16.0	18.5
Mexico	120.0	124.0
Venezuela	23.0	14.0
Greece	12.0	27.6
Israel	21.4	32.0
Portugal	25.7	34.9
South Africa	28.2**	26.4**
Turkey	29.0	50.0
Czech Republic	26.3	28.8
Hungary	22.0	24.5
Poland	31.3	44.7
Russia	86.6	52.5

SOURCE: U.S. Department of Commerce, National Trade Data Bank (1999).
  *1996 data
**1997 data

manufacturing machine tools and instruments are realizing the great potential of these markets. Pharmaceutical firms such as Sterling, Novartis, Pfizer, and Astra are reaping substantial profits selling vaccines and medicines that can be stored without refrigeration when shipped to distant markets. Aircraft manufacturers are designing aircraft especially suitable for emerging markets. For instance, Lockheed Aircraft, whose Hercules turboprop is popular in developing countries, has developed several proto-types for transport planes that can carry bulk commodities at a relatively low cost. Airbus Industries has developed its AXX3 (A380), a double-decker plane for both passengers and cargo, especially for increasing traffic between developed and emerging markets. Opportunities for success in emerging markets are enormous, provided Western firms apply sound marketing principles.

Characteristics of Emerging Economies

It may be helpful to review some general economic and marketing characteristics of emerging economies before discussing entry and negotiation strategies in the following chapters. For this purpose, emerging economies are classified into relatively homogeneous groups on the basis of demographic and economic commonalties (see Exhibit 2.3).

The ability of many emerging economies to engage in international business is frequently constrained by how much they owe to other nations. Useful information on indebtedness, according to four risk groups based on a country's debt service requirements, is shown in Exhibit 2.4. These risk classifications influence a country's ability to borrow from international banks.

Some macroeconomic characteristics of emerging economies are relevant to successful marketing. Most Western companies are accustomed to marketing in a buyer's market (i.e., a market with numerous sellers). Domestic markets in the many emerging economies are characterized by (a) a seller's market in which individual customer concerns are not crucial in consumer goods and (b) a concentrated market in which most personal selling strategies require modifications. Philips Electronics, for example, introduced a two-in-one video CD player in China in 1994. Although this product has no market in the Western world, it was a big success in China. More than 15 million units were sold in the first couple of years. This product has now been introduced in India and Indonesia with big success (Prahalad & Lieberthal, 1998). A number of other companies that tried to use their standardized strategies faced great problems and had to localize their products and marketing strategies. Kellogg and Coca-Cola in the Indian market provide a good example. With an investment of hundreds of millions of dollars, Kellogg was having a tough time weaning Indians from their wheat- and rice-based breakfasts to try its cereals. It had to introduce rice flakes and wheat flakes to match local tastes. Coca-Cola used its global advertising strategies and failed badly in India. After 2 years of losing market shares to Pepsi, the company localized its marketing strategies. In July 2000, Coca-Cola finally decided to use localized marketing strategies in all markets and also in Europe (Barnathan, Moshavi, Dawley, Sunita, & Chang, 1995).

Exhibit 2.3   A Market-Oriented Classification of Emerging Economies

Cluster	Demographic Makeup
Latin American cluster: Argentina, Peru, Brazil	GNP per capita: 20.77* Population growth: 1.40% Urban population: 78.33% Annual growth of industry: 0.27% Economic freedom: 2.82** Life expectancy: 67.33 years
Laggards: Algeria, Bangladesh, Egypt, Morocco, South Africa, Nigeria, Pakistan, Tunisia, Guatemala	GNP per capita: 14.04 Population growth: 2.24% Urban population: 42.22% Annual growth of industry: 2.69% Economic freedom: 2.78 Life expectancy: 61.56
Emerging markets: Chile, Colombia, Costa Rica, Dominican Republic, Ecuador, El Salvador, Honduras, Mexico, Philippines, Sri Lanka, Turkey, Venezuela	GNP per capita: 20.91 Population growth: 1.83% Urban population: 59.08% Annual growth of industry: 2.86% Economic freedom: 3.01 Life expectancy: 69.00
Southeast Asian cluster: Indonesia, Malaysia, Thailand	GNP per capita: 24.37 Population growth: 1.57% Urban population: 33.33% Annual growth of industry: 8.07% Economic freedom: 3.40 Life expectancy: 66.67
Mature markets: Sweden, Switzerland, Austria, Belgium, Denmark, Finland, Norway, Poland, Netherlands, United Kingdom, Ireland, Italy, France, Spain, Greece, Hungary, Australia, New Zealand, Israel, Canada, Japan	GNP per capita: 68.01 Population growth: 0.46% Urban population: 75.71% Annual growth of industry: 2.15% Economic freedom: 3.55 Life expectancy: 76.05
Dynamic growth markets: Hong Kong, South Korea, Singapore, Portugal	GNP per capita: 60.38 Population growth: 0.70% Urban population: 75.75% Annual growth of industry: 8.8% Economic freedom: 4.14 Life expectancy: 74.50
Asian "elephants": China, India	GNP per capita: 7.15 Population growth: 1.35% Urban population: 26.50% Annual growth of industry: 8.75% Economic freedom: 2.25 Life expectancy: 65.00

*GNP per capita: Purchasing-power parity estimates (U.S. = 100)
**Economic freedom: 1 = *Not free;* 5 = *Free* (from the Economical Freedom Index developed for Freedom House)

Exhibit 2.4   Indebtedness of Emerging Economies

Location (1999)	External Debt ($ Billions)
China	159.0*
Hong Kong	48.1
India	98.0
Indonesia	140.0*
Malaysia	43.6
Philippines	51.9
Singapore	N/A
South Korea	142.0
Thailand	80.0
Taiwan	35.0
Argentina	149.0
Brazil	200.0
Chile	39.0
Mexico	155.8
Venezuela	32.0
Greece	41.9*
Israel	18.7**
Portugal	13.1**
South Africa	25.7*
Turkey	104.0
Czech Republic	24.3
Hungary	27.0
Poland	44.0*
Russia	166.0

SOURCE: Central Intelligence Agency (2000).
 *1998 data
**1997 data

Most emerging economies are being liberalized, although many are still far from becoming market economies. This is due to various reasons:

1. Domestic markets of many emerging economies are small in terms of absolute size and purchasing power. This leads to natural monopolies in which the production or imports of a single entrepreneur become more efficient than those of several entrepreneurs. Even with the absence of export restrictions, competition for a share of the domestic market is accompanied by a relatively low return, thereby discouraging new entries.

2. Wholesale distribution in many emerging economies is controlled by manufacturers or importers, thus creating a formidable barrier to entry. New entrants soon discover that although their products may be a better buy, there is no way of distributing the product through existing channels. Wholesalers tend to control the retail outlets in terms of their product portfolios and financing agreements. These wholesalers can dictate the product mix to the retailers in the absence of fair-trade regulations and antitrust laws. These market imperfections result in highly controlled markets in which the buyer must purchase whatever is offered. The power of natural monopolies remains unchallenged in many cases because of their traditional ties to the government and each other.

3. Emerging markets are extremely concentrated in decision making and market potential. Government involvement is more than regulatory; however, it is being reduced gradually. The active economic role played by governments in the emerging economies is evident in the ability of the private sector to accumulate capital required for certain investments, in national and economic security issues, and in subsidizing a sector. The share of state-owned economic enterprises (SEEs) in most emerging economies is quite substantial, although privatization of government-controlled enterprises is under way in many of them. Railways, oil production, coal, steel industries, banking, shipping, and airlines are controlled by the government in many countries. Only recently, India allowed privatization of banking and airlines. The same pattern occurs in Mexico. In Turkey, SEEs control more than 50% of the manufacturing industry, ranging from textiles and ceramics to steel (U.S. Department of Commerce, 1999).

Active participation of the government in economic activities can often be explained by ambitious developmental goals and historical factors. The government is involved indirectly through centralized economic planning, in addition to being directly involved in the economy through ownership of economic enterprises. Government intervention increases concentration in these economies in the sense that business deals are not made with individual buyers, but with bureaucrats in various government agencies. It is a common practice for international marketers to start sales calls with civil servants in the capital city instead of with the actual buyer. As in the old adage that says, "All roads lead to Rome," all major deals in the emerging markets go through the government at one point or another.

Geographic concentration is a reality. For the private sector, 50% of manufacturing occurs in only 3 of 67 provinces in Turkey. More than one fifth of the 40 million people in Egypt live in or around Cairo (U.S. Department of Commerce, 1999). A direct implication of these observations is that the task

Exhibit 2.5   Market Potential in Four Major Emerging Markets

	Mobile Phones		Computers	
	Market ($ Millions)	Increase Since 1995 (%)	Market ($ Millions)	Increase Since 1995 (%)
Brazil	7.3	+750	1.4	+720
China	21.3	+965	4.9	+390
India	0.8	+1,425	0.7	+85
Mexico	3.2	+1,675	1.4	+300

SOURCE: Whelan (2000, pp. 92-95).

of identifying target buyers and assessing competition is made easier. Despite these factors, these emerging markets are progressing at an unstoppable speed. According to *Fortune* (Whelan, 2000, pp. 92-95), the four major emerging markets, listed in the United States as "American depositary receipts" (meaning they are easier to trade and follow U.S.-style accounting standards), have progressed remarkably during the last 5-year period, 1995 to 2000, as illustrated by Exhibit 2.5.

Risk Factors in Emerging Economies

Though emerging economies offer large untapped markets, it is extremely important for a Western manager to be acquainted with various kinds of risks involved in doing business in these countries. Often, Western managers complain about the lack of information sufficient to perform a risk analysis for doing business in another country. Western managers can make use of two types of information available about emerging markets, primary and secondary. *Primary data,* which are more industry specific and focused, can be obtained by contacting international business consulting companies, commercial attachés of embassies in foreign countries, and subsidiaries, agents, or distributors in foreign markets. There are many reliable sources for *secondary data,* such as *The Economist, Euromoney,* and *Institutional Investor,* which publish country risk ratings semiannually or annually. Also, following leads given by major finance and investment houses or banks and tapping into resources of local universities and business schools may be helpful in risk analysis. The framework in Exhibit 2.6 can help a manager perform a country risk evaluation for a company or a product line.

Exhibit 2.6   A Managerial Framework for Risk Evaluation

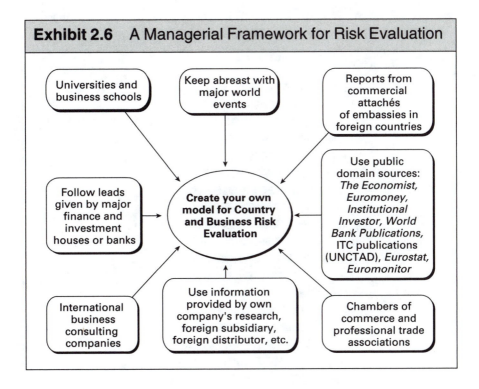

Exhibit 2.7a *Euromoney* Country Risk Rankings

	2000 Risk Rating		*2000 Risk Rating*
United States	94.04	China	57.60
Russia	30.00	Malaysia	59.27
Indonesia	32.82	Czech Republic	60.19
Vietnam	38.40	Poland	61.67
Venezuela	42.08	Hungary	61.83
Brazil	47.41	Chile	63.47
Turkey	48.68	South Korea	63.48
India	52.64	Israel	73.53
Argentina	52.74	Hong Kong	76.27
Philippines	52.96	Greece	79.20
Thailand	54.73	Taiwan	81.76
South Africa	55.63	Portugal	85.17
Mexico	56.89	Singapore	90.18

SOURCE: Newby (2000a, pp. 106-110).
NOTE: *Euromoney* magazine provides coverage and analysis of international business trends and world markets. The following represents their evaluation of various emerging economies. A score of 0 indicates *extreme risk;* a score of 100 indicates *very low risk.*

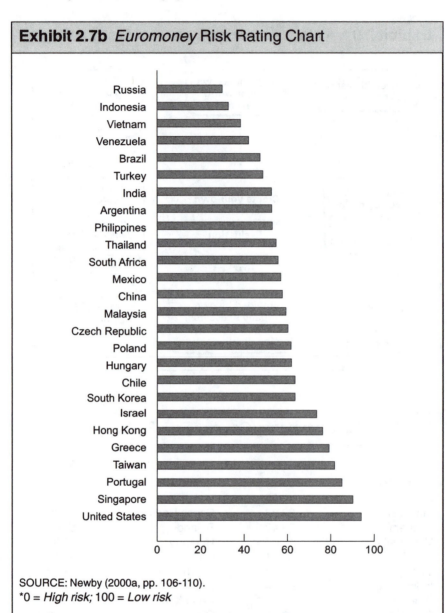

Exhibit 2.7b *Euromoney* Risk Rating Chart

SOURCE: Newby (2000a, pp. 106-110).
*0 = *High risk;* 100 = *Low risk*

The economic intelligence units of *The Economist* and *Euromoney* rate countries on a quarterly basis according to credit risk, which is based on political and economic factors. Exhibit 2.7a illustrates these ratings (Newby, 2000a, pp. 106-110).

Exhibit 2.8   How *Euromoney* Compiles Country Risk Ratings

The *Euromoney* country risk assessment uses nine categories that encompass three broad categories (analytical indicators, credit indicators, and market indicators). The different scores and figures for each category are calculated into the weighted scores as follows: The highest figure in each category receives the full mark for weighting; the lowest receives zero. The score for other figures is calculated proportionately according to the formula: *Final score = (weighting/[maximum figure − minimum figure]) × (figure − minimum figure).* The ranking table shows only the final scores after the calculation for weightings. The categories areas follow:

Political risk (25% weighting). *Euromoney* polls risk analysts, who are asked to give each country a score from 0 to 10. A score of 10 indicates nil risk of non-payment; a score of 0 indicates that there is no chance of payments being made. *Country risk* is defined as the risk of nonpayment or nonservicing of payment for goods or services, loans, trade-related finance and dividends, and the nonrepatriation of capital. This category does not take into account the credit-worthiness of individual counterparties in each country.

Economic data (25%). Based on (a) GNP figures per capita and (b) results of a *Euromoney poll* of economic projections, in which each country's score is obtained from average projections for 1999 to 2000. (For Taiwan, GDP data is used.) The score is calculated from the sum of these two factors, equally weighted. The higher the result, the better.

Debt indicators (10%). Scores are calculated from the following ratios taken from the World Bank's Global Development Finance 2000: (a) total debt stocks to GNP, (b) debt service to exports, and (c) current account balance to GNP. Figures are for 1998. Scoring is calculated on the basis of *(A) + (B × 2) − (C × 10)*, with the lower the score, the better. Because of the lack of consistent economic data for Organization of Economic Cooperation and Development (OECD) and rich, oil-producing countries, these score the full weighting, except when they report debt figures to the International Money Fund (IMF). Developing countries which do not report complete debt data score 0.

Debt in default or rescheduled (10%). A score from 0 to 10 based on the ratio of rescheduled debt to debt stocks, taken from the World Bank's Global Development Finance 2000. The lower the ratio, the better. OECD and developing countries which do not report under the debtor-reporting system (DRS) score 10 to 0, respectively.

Credit ratings (10%). Nominal values are assigned to sovereign ratings from Moody's and S&P's and Fitch IBCA. The higher the average value, the better. Countries without credit ratings score 0.

Exhibit 2.8 *Continued*

Access to bank finance (5%). Score is calculated from disbursement of private, long-term, unguaranteed loans as a percentage of GNP. The higher the result, the better. OECD and developing countries not reporting under DRS score 5 to 0 respectively.
Source: The World Bank's Global Development Finance 2000.

Access to short-term finance (5%). Takes into account OECD consensus groups and short-term cover available from the U.S. Exim Bank and NCM UK. The higher the result, the better.

Access to capital markets (5%). Head of debt syndicate and loan syndications rated each country's accessibility to international markets at the time of the survey. The higher the average rating out of 10, the better.

Discount on forfeiting (5%). Scored from a combination of the maximum tenor for forfeiting and the average spread over countries without risk, such as the United States. Countries for which forfeiting is not available score 0.

SOURCE: Newby (2000b, pp. 109-110); data supplied by Deutsche Bank, Standard Bank, and West Merchant Capital Markets.

As seen in Exhibit 2.7b, Russia is the riskiest country with which to do business, and Indonesia is the second-riskiest. A stronger government in Poland has increased its rating from 56 to 61. *Euromoney* publishes country risk ratings semiannually (March and September), using nine indicators that encompass three broader categories: (a) analytical indicators, (b) credit indicators, and (c) market indicators (Van Duyen, 1994, pp. 177-180). The method of compiling these ratings is explained in Exhibit 2.8.

Institutional Investor publishes country credit-worthiness ratings semiannually (March and September) that are based on information provided by leading international banks, as shown in Exhibit 2.9. The method of compiling these ratings is explained in Exhibit 2.10. A kind of a generic improvement in high-risk countries is under way. Country risk is generally down, whether you're talking about Vietnam or India or all of Latin America. The general shift to a globalized financial system has reduced risk because more countries are trying to attract foreign capital. A banker in the United Kingdom was quoted as saying, "As long as the emerging markets keep waiving the 'Invest Here' signs instead of the 'Yankee Go Home' signs, the confidence level of foreign lenders and investors should keep going up."

Exhibit 2.9   *Institutional Investor* Country Risk Ratings

	2000 Risk Rating		2000 Risk Rating
United States	91.6	Malaysia	59.5
Russia	26.7	China	60.6
Indonesia	27.4	Czech Republic	60.9
Vietnam	28.0	Poland	62.2
Venezuela	37.9	South Korea	63.3
Brazil	45.0	Israel	64.4
Argentina	45.8	Hungary	64.9
Turkey	46.8	Chile	67.2
Philippines	49.4	Hong Kong	68.3
India	51.5	Greece	70.0
Thailand	53.2	Taiwan	78.9
South Africa	55.1	Portugal	83.6
Mexico	56.7	Singapore	87.8

SOURCE: Rowley (2000).
NOTE: *Institutional Investor* is another publication that provides investment and financial intelligence for international business professionals. Like *Euromoney, Institutional Investor* ranks a country's risk on a scale from 0 to 100, with 0 being *most risky* and 100 being the *least risky*.

Exhibit 2.10 How *Institutional Investor* Compiles Country Risk Ratings

The country-by-country credit ratings developed by *Institutional Investor* are based on information provided by leading international banks, money management firms, and economists. They have graded each of the countries on a scale of 0 to 100, with 100 representing those with the *least chance of loan default* or that offer *the best investment risk*. The names of the respondents to the survey are kept strictly confidential. Participants are not permitted to rate their home countries. The individual responses are weighted using an *Institutional Investor* formula that gives more importance to responses from institutions with greater worldwide exposure and more sophisticated country analysis systems.

SOURCE: Rowley (2000).

Most of these emerging markets have thus become centers of outsourcing for Western companies. It is quite easy to develop a quality supplier network to sell in the domestic markets of these suppliers as well as in the global market. At present, about 40% of the world software development is being done in India. Most multinational companies (MNCs), from Intel to Microsoft, are moving their R&D activities to India. Most of the branded clothing companies are now producing in India, Pakistan, and Bangladesh. Motorola, Intel, and Philips are producing their semiconductors in Malaysia and Taiwan. Companies that work with localized product and marketing strategies are doing excellent business in these markets. Unilever in India, Philips all over Asia, Carrefour in South Korea, and WalMart in Mexico are just a few examples.

Major Concerns in Emerging Economies

Lack of Infrastructure

The term *infrastructure* covers services from public utilities (power, telecommunications, piped water supply, sanitation and sewerage, solid waste collection and disposal, and piped gas), public works (roads, dams, and canals), and other transport sectors (urban and interurban railways, urban transport, ports and waterways, and airports). Many Western managers assume that emerging economies have little or no infrastructure and hence it is not worthwhile to spend time and resources in exploring markets in these countries. Many emerging economies have yet to extend basic facilities such as telephone lines, roads, and electricity beyond the capital city. Some markets already have well-established local distribution systems (e.g., India, Brazil, and Malaysia) in which retailers are even willing to pay in advance to get the products that are in demand. China and Russia are perhaps the only two countries that lack fully developed distribution systems.

A Western manager should consider the nonexistence of infrastructure in China as an untapped opportunity to do business. Western firms in this case build up an infrastructure most suited to their product and strategy needs. The availability or nonavailability of distribution and other infrastructure would definitely influence the type of local partner/distributor a foreign firm is looking for. Also, Western firms can think about investing in international equity markets for infrastructure-related bonds and stock issues of emerging economies. For example, according to the *International Capital Markets Report 2000* (IMF, 2000b) in 1999, private financing to emerging markets in terms of bond and security issues accounted for $110.2 billion. General Electric Corporation, an international conglomerate, has an active interest in infrastructure projects in developing countries and issues securities in the U.S. and European markets through its subsidiary, General Electric Capital Corporation, for investing in selected

---

Exhibit 2.11 The Importance of Infrastructure to
                   Commerce and Foreign Investment

An Example From China

Lack of infrastructure can become a major hurdle for a growing economy. China still suffers from infrastructure bottlenecks. Its intercity transport system, which is linked to the supply of raw materials, coal, and electricity, is one of the thinnest in the world. So transport shortages result in power shortages, because coal accounts for 70% of China's power generation. Raising capital for infrastructure improvements is a major task. It is estimated that at least $750 billion will be required over the next decade for these investments. Legal and regulatory changes are needed to generate financing mechanisms for infrastructure projects.

SOURCE: *World Bank, Country Briefs: China* (2000).

An Example From India

For emerging economies wishing to participate in global high-tech markets, reliable and plentiful power infrastructure will have to be developed. India emerged as a provider of reliable software solutions and skilled software engineers to the international information technology (IT) industry. However, India faces the problem of power shortages. To support the growing needs of software and IT-enabled service industries, such as call centers, India needs to double its electricity-generating capacity during the next decade. The cost of this investment is estimated to reach $250 billion.

SOURCE: *Financial Times Survey:* India (2000).

---

infrastructure projects. For small and medium-sized Western firms, working with local distributors or partners in the foreign market will be a more appropriate strategy to overcome infrastructure-related hurdles. The importance of this issue is illustrated in Exhibit 2.11.

Environmental Issues

Western firms are used to competing on price, quality, delivery, and reliability dimensions. More recently, a new dimension has been added: the environmental or social responsibility. Although environmental laws in emerging economies are not as stringent as they are in developed countries, Western firms interested in doing business in emerging markets over the long term should be aware that the situation is changing fast. This became apparent in the North American Free Trade Agreement (NAFTA), signed by the United States, Canada, and Mexico, which included sustainable development as a specific objective. *Sustainability* is a concept that strives to balance economic growth with environmental management. It asserts that economic and industrial development is essential if people in developing countries are to rise out of poverty and that this development can be accomplished without destroying the environment: Long-term economic growth ultimately depends on the integrity of the ecosystem. Mexico is an important emerging economy that is developing environmental regulations as stringent as those in the United States or Canada, and the benefits perceived by Western managers of not having costs related to environmental protection while manufacturing in Mexico will be lost completely.

Environmental awareness is also rising in other emerging economies, and the governments may have to pass laws under public pressure to protect the environment. The United Nations held the Earth Summit Conference on the Environment in 1992, in Rio de Janeiro, to discuss how the stewardship of dwindling natural resources was to be apportioned between developed and developing nations. Yet despite much discussion at the conference, the critical question of how to raise the estimated $125 billion per year required to clean up environmental problems in developing countries remained unanswered (Sung, 1992, pp. 34-35). To address those issues and assess the accomplishments and global changes since 1992, the World Summit on Sustainable Development will be held in South Africa in 2002.

To overcome emerging economies' inability to fund preservation projects, nongovernmental organizations have initiated a new form of conservation agreement—debt-for-nature swaps—which can occur in various forms. One example of this swap involves the central bank of a less-developed country converting foreign debt into local currency or local bonds, which are then held by local environmental groups for investment in preservation projects (Chambers, Chambers, & Whitehead, 1993, pp. 17-21). By being involved in environmental preservation attempts, corporations can build goodwill with the public and attract more customers. The Overseas Private Investment Corporation (OPIC) established the privately owned and managed Environmental Investment Fund to invest in new or expanding business enterprises in emerging economies that use natural resources on a sustainable basis or practice sound environmental management. Money will be used by private businesses in emerging economies that demonstrate positive, mutually reinforced relationships between profitable economic development and environmental protection (Delphos, 1992, p. 29).

Farsighted Western managers will take environmental issues into consideration when doing business in emerging economies. They will consider the full scope of the value chain, which includes recycling when the customer wants to dispose of the used product. Reverse logistics and recycling will play a major role in the long term in doing environmentally friendly business in emerging economies.

Ethical Issues

The desire to gain entry into an emerging market may tempt Western managers to offer bribes or otherwise "grease palms" of government bureaucrats, politicians, or corporate buyers making purchasing decisions. Undoubtedly, though unethical, bribery and corruption are a reality in many emerging economies.

As seen in Exhibit 2.12, most emerging economies can be called corrupt, having ratings below 5.0. The U.S. government considers bribing foreigners for business deals or contracts to be illegal under the Foreign Corrupt Practices Act (FCPA). The FCPA prohibits American companies or managers from offering bribes of any kind for business to officials in foreign countries. American managers have complained that although the FCPA is good for fostering healthy and ethical practices in international business, it puts them at a competitive disadvantage compared with Japanese and European competitors, who are not restrained by similar laws in their home countries. Clearly, however, it would be in the best interest of the entire world if no bribes were offered or accepted in business dealings.

But before a Western manager passes judgment on business practices in another country, he or she must be aware that the perception of bribery is culturally relative and socially conditioned. Recognize that in many cultures, gifts and payments are essential parts of building relationships, and sometimes the line between a bribe and a gift can be blurred. Such delicate situations must be dealt with carefully and with tact.

With respect to ethical issues in international business, there are two extreme positions: relativism and universalism. *Relativism* is based on the view that rules are basically local and do not apply elsewhere. *Universalism,* on the other hand, favors the view that most rules cross borders and apply everywhere, because they are based on universal moral principles. In between lies the third possible alternative, which is a pragmatic and respectful view of how ethical behavior can be developed in a cross-cultural context. It implies that given the legality and legitimacy of a definite action, we need to develop specific ethical concerns and attitudes related to a particular situation (Ghauri & Usunier, 1999).

Exhibit 2.12 Corruption Perception Index

Country	2000
China	3.1
Hong Kong	7.7
India	2.8
Indonesia	1.7
Malaysia	4.8
Philippines	2.8
Singapore	9.1
South Korea	4.0
Thailand	3.2
Taiwan	5.5
Argentina	3.5
Brazil	3.9
Chile	7.4
Mexico	3.3
Venezuela	2.7
Greece	4.9
Israel	6.6
Portugal	6.4
South Africa	5.0
Turkey	3.8
Czech Republic	4.3
Hungary	5.2
Poland	4.1
Russia	2.1

SOURCE: Transparency International (2000).
NOTE: The Corruption Perception Index relates to perceptions of the degree of corruption as seen by businesspeople, risk analysts, and the general public. It ranges from 10 (*highly clean*) to 0 (*highly corrupt*).

Importance of Negotiations in Emerging Economies

Previous studies conclude that Western firms are facing many difficulties in doing business in the emerging economies. Transnational firms, especially from Western countries, have difficulty understanding the needs, behavior, and evaluation criteria of emerging market buyers. It is admitted that both parties have problems in negotiating projects and deals. Sound proposals that could have been beneficial to both parties have often been disrupted and dropped during negotiations (Ghauri, 2000).

Two elements must normally be present for negotiations to take place: (a) common interests and (b) issues of conflict. "Without common interests, there is nothing to negotiate for, without conflicting issues nothing to negotiate about" (Ikle, 1964, p. 20). In other words, although the parties might have a number of conflicting issues, both of them would hope to achieve a common objective (i.e., a transaction). Therefore, *negotiation* is defined as an interactive process of resolving conflicts and reaching agreements to provide terms and conditions for the future behavior of the parties involved. Little research has been carried out on international business negotiations, despite the increasing importance of international business. In the past, the ability to negotiate was considered innate or instinctive, but studies have shown that negotiation as a technique can be learned.

Basic to understanding negotiation is the concept of *process*. Most professionals and academics agree that negotiation is an activity fraught with difficulties. Very few negotiations exactly replicate the previous experience, especially when they are held with different parties coming from different countries and cultures. However, we can identify some elements of the process that constitute business negotiations and the factors that influence these negotiations. Because this is an essential part of doing business abroad, we have devoted all of Chapter 7 to the process of international business negotiations, with a special reference to emerging markets.

3

Internationalization as a Business Strategy

Factors Affecting Internationalization

Domestic and international business involve similar types of activities, with the main difference being that in international business, transactions take place in more than one country and market environment. This apparently minor difference causes the complexity and diversity in managing international business operations. The concepts of international business and international marketing are universally applicable, but the environment within which marketing plans must be implemented is different from market to market. The unfamiliarity and uncertainty in emerging markets demands rather unique handling and a variety of strategies to enter and to operate in these markets. The environment includes market structure, political and legal forces, economic forces, level of technology, structure of distribution channels, and cultural and social characteristics. According to Cateora and Ghauri (2000), marketing involves managing both controllable and uncontrollable elements, as illustrated in Exhibit 3.1.

Uncontrollable and Controllable Elements

In Exhibit 3.1, the outer circles show various uncontrollable elements of international markets. Uncontrollable elements are present both in domestic and international business. However, the scope and depth of these elements in international business make international transactions more

Exhibit 3.1   The International Marketing Task

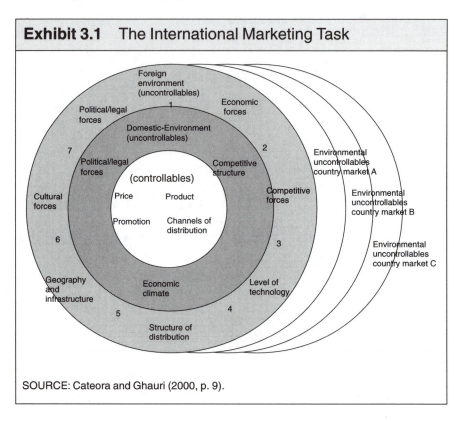

SOURCE: Cateora and Ghauri (2000, p. 9).

complicated and are the internal decisions and marketing mix of the firm. Western businesses may find the uncontrollable elements of each foreign market complicated and compliance difficult. Moreover, these elements are very dynamic, involving dramatic social, economic, political, and cultural changes with increasing uncertainty. This uncertainty can be reduced significantly by carefully studying the operating environments of each country the firm is planning to enter. Competition, economic restraints, government rules and regulations, infrastructure, and cultural factors are some of the uncontrollables that firms have to manage in foreign markets.

The task of a marketer is to adjust and mold the controllable elements of his or her strategies—product, promotional strategies, distribution, and pricing policies—to the uncontrollable elements of a particular market. As illustrated by Exhibit 3.1, these uncontrollable elements differ drastically from market to market, and the marketer has to face a new set of uncontrollables when he or she goes to a new market. Some aspects of the international environment can be directly dealt with using basically identical marketing strategies, and experience in some regions can be helpful in addressing problems in another. Not only do marketers need to manage and adapt to these uncontrollables in foreign markets, they also have to handle and adapt to the domestic uncontrollables, the second circle in Exhibit 3.1. A political decision at home (the domestic market) or an economic recession or boom at home may directly influence a company's international operation. For example, when the U.S. government, in its foreign trade policy, decided to grant most favored nation status (MFN) to China, a lot of opportunities were created for U.S. companies to enter into this huge market. In the same way, if economic conditions at home deteriorate, it may lead to restrictions on purchasing/imports from abroad to strengthen the domestic economy but perhaps influence competitive position of some of the domestic companies.

The following sections discuss external and internal factors that can affect the internationalization of the firm.

External Factors

Market, production, and environmental factors are some of the uncontrollable elements, as discussed above. These factors cannot be influenced by management decisions, but they affect the selection of a particular entry mode.

Target Market Factors

The present and projected size of a target market is a primary determinant for the type of entry. Small markets favor entry modes with a low break-even sales volume, such as indirect exporting, licensing, or contractual arrangements. Large markets with high sales potential justify entry modes with a high break-even sales volume, such as subsidiary operations or joint ventures. Another dimension to be considered is the availability of suitable agents or distributors. If there is an inefficient and/or inadequate marketing infrastructure, the market may be reached only through a branch or subsidiary entry mode.

Production Factors in the Target Market

If production costs (raw materials, labor, energy, etc.) and the economic infrastructure (transportation, ports, and communications) are favorable, local production can be beneficial. Local manufacturing is not appropriate when production costs are high and infrastructure is poor. When Nestlé opened a powdered-milk and baby-cereal plant in China, it developed its own distribution network, called "milk roads," between 27 villages and the factory collection points. As a result, the farmers had an incentive to produce more milk, and the district's herd grew from 6,000 to 9,000 within a few months (Rapoport, 1994).

Exhibit 3.2   We Want to Be Friends, But What About Our Governments?

Another dimension to be considered in international business is the political relationship between the domestic and foreign governments. The business executive going abroad must be aware of these relationships. In some emerging countries (e.g., previous British and French colonies), mixed feelings exist toward former colonial governments, complicating the assessment of uncontrollable elements. Some countries arrange for special delegations to smooth the relationship at the government level in the early stages of business relationships. The king and queen of Sweden were among the first delegates for Swedish business firms when China opened its doors to Western firms and technologies. When a large Swedish firm was competing for the contract to build an atomic reactor in Brazil, the king and queen of Sweden visited the country before the negotiations began, thus reminding the people that the royals were relatives (the Queen was born in Brazil).

Environmental Factors

The economic, political, and sociocultural character of the target market can affect the choice of entry mode (as illustrated by Exhibit 3.2). Many products are luxurious in a market with a low level of economic activity or skewed economic activity, in which most people live modestly or on a survival level. In many countries, there are dual environmental conditions. These dual economic structures, the coexistence of modern and traditional sectors in the economy, create additional challenges for foreign firms. China, India, and Pakistan are good examples of this idealism, in which people living in the cities (some 25% to 30% of the total population) demand modern Western-style products, while the traditional sector, living in the country, demands more indigenous and simpler products. There are two distinct market segments; each can prove profitable for a foreign company but may demand different marketing programs (Cateora & Ghauri, 2000). Moreover, external or bilateral economic relations influence the complexity of the environmental impact of a company's entry strategy into a particular market.

Internal Factors

Product, resource, and commitment factors also influence a firm's choice regarding establishment of foreign presence.

Product Factors

Highly differentiated products can be priced rather freely and still remain competitive in the market despite high unit transportation costs and import duties. In such cases, an export strategy is favored. Volvo in Thailand, for example, has been positioned as an expensive car priced at more than 1 million baht. This premium price is used to promote a sense of prestige and status to the consumer. Poorly differentiated products must compete on a price basis, which pushes companies toward some form of local production. Technology-intensive products give companies an option to license technology in the foreign market rather than use alternative entry modes.

Resource/Commitment Factors

A company's entry mode options increase as its resources in management, capital, technology, production, and marketing skills become more abundant. In contrast, the company with limited resources is constrained to use entry modes requiring a relatively small resource commitment. Changes in internal factors, particularly growing commitment to foreign markets, are the principal forces shaping a company's international evolution. In the case of smaller firms or firms with limited resources, one way is to find a stronger partner in the domestic market, a partner that has resources or already-established international operations. This was the case when "Breathe Right," the company that makes nose strips for better breathing, formed a partnership with 3M to go international. In such a partnership, both companies gained. Breathe Right could get its products into the global market faster and cheaper, and 3M could introduce a new product in its already-established international distribution channels, with a minimum marginal cost.

The above external and internal factors create an impact on the internationalization of the firm. A continual assessment of the firm's readiness and preparedness for internationalization may be helpful to managers in formulating foreign market entry strategy. Later in this chapter, a checklist for organizational readiness for internationalization and a decision-support methodology for market entry planning are discussed in detail.

Managerial Challenges

International business managers have to constantly face many challenges to develop a foreign business strategy. The following are key challenges:

1. How to identify the right international market(s) for the product or service. This will involve assessing product-market fit and deciding whether the product has to be adapted to suit foreign market environments.

2. How to develop foreign market entry strategies that give them access to these markets. This must include tactics designed to beat domestic competitors who have a better understanding of native markets, and tactics designed to beat other competitors from foreign countries who are in the markets or trying to enter them.

3. How to develop establishment and expansionary strategies in foreign markets once entry is gained.

4. How to create a renewal and change strategy for the business in the foreign country such that competitors cannot imitate them.

Managers also have to develop, nurture, and maintain a network of relationships in the international environment to make their firms successful in foreign markets. The key relationships that an international business manager has to manage are (a) relationships with foreign governments, government officers, bureaucrats, and policymakers, (b) relationships with employees and their families who expatriate and feel far from the home country, (c) relationships with foreign partners, distributors, freight forwarders, banks, and all other such important intermediaries, (d) relationships with communities in the foreign market in which business is transacted, and (e) relationships with foreign customers. In addition, it is important to be sensitive to local culture and traditions, as emphasized in Exhibit 3.3.

The Challenge of Going International

The nature and pattern of international trade flows are changing rapidly. Through the 1980s and 1990s, international trade has been moving more and more from raw material and agricultural products to manufactured goods and services. This is one of the reasons that industrialized Western countries' share of world trade has been increasing. The transition from socialist to market-driven economies, the liberalization of trade and investment policies, privatization of most state-owned industries, and regional market alliances have changed the way countries and companies will trade in the 21st century. According to the U.S. Chamber of Commerce (2000), 75% of the expected growth in the next two decades will come from developing and emerging markets. Moreover, the big emerging markets will be a larger market than Europe and Japan together by 2010 (Cateora & Ghauri, 2000). According to this estimate, there is an accelerated growth in demand for goods and services in these markets. The imports into these markets have already exceeded $1 trillion ("Big Emerging Markets," 1994).

On the other hand, a number of historical, cultural, and institutional factors and recent events in 2002 have made Western (especially U.S.) firms less "export oriented" with respect to other industrialized nations, such as Japan. Many managers do not consider exporting because they

Exhibit 3.3   Some Suggested Managerial Prerequisites for International Business

Cultural Sensitivity
Managers must make every effort to educate themselves and their employees to have a good understanding of the foreign culture in which business is done. It is understandable that not every manager can learn the language of the foreign market. For such cases, we suggest that managers familiarize themselves with good literature (e.g., short stories), history, and economic geography of these countries.

Patience
This is a universally recommended virtue, especially true for managers who cannot discern between "aggressiveness" and "arrogance." Some emerging markets, especially those in Asia, require a lot of patience on the manager's part before a deal can be closed or returns on investment can be realized.

Understanding the Negotiation Strategy of the Foreign Buyer
We have recommended that managers who are given international business assignments be trained in negotiation strategy planning and execution. However, an important issue which is often ignored in negotiation training is gaining the ability to understand the negotiation strategy of the buyer, which becomes more complex in an international setting. Most managers fail to make any effort in training themselves in this area, but if pursued, it can lead to significant leverage and returns.

think it is too risky, complicated, and unprofitable. Others are simply indifferent to exporting and unwilling to invest management time and money. Empirical evidence indicates that lack of information on foreign markets, buyers, marketing practices, competition, language, and unfamiliarity with the procedures of exporting hold firms back from exporting.

Firms often face difficulties in one or more of these historical, cultural, and institutional dimensions. Exhibit 3.4 identifies the stages of internationalization and primary impediments to exporting (Cavusgil, 1986).

Firms should overcome barriers at each stage before moving to the next stage in the export process. Research indicates that exporting needs vary in accordance with the company's stage in the internationalization process. The firms at active or committed stages are more dependent on exports than are the firms at nonexporting or reactive exporting stages.

Doing business with emerging economies brings with it several challenges for the company (see Exhibit 3.5). New tasks, unfamiliar environments, and greater uncertainty mean that the company needs

(Text continues on page 49)

Exhibit 3.4   Classification of Exporters

Stage in the Export Process	Profile of Firms in This Segment	Primary Impediments in Exporting	Illustrative Assistance Programs of U.S. Department of Commerce
Nonexporter Indifferent/Reactive	Tend to be small, serving a limited domestic market. Not likely to possess any differential advantages such as a unique product. Not likely to be in a technology-intensive industry.	Not export capable or simply indifferent to exporting.	
Exporter	Security oriented, risk averse management. Involved in exporting only to the extent of filling unsolicited orders. Suffer from uncertain/unfavorable expectations regarding the effects of exporting on company goals. No commitment to exporting in terms of systematic exploration, export policy, or personnel.	Marketing management	Export motivation programs: information on the benefits of exporting to the accomplishment of the firm's goals.
Experimental Exporter	Actively exploring export opportunities. Active in gathering export-related information from a variety of sources. Favorable expectations regarding profitability of exporting. Management has high aspirations for growth.	Marketing research (Informational)	Export information programs: efforts to better inform the firms about how to export; where the best markets are for their products; who the most promising buyers and distributors are.
Active Exporter	Has greater stakes in exporting: Export sales exceed 10% of output. Usually experience with respect to one or more export markets. Most likely to be in a technology-intensive industry possessing additional facilitating advantages.	Organizational goals and resources	Specific sales and representation leads for U.S. products abroad; assistance in making successful bids for major overseas export contracts.
Committed Exporter	Foreign market opportunities receive equal attention and emphasis. Interested in entering additional foreign markets. Very favorable expectations of exporting and its effects on profits and growth. Regularly plans for export markets. Has a well-developed export structure.	Competitive and public policy	Creating opportunities for U.S. firms to publicize, advertise, and exhibit their products abroad; and opportunities for managers to meet directly with foreign buyers and representatives.

Exhibit 3.5   Minimizing the Impacts of Global Marketing Challenges

Challenge	Impact Minimized by
Distance: Separation of buyers and sellers by great geographic distances may create difficulties in communications and physical distribution. The exporter, for example, has to rely upon a large number of intermediaries. These may include a domestic carrier, an international freight forwarder, a foreign distributor or agent, and local transportation companies. The delivery may take longer and the export transaction may be financed over a longer period.	- Advances in transportation technologies. - Development of multimedia, information superhighway, video conferences, and such advanced but economical communication technologies. - Increase in information available about emerging markets and business conditions there. - Increase in the amount and reliability of the information available about a foreign partner, distributor, freight forwarder, and so on.
Multiple Environments: A company seeking a supplier in a foreign country is faced with a new set of public policy, competitive, resource, and market environment constraints. Different political regions, barriers to trade, higher inflation rates, and greater government involvement in economic affairs, concerning termination of local distributors are just some of the environmental difficulties involved in doing business with another country.	- In-depth research of the political, economic, social, and competitive environment of the countries of interest. - Knowledge of expert opinion on the risks of doing business in or with such countries. - Awareness of cultural norms, traditions, beliefs, etc., of foreign country.
Multiple Currencies: Apart from administrative cost of handling transactions in various currencies, exchange rate fluctuations pose special difficulties. Exchange rates, the value of one currency expressed in terms of another, are subject to fluctuation	- Availability of financial instruments like forex hedges, options, futures, etc. - Signing contractual agreements at a predetermined exchange rate.

Exhibit 3.5   *Continued*

Challenge	Impact Minimized by
as demand for various currencies changes. Therefore, quoting prices in the foreign currency or estimating profitability of an export transaction are difficult, especially for selling to countries that are experiencing high levels of inflation.	
Conflicts With Home and Host Countries: On one hand, home countries accuse their own companies of taking employment, R&D, and taxes out of the country (e.g., some union officials have labeled the U.S. multinationals as "runaway" corporations). On the other hand, the direct investment presence of a company in a host country makes it more vulnerable politically.	- Avoiding countries with adverse relations with home country as target markets. - Creating a positive image in the host country through managing relationships with the host government, communities, and customers.
Social and Corporate Culture Differences, Business Customs, and Language: Stepping into a different social and cultural environment, the international manager encounters one or more foreign languages, different values and beliefs, changing lifestyles and norms, varying aspirations and motivations, and a new set of consumption, use, and shopping behaviors.	- Understanding the social and cultural aspects of foreign country before making business decisions, especially so for marketing. - Involving an employee with foreign country origin in negotiations. - Training managers in intercultural and international business negotiations.

to assume additional and greater risks. The job of international marketers is much more challenging than that of domestic marketers because of the cultural disparities and also the variance in demand patterns and behavior of firms and authorities in different markets. Exhibit 3.5 summarizes some of the challenges encountered by firms engaged in international marketing.

First, there is geographic as well as psychic distance. The geographic distance makes physical distribution more difficult, and psychic distance creates communication problems. Second, firms have to deal with multiple environments, such as public policy, traditions of trade, barriers to trade, and competitive forces. Third, firms engaged in global marketing have to deal with multiple currencies and exchange-rate variations; and transactions in various currencies entail administrative costs and difficulties. Fourth, firms engaged in international marketing are often in conflict with their home governments, because they take employment opportunities and other resources out of the country. These firms are also often in conflict with host governments with regard to remittance of their profits back to their home countries or head offices, ownership of local facilities, and competition with local firms. Finally, cross-cultural interaction also creates challenges for international businesspersons. Differences in language, business customs and ethics, lifestyles and values, and other cultural dimensions often cause uncertainty and a psychic distance. This type of distance is related to how we perceive a certain market and is different from physical distance. For example, for a U.S. firm, in psychic distance terms, the United Kingdom is a closer market than Brazil or even Mexico.

Many authorities contend that Western businesspeople are ill prepared to conduct business in any culture other than their own. They are unfamiliar with the "hidden dimensions" that frequently play a fundamental role in international business transactions. Different cultures require different behavior patterns by a firm, because strategies, structures, and technologies appropriate in one cultural setting may fail in another. Therefore, one of the primary challenges of international business transactions is to operate effectively in a multicultural setting, as explained in Exhibit 3.6.

A foreign firm will be affected by an indigenous culture depending on its level of involvement in the particular market. The greater the involvement, the greater the reliance on cultural growth and survival, and the greater the need for understanding the cultural environment.

Exhibit 3.6   The Importance of Cultural Awareness in Business

Among the many obstacles making international marketing a difficult and time-consuming task are the intricacies implied and caused by local culture. Consumers in one country are clearly not the same as consumers in another. While the mistakes made by other marketers are often amusing, they are often a costly and frustrating part of doing business abroad.

Example One

A well-known North American brewer engaged in a special promotional campaign during the 1994 World Cup soccer tournament. Among other activities, the company had flags of all the countries qualifying for the World Cup Finals imprinted under the bottle cap of their leading brand of beer. Among the numerous flags portrayed was that of Saudi Arabia, which depicts a holy verse from the Koran, the holy scripture of the Muslim religion. In response to this, Muslims from all over the world reacted angrily to the fact that a holy verse was associated with alcoholic beverages. Subsequently, the brewer had to recall all its bottles and discontinue the promotion. A simple cultural oversight led to considerable embarrassment and customer disappointment.

Example Two

A U.S.-based company in the business of telephone directory production set up a joint venture in Turkey with a Turkish firm. The new firm prepared and printed special telephone directories for every city in the country. In the new telephone directory for Bolu, a city located halfway between Ankara and Istanbul, a prominent businessman's last name, "Tarak," was misprinted as "Yarak." "Tarak" means "comb" in Turkish, while "Yarak" is the Turkish slang for the male genital organ. As a result of this error, the prominent businessman of Bolu was, much to his displeasure, the subject of jokes for some time thereafter.

Although typographical errors are common in the printing business throughout the world, it is important to be sensitive to the characteristics of the language of the country of interest. In this case, special attention should have been paid both during the typing and proofreading stages of the printed material, since the core business of the joint venture was printing. Partly as a result of this mishap, this company is no longer in the yellow pages business in Turkey.

Example Three

Daf Trucks, a major Dutch vehicle manufacturer, believed that there were opportunities for expansion outside Europe. After comprehensive desk and field research, the company decided to enter the Saudi Arabian market with its standard line of trucks. However, after several years of hard work and marketing effort, sales proved to be very disappointing. Subsequently, a thorough investigation of truck-buying behavior in the Saudi market revealed some remarkable facts. First, it appeared that Saudi truck owners have a great loyalty for the leading brand of German trucks—Mercedes. Second, it became

Exhibit 3.6 *Continued*

apparent that Saudi buyers prefer trucks that have "torpedo" type fronts to those with "flat" fronts. Third, although Daf set up an extensive dealer network with modern service facilities, it became evident that truck owners preferred the services of the older, smaller service stations that they were already familiar with. The older, smaller service stations were perceived as more flexible and employing more friendly mechanics. By contrast, the service stations that Daf had established were seen as too informal and inflexible. Finally, the new Daf trucks were equipped with two front seats, instead of the four that were standard in the German models. Saudi truckers have a habit of carrying a number of passengers and family members in their driver cabs and the limited seating made that factor a disadvantage for the company.

Strategic Alignment for Internationalization

All companies large and small need to have a well-thought-out strategy for going international. This strategy should be aligned to a company's own organizational capabilities and environments and the capabilities of the other organization or company with whom it is building a partnership for entering a specific market. A company can complement its own capabilities with that of other organizations, such as banks, freight forwarders, different government offices, trade associations, and market-research companies. A good alignment among these two capability sources will facilitate the process of going international and formulating an efficient marketing strategy. This is further explained in Exhibit 3.7.

Company Capabilities: Finding a Fit

It is a well-documented fact in management literature that poor performance results when a company fails to align its capabilities with its business strategy. Whenever a company decides to internationalize its business, it should reassess its capabilities or strengths and weaknesses and try to find a fit between its capabilities and the internationalization process. This may involve an evaluation of the company's resources, technology, business processes, and products or services that the company wishes to sell from the target foreign market perspective. We recommend five key areas that a company must investigate before committing resources to exporting or other forms of internationalization. These five areas and appropriate questions to be asked are as follows:[1]

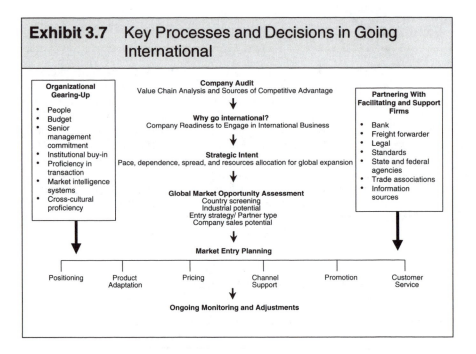

Exhibit 3.7   Key Processes and Decisions in Going International

1. **Business Background**
   a. How long has your firm been in business?
   b. How many full-time employees does your company have?
   c. What were your gross sales last year?
   d. What was the growth rate of your company over the past 3 years?
   e. Which of the following best describes your sales and distribution activity: manufacturers' representatives only; direct sales force only; or a combination of sales force, representatives, and distributors?
   f. Which of the following best describes your scope of marketing: few local customers, few regional and national customers, large base of local customers, large base of regional customers, or large base of national customers?
   g. What is the current strategic emphasis of your company: maximum profitability and return on investment (ROI), equal emphasis on profitability and market share, strong emphasis on growth in domestic market share, or strong market share in key global markets?
   h. What percentage of your total company sales should be represented by foreign market sales within the next 3 to 5 years?
   i. Which of the following best describes your firm: currently not exporting; exporting by selling to middlemen in your home country; exporting directly to foreign agents, distributors, and customers; exporting through company-owned sales organization; or exporting through subsidiary(ies) in foreign markets?

    j. Do you have access to external funds for expansion or working capital purposes?

    k. Does your staff have adequate knowledge of foreign cultures and business customs?

    l. How extensive is your staff's previous international business experience?

    m. How familiar is your management with the language and culture of the target market?

2. **Motivation for Going International**

    a. Do you wish to export because you have excess production?

    b. Do you wish to export to fill unsolicited orders only?

    c. Do you wish to export to benefit solely by stabilizing seasonal market fluctuations?

    d. Do you wish to internationalize to expand into key world markets?

    e. Do you wish to internationalize to enhance your firm's competitiveness by acquiring market knowledge?

    f. Do you wish to export to extend the life cycle of existing products in foreign markets?

    g. Do you wish to internationalize to supplement domestic sales with occasional export sales?

    h. Do you wish to internationalize to reduce risks by selling in diverse foreign markets?

    i. Do you wish to internationalize to exploit the firm's unique technology and know-how?

    j. Do you wish to internationalize to improve ROI for the entire company?

    k. Is internationalization a part of your long-term expansion strategy?

3. **Top Management Commitment**

    a. What view does the top management take concerning risk factors involved in getting into foreign markets: not willing to jeopardize current profits and ROI, will sacrifice current profits and ROI moderately, will sacrifice current profits and ROI significantly, or will sacrifice more than 20% ROI and profits?

    b. How does your management intend to sell overseas in the next 3 to 5 years: selling through middlemen located in United States, selling to or through agents or trading companies in foreign markets, selling directly to distributors in foreign markets, selling through at least one marketing subsidiary in key markets, or selling through marketing subsidiaries in major foreign markets?

    c. What will be the size of funds that will be set aside to develop foreign markets in each of the 3 years on average: less than $5,000 per year, between $5,000 and $25,000 per year, between $26,000 and $50,000 per year, between $51,000 and $100,000 per year, or more than $100,000 per year?

    d. How much time is senior management willing to allocate to international expansion efforts: occasional or sporadic as required, up to quarter-time of one person, up to half-time of one person, up to full-time of one person, more than one full-time person?

    e.   How will you develop your management plan for foreign markets: no formal planning; at most through an annual budget; through marketing plans developed for specific needs or projects; by periodic marketing plans developed for total international operations; through periodic marketing plans developed for the total and for each market; or regular marketing plans for the total, each market, and each product?

    f.   What will be the size of funds that will be allocated in each of the first 3 years for market research, market analysis, and competitive analysis?

    g.   At which level will international personnel in your company be compensated: the most affordable level we can pay with our resources, a level compatible with third-level management in the company, competitively with the rate for equivalent positions in industry, or higher than the rate for equivalent positions in industry?

    h.   How long is top management willing to wait before achieving a break-even point on their foreign market investment? Is the top management commitment long-term?

    i.   What attitude does the management take toward long-term contractual relationships with overseas partners?

    j.   How does top management envisage exporting: occasional activity, regular activity but no targeted export sales, regular activity with moderate levels of targeted exports, or regular activity with aggressive levels of targeted exports?

4. Product Strengths

    a.   Does your product require extensive training to operate or use?

    b.   Does your product require considerable support after the sale?

    c.   Is your product versatile? Does your product fulfill different needs?

    d.   Is your product bulky? Are shipping costs for your product high?

    e.   Is your product category enjoying increasing market demand in domestic country?

    f.   Is your product unique, differentiated, or technologically advanced?

    g.   Is the production process exclusive to your firm?

    h.   Do your company R&D levels exceed industry average?

    i.   Is your product competitively priced in the domestic market?

    j.   Does your product have significant advantages over competing products?

    k.   Does your product require extensive inventory investment by distributors?

    l.   Does your product require special domestic license to export?

    m. Does your product require special storage?

5. Market-Specific Strengths

    a.   Do you think your product will be well accepted in the foreign market?

    b.   Will the climate in the target country restrict the life or use of your product?

    c.   Are tariff levels low for your product?

    d.   Can your product be shipped or disassembled to obtain lower duties?

    e.   Will patent or trademark protection provide any advantage in the target market?

    f.   Does your product face significant obstacles and high costs in complying with standards and regulations of the target market?

    g.   Are there any existing substitutes for your product in the target market?

    h.   Will you be able to price your product competitively in the target market?

    i.   Are there any serious nontariff barriers to import your product by foreign market?

    j.   Can product and/or packaging be made suitable to foreign customers?

    k.   Can manufacturing make any adaptations to enhance product appeal?

    l.   Are product category sales in a growth stage in the target market?

    m. Is it difficult or easy to locate qualified distributors to promote and distribute your product?

    n.   Can the credit terms and delivery requirements of the target market be met?

    o.   Are there a number of strong, entrenched competitors in the target market, each having a significant market share?

    p.   Is there a favorable attitude in the target country toward products made in your country?

Sometimes, just finding a fit between company capabilities and internationalization may not be enough; some key capabilities have to be leveraged by adapting these to the foreign culture. Exhibit 3.8 represents the strategic intent of a firm that wants to grow and become more profitable and what capabilities it needs to align to become successful. To develop new customers and businesses, the firm decides to explore foreign markets. Though many academicians agree that most firms go through the evolutionary process of internationalization (i.e., exporting to foreign direct investment), the pace of global changes has made it necessary for firms to skip some stages in the internationalization process, depending on the firm's strategic intent.

Company Competitiveness

Regardless of size, survival of a firm depends on the managerial ability of setting new directions and achieving goals based on the requirements for competing in a global community. Continuous improvement is critical in the search for world-class status, but before a company can think of an improvement program, it must develop a profile of its current status, analyzing strengths and weaknesses and formulating strategies for addressing the identified weaknesses.[2] The importance of performing a competitive assessment internationally has grown in recent years, as indicated by a study of U.S. manufacturing companies by A.T. Kearney (Steingraber, 1992, pp. 14-15). The study found that in 1982, fewer than 5% of U.S. manufacturing companies could claim that one of their top five competitors

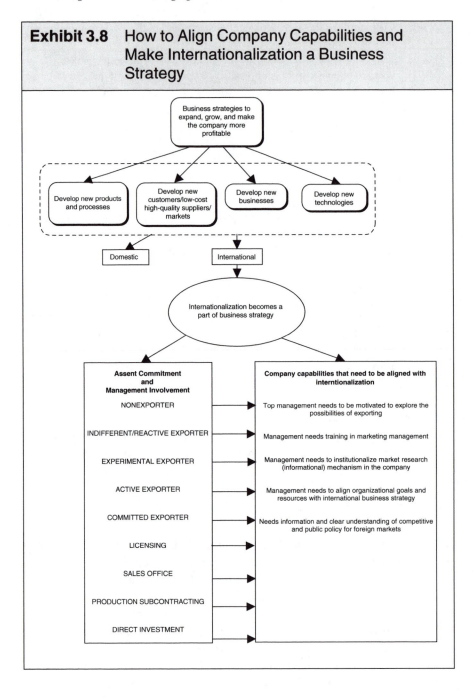

Exhibit 3.8   How to Align Company Capabilities and Make Internationalization a Business Strategy

in the U.S. was from abroad. By 1987, 30% of U.S. manufacturers identified three of their top five domestic competitors as foreign companies. In 1992, 45% of U.S. manufacturing companies expected three or four of their top five competitors to be from outside the United States. These changes demonstrate the necessity of a global outlook for managers.

A manager may follow three steps to measure business performance:

1. Determining current performance levels in all areas of the corporation and then benchmarking with competitors will help managers in determining how their businesses are performing vis-à-vis the competition. The importance of measuring business performance can be emphasized with the popular management saying "If you cannot measure it, you cannot manage it!"

2. Identifying, developing, and implementing both long- and short-term strategies must be developed to address areas requiring attention.

3. Implementing a continuous improvement program that cuts across all aspects of the enterprise is necessary to increase productivity and place the company in a much improved competitive position.

Competitive analysis can follow either a horizontal or a vertical approach to diffuse through the whole organization. Thus, it can analyze the company by its functional areas or through its processes. Another approach could be matching processes with functions to get a cross-functional matrix. The essence of this approach lies in its use with companies in the transition phase from a function-driven organization to a process-driven organization. Analysis through the coupling of vertical functions against horizontal processes provides the company with feedback on its transformation process. Competitive assessments may include the functions and processes illustrated in Exhibit 3.9.

The global competitiveness of the company is not only dependent on how well the functions and processes appearing in Exhibit 3.9 are managed but also on specific capabilities it uses for gaining a competitive advantage abroad. These capabilities can be one or more of the following:

- Product or process technology that is unique to the company
- Logistics and distribution capabilities to meet high customer service levels
- Smaller or compressed new-product development and introduction cycle times

Managers may find some other areas not discussed above in which their firms can gain competitive advantage. However, we assert that it is extremely important to perform a competitive analysis of the company and that this should be done internationally, not domestically.

Exhibit 3.9   Functions and Processes That Can Be Used in Competitive Assessment

Vertical Functions
Human resources
Accounting
Finance
Technology
Product design
Manufacturing
Marketing and sales
Logistics
Customer service

Cross-Functional or Horizontal Processes
New-product management
Inventory management
Quality Management
Labor/management relationships
Relationship management
Information management
Budgeting
Financing
Cost reduction
Management of structure
Safety processes
Management of customer payment

Support Functions
Image
Customer franchise
Networks and alliances
Global configuration

International Integration
Through Information Technology

Global connectivity, which is essential for firms to do business internationally, has been facilitated by the Internet. In the future, the importance of networks like the Internet in business will continue to grow and evolve into systems that are based on multimedia and the information superhighway (see Exhibit 3.10 for an example).

Exhibit 3.10 The Internet and Emerging Markets

E-mail has become an important tool for communications and networking. Ted Sickles, manager of data networking at Rockwell International, recalls the following incident when he was visiting a Rockwell site in London in May 1993:

> I checked my e-mail, and along with the more routine messages, I found a request from a person somewhere in China asking for information about a particular chip that Rockwell manufactures. I didn't know anything about that topic, but I used e-mail to forward the message to the appropriate person back in Newport Beach, California. He contacted the Rockwell support people in Japan, and they were able to reach the person who made the original query with an answer via the Internet. There's no way to provide that kind of responsiveness without global connectivity.

SOURCE: Cronin (1994, pp. 90-91).

The Internet is gradually transforming itself into a worldwide network that will become the informational "nervous system" for future international businesses. The revolution in information and communications technology has made it feasible for companies to integrate the entire supply chain or value chain globally. However, many managers think that integrating the value chain by using information technology is not a feasible idea, because they believe that (a) the integration of the supply chain would require a total redesign of existing operational support systems, (b) supply chain integration is a multiyear, multimillion-dollar exercise, and (c) it may disturb already-existing relationships among different parties in a particular supply chain system.

In practice, however, businesses are noticing the following:

• Today's technologies (EDI, Oracle-type databases, C++ type languages, knowledge-based systems, logic, etc.) can provide a full view of the supply chain activity, and it is possible to use this to regulate flows through the pipeline, as demonstrated by corporations such as Xerox and DEC.

• Organizations do not have to go through a major process-rewriting exercise. Small modifications in the existing systems can be used to achieve major gains toward integration. For example, Xerox and DEC have made all company data from existing systems available at every other point, on a distributed basis, thus making material flows transparent throughout the organization.

• Information technology for export purposes is becoming common, and companies will have to invest in additional infrastructure to develop and maintain large communications networks in order to implement integration through information technology.

• Multimedia computers will make two-way audio, video, and text transfers extremely fast and inexpensive, thus catalyzing the process of the global integration of value chains.

• More and more companies are forced/induced by each other to incorporate information technology into their systems. If your suppliers or distributors are switching over to information technology to achieve efficiencies, you simply have to follow suit if you do not want to lose that supplier or distributor.

The use of multimedia technology and information technology has become more and more popular in business. We believe that these two will become the critical technologies that will facilitate the integration of the firm's value chain. Multimedia presentations will be used frequently for joint problem solving, communicating new ideas, global training programs, and even video conferences between employees separated by large geographical distances. This technology will also facilitate the global sharing of expertise. Problems posted on an electronic bulletin board will be read and solved by employees in other parts of the world. The information technology will provide worldwide access to information resources without forcing companies to lock investments in proprietary electronic networks. It will also facilitate the creation of global databases accessible to employees all over the world. This may lead to enormous advantages for the firm, because management will be able to access pricing and cost differences in various parts of the world in real time. Management can also continuously monitor material flows all over the world and do consolidated buying if the same material is needed in two or more different parts of the world. Exhibit 3.11 captures the future role of multimedia and the information superhighway in international business.

The same technologies will also be used to design management control systems in four categories: beliefs systems, boundary systems, diagnostic systems, and interactive control systems.[3]

Belief systems are used to provide momentum and guidance to opportunity-seeking behaviors from employees so that they constantly think of making the firm's business more profitable, effective, and efficient within the framework of shared beliefs that define basic values, purpose, and direction.

Exhibit 3.11 The Future Role of Multimedia and the Information Superhighway in International Business

TWO-WAY SOUND AND VIDEO

- CEOs and managers will use new technologies for global video conferencing with employees.
- New ideas will be able to be expressed and dispersed at a very high rate.
- Computers will continue to provide new methods for management and problem-solving techniques.
- Multimedia programs will provide more effective training programs.

GLOBAL DATABASES

- Global databases will allow managers to monitor and simulate continuous material flows.
- Managers will be able to forecast areas where synergies may be achieved through consolidation.
- Computers will continue to provide new methods for management and problem-solving techniques.
- Expertise may be shared globally through bulletin boards, e-mail, and other information systems.

REVERSE FEEDBACK

- Increased feedback will allow organizations to learn and continuously improve their processes.
- Customers' expectations can be monitored and met more efficiently.
- Increased feedback will minimize forecasting and "guesswork."
- Procurement planning and cost-price decisions will benefit from increased information flows.
- Managers will be able to adapt more quickly to changes in customer preferences.

Boundary systems are formally stated limits and rules that must be respected and are used to allow employees to express creativity in improving work and business conditions, within limits of freedom.

Diagnostic control systems are feedback systems used to monitor organizational outcomes and ensure that preset standards of performance are met.

Interactive control systems allow managers to focus the organizational attention on uncertainties that can have a major impact on the firm's future, thereby triggering new initiatives and strategies from employees. Managers personally involve themselves with employees in these kinds of control systems and continuously try to foster creativity and innovativeness within the organization.

We expect that in future (as shown in the shaded areas of Exhibit 3.12), multimedia and information superhighway technologies will be directly and indirectly used to design management control systems in the above-mentioned four categories.

As seen in Exhibit 3.12, managers in the future will make extensive use of audio, video, and textual media to communicate with employees separated by geography. We hope that the reader envisions an organization in which employees solve problems and share creative and new ideas across distances almost in real time. The management will be able to communicate any change in organizational strategy or vision and organizational limits of freedom to all employees simultaneously.

The above discussion should convince a Western manager that managing a global company becomes much easier with the use of information technology. Distance will no longer hamper the process of value chain integration. Exhibit 3.13 illustrates how a future Western company may do business in the emerging markets.

• The hypothetical company will source high-labor-content parts from China as long as it keeps offering the competitive advantage of lowest-cost production. At present, a number of companies, such as Nike and IKEA, are reaching this stage. Nike, for example, does not own any manufacturing facilities. Factories in China, Vietnam, or Indonesia are geared toward Nike standards. A typical Nike shoe is made up of 52 different components coming from five different countries and different companies. The new production system is a network of logistics; not only does all the material have to come together, it has to come together at the right time. Moreover, designs and models are changed every week, which has to be conveyed to suppliers and manufacturers in all of these countries and companies. This type of efficiency and speed can be achieved only with the help of information technology (Cateora & Ghauri, 2000, p. 5).

• The software needed for the product may be sourced from India, where software expertise is available cheaply. The company management wants to control the critical technologies and source technology-intensive components from the United States.

• The logistics of the company are managed by a third-party logistics company under a long-term contract or alliance with the company. The logistical structure is a seamless distribution network, and any employee of the hypothetical company anywhere in the world will see the same documents

(Text continues on page 66)

Exhibit 3.12 Designing Global Management Control Systems Using Multimedia and the Information Superhighway

	Belief Systems	Boundary Systems	Diagnostic Control Systems	Interactive Control Systems
Nature of Systems	Explicit set of shared beliefs that define basic values, purpose, and direction	Formally stated limits and rules that must be respected	Feedback systems used to monitor organizational outcomes and correct deviations from preset standards of performance	Control systems that managers use to regularly and personally involve themselves in the activities of subordinates
Purpose	Provide momentum and guidance to opportunity-seeking behaviors	Allow individual creativity within limits of freedom	Provide motivation, resources, and information to ensure important organizational strategies and goals will be achieved	Focus organizational attention on strategic uncertainties and thereby provoke the emergence of new initiatives and strategies
Information Technology Application	Management uses audio, video, text, e-mail, etc. of multimedia technology to communicate beliefs through the network.	Management communicates the formal organizational rules and limits and changes thereof electronically to employees all over the world.	Management uses planning, expert systems, and decision support systems extensively with feedback mechanisms.	Management regularly interacts with global employees through audio, video, text, etc., of multimedia

Exhibit 3.12 *Continued*

	Belief Systems	*Boundary Systems*	*Diagnostic Control Systems*	*Interactive Control Systems*
Multimedia and Information Superhighway	For many employees a common electronic system may be installed, thus making the system economical.	The system may be designed (for quantitative measurements) so that whenever a threshold is reached by a behavior or performance measure a beeper or alarm is set off.	Human intervention, monitoring, and control make the system "intelligent," thereby correcting any deviation from intended outcomes.	Technology getting fresh ideas for improving the firm's business, by focusing the employees' attention on major issues or problems faced by the firm.

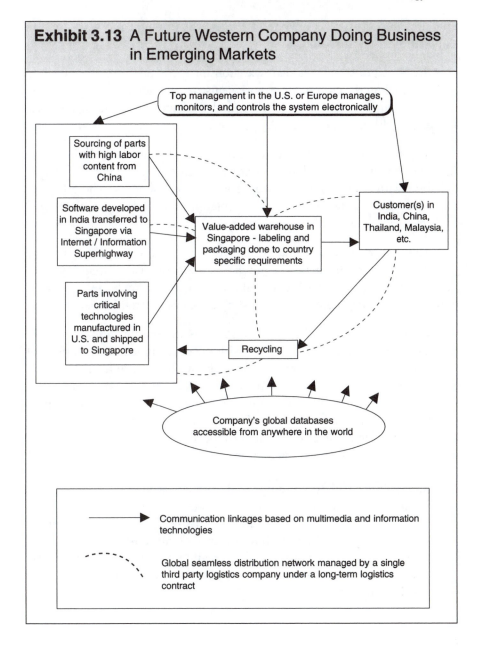

Exhibit 3.13 A Future Western Company Doing Business in Emerging Markets

and similar processes as anyone else does, thus minimizing waste due to duplication and translation.

• In Singapore, value-added warehousing activities are performed in which, based on the customer's requirements, an individual or unique configuration is put together. The labeling and packaging is done in the local language of the customer, depending on the customer's geographical location.

• Top management continuously monitors and controls the value chain from the United States and makes critical decisions, when required, in consultation with local managers located in various countries. The company maintains global databases so that information is available on a distributed basis from anywhere in the organization.

• The customer remains the primary driver of the value chain, and the moment the customer makes a purchase, the entire value chain cycle of activities is triggered. This leads to almost real-time knowledge of demand patterns for management, and forecasting errors can be minimized.

• The scope of the value chain is complete with recycling and disposal of used parts and is done in accordance with the environmental regulations of the local country. A reader may wonder why we have included recycling in this hypothetical picture: Environmental concerns will become more and more important all over the world in the future, and businesses will not be able to ignore environmental costs. Western managers must keep recycling in mind and design a reverse logistics channel up front, when first creating a logistics channel in an emerging market.

Managers of small to medium-sized companies may wonder whether such a scope of global activity is really feasible for their companies. The answer is "yes"—if the small and medium-sized companies succeed in forming alliances with the right kind of firms doing business in their core competence areas. They will succeed in creating a global virtual organization that will essentially function in a similar fashion as the one shown in the hypothetical example in Exhibit 3.13.

Notes

1. This kind of assessment is called "Company Readiness to Export" (CORE) and was developed and copyrighted by Dr. S. Tamer Cavusgil, Michigan State University. A software version of this assessment based on expert systems or artificial intelligence logic is available at nominal costs at the International Business Center, Michigan State University, East

Lansing, MI. Please contact by phone (517) 353-4336 or fax (517) 432-1009 to obtain more information about CORE.

2. The authors wish to thank Tunga Kiyak and Parth Gandhi, MBA class of 1995, Eli Broad Graduate School of Management, Michigan State University, East Lansing, MI, for providing us with their research on competitive assessment.

3. The nature of systems and purpose has been adapted from the following source: Robert Simons, "How New Top Managers Use Control Systems as Levers of Strategic Renewal," 1994, *Strategic Management Journal, 15,* pp. 169-189. The shaded area shown was not present in the original source, and it depicts how we feel information technology can be used to develop control systems for the organization economically.

4

Export Marketing and Sourcing in Emerging Economies

The emerg ing markets share remarkable features in terms of economic potential; they have large markets, young labor forces in abundance, and are thus attractive for both selling and sourcing. Moreover, most emerging markets have major political influence in their regions and are regional economic drivers. Whether seeking to do business in developed countries or in emerging economies, the first market research initiative a firm has to undertake is identifying a few countries that are the most attractive for doing business in. This can be done by looking at various characteristics of the potential market. Information is the key component in developing a strategy to do business in emerging markets. Market research is the systematic gathering, recording, and analyzing of information useful in marketing decision making (Cateora & Ghauri, 2000). Below is a list of some key characteristics a manager must assess to determine the attractiveness and suitability of an emerging market.

1. History of Country Risk. We recommend that a manager look at the country risk ratings for at least the last 3 years and at projected risk ratings for the future. As outlined in Chapter 2, country risk ratings can easily be obtained from *The Economist, Euromoney,* and *Institutional Investor.* Managers may also choose to make their own country risk evaluation models. Countries with high risk ratings should not be considered for business.

2. GDP Growth Rate. One common characteristic of most emerging markets is their high gross domestic product (GDP) growth rates in present and future projections. Emerging economies (especially huge ones like China) will need to generate demand for foreign businesses, especially in infrastructure. Countries experiencing low risk (according to risk ratings in Chapter 2) and high economic growth rates are very attractive for doing business in.

3. Per Capita Income on Purchasing-Power Parity Scale. Markets require not only people, but people with money. Therefore, a Western manager should examine the per capita income of a country to determine the level of its economic development. We suggest that for a Western manager, the best comparison to make between per capita incomes is according to a common purchasing-power parity scale. This way, a clear view can be obtained of exactly what a customer can buy and at what cost in his or her country and in the foreign market in question. However, it may not be a good idea to automatically eliminate countries showing low per capita incomes even on a purchasing-power parity scale. This is because certain countries, although low in per capita income, may be historically specialized in a particular industrial activity that creates a focused product demand (an example is the textile machinery industry in India). Also, in some emerging markets in which aggregate statistics indicate a low per capita income, there may be a high-income segment that represents an attractive market (an example is the burgeoning upper-middle class of India, which approximates 300 million people who can afford most Western goods).

4. Share of World Trade. This statistic is commonly available and gives an indication of the intensity of international trade activity going on in a country. It is worth conducting research on the performance of key industries responsible for the increase or decrease in the share of world trade by a country.

5. History of Economic Liberalization. As discussed in the classification of emerging markets in Chapter 2, knowledge of when and how the emerging-market government began economic liberalization will indicate the following facts to the manager:

- How familiar the market is to Western management, marketing, and products. For example, Singapore and Hong Kong, which emerged during the 1980s, are far more familiar to Western management, marketing, and products than is India, which emerged in the 1990s.

- Economic liberalization is often seen as an irreversible process, even if the government changes.

6. *Is economic growth and development projected to be sustainable in emerging markets?* This question becomes extremely important to address, because the long-term future of business in a foreign company will depend on sustaining economic growth and development by the emerging economy. There are several sources: World Bank, United Nations Conference on Trade and Development (UNCTAD), *The Economist,* and the National Trade Data Bank (NTDB) of the U.S. Department of Commerce provide historical data as well as estimates for some future years. For example, the "10 biggest emerging markets" are expected to show very rapid economic growth in the next 20 years, and this makes them attractive for business.

7. *Foreign Trade Policy Drivers of the Emerging Economy.* Most emerging-market governments are providing enormous incentives to Western businesses for foreign direct investment and development of basic infrastructural capabilities. If an invitation to foreign businesses is a foreign trade policy driver, then the Western manager must expect much more cooperation from the emerging-market governments. Many times, Western managers can even use these policy drivers by negotiating favorable terms and conditions. For example, when Cargill opened an office in India in 1991, it was attacked by local farmers who perceived it as the "ugly multinational." However, the government of India took steps to protect Cargill's facilities from such future attacks to restore confidence in other Western investors' minds about safety and stability in India.

8. *Most-Promising Industries and Import Statistics.* A knowledge of high-growth or most-promising industries in a potential country market may help a manager in selecting a country if the firm's business is in one or more of those industries. The NTDB of the U.S. Department of Commerce provides a list of the most-promising industries in various country markets all over the world. Though this information may come purely from a U.S. point of view, it may still be used as an example by Western managers to select countries with the most-promising industries related to their businesses.

It may also be necessary to examine the size and growth of each country's import of products or product lines that are similar to the firm's business. The countries that do not import very significant quantities of products may be eliminated. However, on many occasions, small imports do not always indicate insignificant markets. Therefore, a manager must try to understand and inquire as to the true reasons behind a country's limited imports. Sometimes, the stagnation of imports is imposed by a country's trade restrictions. In such a case, it will be necessary to keep up-to-date on further developments about these restrictions because they are often removed. In addition, it is a good idea to check the sources of the target country's imports. Countries whose imports are clearly dominated by one or two supplying countries should be dropped.

9. *Attractions for Gaining a Competitive Advantage From a Western Perspective.* Managers must also seek only those countries that offer a competitive advantage in the long run. A competitive advantage may come in the form of huge untapped markets or by gaining a foothold in a promising region by establishing a presence in one key market. For example, when the U.S. manufacturer of home appliances, Whirlpool, decided to create an Asian presence, it chose to buy Kelvinator of India as a first step. Whirlpool has decided to expand its markets all over Asia, starting with India.

10. *Facilities Available for Foreign Businesses.* If significant investments are planned in that region, a Western manager must never ignore the infrastructure and facilities available in a foreign target market. Many emerging countries still lack basic facilities such as transportation and distribution, communication, and electricity. Also, an educated workforce in a foreign market may prove useful because it is more productive.

11. *Major Cultural Factors to Be Considered in Doing Business.* A country's social, educational, and religious systems critically influence its marketing system. These cultural variables have a crucial impact on product policy and are considered by many to be the biggest barriers to doing business overseas. Yet many Western managers fail to include these variables in their research. The reason for this may be due in part to the problems of trying to quantify cultural characteristics. However, more common and more serious is the tendency of Western managers to view a foreign culture in the same framework as their own culture.

12. *Foreign Trade Policy Priorities of U.S./European Union Governments.* Many Western governments are designing national export strategies to promote exports from their countries. There are many informative reports on international business available from such export-promotion governmental and semigovernmental agencies, and these may help a manager select a foreign market on the basis of reliable information. Also, foreign trade priorities of Western governments may lead to availability of funds and other crucial information for certain markets, and a manager must make full use of these to select the foreign market. If this support from home government

is a national trade priority, then the number of facilitating factors for exporting becomes enormous. Generally, the tools and techniques for research remain the same for emerging and developed country market research, but the environments in which they are applied are different. The problems of implementing marketing techniques may thus vary from country to country.

Guidelines for Export Marketing to Emerging Economies: Bidding for Global Tenders

Many opportunities in emerging economies come in the form of global tenders for infrastructural projects (power, telecommunications, roads, ports, airports, etc.) and bulk purchases of commodities and equipment. Typically, a two-step bid process is followed by emerging economies: the technical bid and the commercial bid. Technical bids may entail preparing a feasibility report, which then may be approved by the buyer, enabling the bidder to qualify for commercial or price bidding.

It is helpful to conceptualize the marketing process to emerging economies in six phases (see Exhibit 4.1). The process is typical of the experience encountered by a Western firm selling to private and government sectors. It is much more descriptive of the unusual, rather than routine, major purchases made by emerging economies.

Phase 1: Scanning

Marketing to emerging economies begins with the identification of new opportunities. Most aggressive firms develop sophisticated market intelligence systems to monitor worldwide sales opportunities on a continuous basis. Information from a variety of sources is sought and evaluated. Internally, traveling managers, subsidiaries, and overseas representatives feed information to a central office. Externally, useful information about new opportunities may be gathered from the Agency for International Development, the World Bank, foreign embassies, international banks, industrial organizations, and other firms. Many publications, such as the bimonthly periodical *Worldwide Projects,* are also helpful.

Although most emerging economies are made up of nonsocialist countries, buyers from these countries must still comply with an annual economic plan or, for example, the yearly implementation of a 5-year development plan. These plans differ in detail and directiveness from country to country. Nevertheless, most plans are substantially directive, although they may be called "advisory" for political reasons.

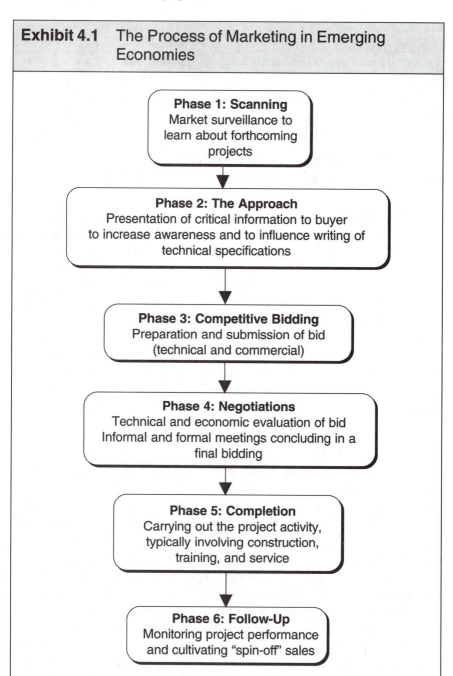

Exhibit 4.1   The Process of Marketing in Emerging Economies

Phase 1: Scanning
Market surveillance to learn about forthcoming projects

Phase 2: The Approach
Presentation of critical information to buyer to increase awareness and to influence writing of technical specifications

Phase 3: Competitive Bidding
Preparation and submission of bid (technical and commercial)

Phase 4: Negotiations
Technical and economic evaluation of bid Informal and formal meetings concluding in a final bidding

Phase 5: Completion
Carrying out the project activity, typically involving construction, training, and service

Phase 6: Follow-Up
Monitoring project performance and cultivating "spin-off" sales

Understanding the process of plan preparation and becoming familiar with the plan itself is the first step in successful marketing in emerging economies. It is through the planning process that most emerging economy governments announce their import priorities and investment plans. English texts of annual plans are usually available.

Industrial-sector programs are usually integral parts of development plans. These are important documents for marketing planning. Note that in many nations, plans can change with governments. Thus, the international marketer must be familiar with the programs of political parties. That is where policy guidelines for annual plans can be found.

The situation is not much different for sectors outside the scope of annual plans or when plans are not directive. Almost all private and government enterprises are forced to operate with high financial leverages, given the insufficient capital accumulation in these countries. Most financing originates from private or state-owned banks and direct or indirect government subsidies. Government subsidies, such as tax rebates and low-interest credit, are more directive than the plan in most cases. It is almost impossible to realize an investment in many emerging economies without such incentives. Therefore, government interference and control are quite dramatic even in those sectors that appear not to be regulated by plans.

Western marketers must also stay abreast of sales opportunities through their overseas representatives or agents, especially in major markets. These representatives are local businesspeople who ordinarily work on a commission-on-sales basis. They are familiar with the realities of the market and are in a position to evaluate the plans and programs efficiently and identify sales opportunities. In addition to monitoring the market, they provide valuable assistance in lengthy sales negotiations.

There are two types of representatives: exclusive and nonexclusive. Exclusive representatives are the only representatives for a company in a country. They are compensated whether or not they have anything to do with the sales. Experience shows that in concentrated and relatively small markets, obtaining a nonexclusive representative may be counterproductive. Some companies make use of "scanners," who are not formally representatives but provide information about future contracts.

Several considerations are relevant in selecting an exclusive representative. First, exclusive representatives may attempt to represent more than one company. The international marketer should be careful in selecting representatives to ensure there is no conflict of interest. An exclusive representative may be an agent for several companies in related businesses to secure a certain level of sales commissions. Second, most representatives have their own businesses and essentially run a "one-person show." There is always a majority shareholder or a family known to the locals as the owner(s), even if a professional manager runs office operations. The personal history and reputation of this person or family is extremely important. A representative's business is based on reputation and contacts. Therefore, it is always advisable to check on the history and degree of success of the representative with other clients. Third, corruption is a reality in most emerging economies. The Western marketer would be in a difficult position when confronted with such a sensitive issue without the help and commitment of an exclusive representative.

Phase 2: The Approach

The marketer must approach the buyer with relevant information and attempt to influence the writing of a tender specification, which usually takes the form of a feasibility report, once the opportunity for a specific project is identified. The marketer's aim is to present information on production and technological capabilities, solvency, and the likelihood of successful completion of the project. This is done to establish familiarity and confidence and to reduce any perceived risk on the part of the potential buyer.

An important objective of the marketing effort is to achieve a "first-mover" advantage. A marketer who can preempt competitors and be first in supplying relevant information to buyers will have a head start in the selling process. Marketers can tie up prospective buyers through several strategies: (a) a technical solution to buyers' problems, (b) social linkages between buyers and sellers, (c) financial linkages in terms of provisions for financing the project, and (d) other informational linkages. In the final analysis, the choice of a supplier boils down to human judgment. Hence, the importance of informal social contacts cannot be overemphasized (see Exhibit 4.2).

Jansson (1986) compares the creation of first-mover advantage to the spinning of a web, in that the buyer is encircled while the competitors are closed out. Growing interdependence between buyers and sellers, strengthened through the four types of linkage, facilitates successful bidding. In the absence of a first-mover advantage, marketers should carefully consider any further allocation of time and resources to the particular project. At this point, considerable marketing efforts have already been expended in identifying and cultivating new opportunities. Any additional expenses may be useless if a competitor already has the first-mover advantage.

Consideration of the following issues may be helpful in determining the desirability of any further commitment to the project:

- Can any information be provided to the buyer that would place you in a stronger position?
- What level of previous influence do you have with the buyer?

Exhibit 4.2   Strengthening Buyer-Seller Linkages

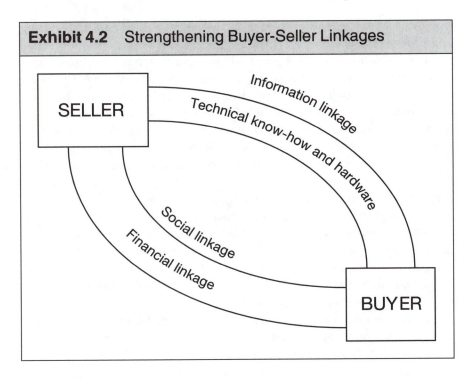

- Even if the product offerings are comparable, can you offer a more attractive financing option to the buyer?
- Can you gain a competitive edge by using domestic materials or by directing end products into export markets?
- Is there an opportunity to tie up the buyer in order to supply managerial/technical services and other products once the operation is completed?

A major objective of the first-mover is to affect the tender specifications before they are finalized in a feasibility report. The marketer must find out who is responsible for the delineation of tender specifications and then supply technical and other information to the buyer's project team. It is not unusual for marketers to assist buyers with various project-related studies at this stage.

There are several reasons why feasibility reports precede the actual solicitation of bids. Often, the buying organizations have to submit a feasibility report to take advantage of various incentives and obtain credit from local and international sources. Government generally requires a feasibility report to show compliance to plans and overall economic objectives. Favored projects include building infrastructure; improving the balance of payments, either by import substitution or by creating export opportunities; creating employment opportunities; having high added value; and transferring appropriate technology.

Most feasibility reports are prepared for a specific type of investment with detailed specifications. Although competitive bidding is an accepted practice, many prospective bidders are eliminated because technical specifications are often prepared for a specific group of suppliers. In some cases, selection of suppliers precedes the preparation of a feasibility report. This means that sales efforts must begin prior to the preparation of feasibility reports.

A feasibility report is a technical documentation of the proposed project. A considerable amount of expertise and technical know-how is required to prepare this report. Usually, the managerial expertise can be found locally. The technical expertise, on the other hand, is usually unavailable, and the customary approach is to consult published reports or international consultants. Because many projects are duplicates of similar investments in industrialized economies, visits to overseas sites by the buyer's project team are also common. Potential clients can be invited to tour the marketer's facilities in the home market and elsewhere.

The local exclusive representatives usually lack technical know-how, and they may not have the authority to make commitments on behalf of the foreign vendor. When the prospective project warrants, a team must be in direct contact with the potential buyer during the preparation of the feasibility study. One way of accomplishing this is for sellers in the West to have ad hoc project teams for emerging markets that can be organized quickly and hence avoid missing potential opportunities.

It is not unusual for an international consulting firm to be assigned to the preparation of the feasibility report for large-scale projects. Usually, this is a loan requirement for large-scale projects financed through international financial markets. However, the use of a consulting firm does not necessarily guarantee a better report, because most international consultants are unfamiliar with the particular market. The firm may overlook major factors or rely on incomplete information. Furthermore, political and business considerations force international consultants to act as mediators in most cases. Consulting firms will rarely be willing to make radical suggestions, because decisions relating to large investment/import projects may result in power struggles and political controversies in emerging economies.

Phase 3: Competitive Bidding

A tender is published, and bids are solicited from all interested vendors once the technical specifications are set. Technical terms and conditions are followed by the so-called administrative terms and conditions (ATC) for large-scale projects. Various legal, financial, and administrative issues are spelled out, and procurement procedures are revealed.

A critical decision by the international marketer at this stage relates to the amount of time and other resources to be invested in preparing the bid. It is expensive to produce bids, particularly for large projects, but it is hoped that the likelihood of a successful bid has been strengthened by tying up the buyer in the previous stage.

Purchasing by the government or state-owned economic enterprises (SEEs) is regulated by law in most emerging economies. This is helpful to the supplier because the organizational buying process and the authority and responsibility of each buying unit are clearly described in such laws. The regulations relating to government procurement state how requisitions are to be placed, who will have decision-making authority, and how the decision will be implemented. The international marketer must become familiar with these regulations. However, it should be noted that governments and SEEs are not always obliged to follow the law. This is true especially for certain clauses specifying the conditions under which a contract can be awarded.

There are no such regulations in privately owned corporations. The organizational structures of these corporations are usually centralized. Occasionally, shares of even the largest corporations are controlled by a few individuals or families. Therefore, the international marketer does not have to look far in identifying key decision makers.

This identification is often more difficult with government/SEE purchases. International marketers may be surprised to discover that they must talk to a dozen people from different echelons and divisions of an agency or agencies. Some agency personnel may even pretend to be real decision makers. A local representative may provide helpful inside information in this regard.

Some international marketers concentrate their efforts on the person who appears to be the final decision maker and neglect or even avoid others in the process. Due to cultural reasons, this strategy backfires in many emerging economies. Bureaucrats at lower levels of the hierarchy are generally frustrated and alienated because of low pay, underemployment, elitism, and other factors. Hence, being bypassed by a foreign supplier may be insulting. A major sales opportunity was lost by a U.S. textile company because of this oversight. An expert in the state planning organization argued that the supplier's technology was inappropriate and convinced the minister of finance, who was negotiating the financing, not to award the contract, even though the minister of industry and the general manager of the buying corporation were convinced it was the best offer.

Phase 4: Negotiations

Submitted bids are evaluated by the buyer from both technical and economic perspectives. Typically, bids are shortlisted, and some vendors are invited for further discussions, which usually marks the beginning of lengthy negotiations. These meetings provide opportunities for marketers to present additional explanations and details. These can be crucial in terms of their impact on the outcome.

Due to increasing international competition, the emerging economies drive a hard bargain. Emerging economy buyers may play Western suppliers against each other through bilateral or multilateral agreements. Applying uniform import taxes, pooling commodity imports, and cartel-type agreements are common. Pooling import purchases, such as fertilizers and tractors, for commodity production from multinational corporations is an example of such agreements. For example, when China was negotiating a project with Ericsson, the Swedish telecommunication company, they were at the same time negotiating with Ericsson's competitor Nokia, the Finnish company. They even booked them in the same hotel, moving from session to session with the two companies, and often using arguments such as "If Nokia can do it, why can't you?" (Ghauri & Fang, 2001). Many emerging economies lack the necessary foreign exchange to finance purchases. Total financing by the seller is a common practice now in large-scale projects. Tight international money markets and the low credit ratings of many emerging economies force them to look for the best payment terms. Japanese firms are quite successful in competitive bidding because they provide complete financial packages to emerging economies.

Limitations in certain products or process attributes may be overcome by strengths in financial terms, such as low interest, total financing, long maturity, and grace periods. Cooperation with financial institutions becomes a necessary ingredient for most negotiations. At the same time, these countries are increasingly engaging in countertrade deals, in which part of the import is paid for with goods rather than cash. Most countries now require countertrade purchases from their foreign suppliers.

The balance of trade continues to be a serious problem for most emerging economies. Their desire to improve their export situation enhances the seller's bargaining power. A contract for the construction of a vegetable-processing plant was granted to a French firm because the technology it offered, although expensive, was capable of producing goods that could be exported to the European community.

Some emerging economies are attempting to alter existing economic ties and establish alternative trade channels. The increasing aggressiveness of Eastern Europe in international markets provides additional bargaining power for most emerging economies. Western manufacturers limit the buying options of emerging economies. A large project involving machine tools was not awarded to a U.S. bidder because the manufacturer insisted on exclusively providing parts and supplies needed later. In contrast, Japanese bidders included a comparison of alternative sources from a variety of countries.

In certain countries, it is necessary to deal with intermediaries close to the government to accomplish any business deal. Their commissions (usually around 5% to 10%) are paid almost automatically. "Lubrication" or "grease payments" are a way of life in most emerging economies, even though they are considered unethical by some. International marketers should be prepared to take positions on such issues and make their positions known from the outset. Although such payments are considered bribes by Western standards, intermediaries believe them to be payments for their services.

Local representatives will be able to advise the international marketer on such matters, and establishing cordial relationships with the negotiating party may help to reduce this expense. Because many cultures mix interpersonal relations with business, a company with established, friendly relations may not have to deal with corruption at all.

The supplier's ability to use local resources is an additional feature attractive to most emerging economy buyers. Sellers who can demonstrate that their offers create additional jobs and added value will have greater bargaining power, particularly with government purchasers.

Note that historically, buyers from emerging economies did not place a high value on quality, especially when imported products were intended for sale within the domestic market. Therefore, emphasizing quality was not likely to increase the seller's bargaining strength in the case of a price disadvantage. But now, quality consciousness is gaining momentum in emerging markets, and therefore quality considerations should not be ignored. In many cases, sellers should try to provide the best quality at lower prices. For some products, however, quality is not the most important issue. For instance, Italy is the preferred supply source for aluminum die-casting because of its low price. However, the silesium content of the material is low, and the metal is basically recycled and therefore "tired." Nevertheless, buyers are willing to sacrifice quality for price.

Sellers have a stronger bargaining position in cases in which procurement is related to export-oriented programs and when any assistance is needed in marketing the final product. Often, emerging economies are unable to market what they produce because they cannot penetrate the international distribution channels. The seller who has some control over such channels or who can secure the cooperation of a trading company or a broker has considerable bargaining power in negotiations. *Sogo shosha,* Japanese general trading companies, have been instrumental in finding markets for emerging economy products primarily because of their global networks.

Finally, an important element strengthening the seller's bargaining power is the managerial expertise provided in postinvestment operations. Many emerging economies are hesitant to acquire turnkey agreements for various reasons.

First, these countries feel they do not have the managerial expertise needed to run the operation successfully. Second, even if the operation can be handled, marketing becomes a problem. Third and most important, buyers from emerging economies feel that they are sold inappropriate or outdated technology. As a solution, turnkey-plus or build-own-and-operate arrangements are favored by many emerging economies. The supplier guarantees to buy part of the end products or makes an equity investment in this arrangement. The seller may be asked to provide the managerial expertise needed to run the operation. The developing country partner agrees to buy the seller out after a specific period. In this way, the burden of choosing the right kind of investment is placed on the seller. The seller's risk is greater in such an agreement, but his bargaining position is strengthened. International marketers who are willing to take such risks are better equipped for penetrating emerging markets.

Phase 5: Completion

Once a certain supplier is selected, delivery, installment, and the initiation of different components takes place. Typically, a temporary project organization is formed to complete this assignment. Most projects in emerging economies involve a combination of construction, personnel training, project management, and service. The smoothness of the implementation will be critical to the supplier's long-term success. A supplier can experience numerous problems and delays in coping with local subcontractors, local authorities, import regulations, union procedures, and other constraints within the local environment. Successful suppliers will expect such problems and take active steps to deal with them.

Phase 6: Follow-Up

Successful completion of a project usually generates a considerable number of spin-off sales. Opportunities exist for selling a service contract, parts and equipment, software, and other supplementary products. Hence, it is desirable to maintain contact with the customer to ensure satisfaction and to learn about developing projects. A company must maintain a reasonable

---

Exhibit 4.3   Guidelines for Marketing to Emerging
Economies

- Follow development plans, yearly programs, government programs, and programs of political parties closely. These are easily accessible in public domain information sources.
- Become familiar with government incentives for investments. These will determine future demand.
- Select a good exclusive local representative. Make sure that he or she does not represent competitors, has an area of specialization, and is reliable.
- Become familiar with the process of preparing a feasibility report.
- Provide technical know-how during the preparation of technical specifications.
- Maintain close contact with domestic and international consulting organizations who may be preparing technical specifications or feasibility reports. Keep in touch with local technocrats and engineers. They are small in number and easily accessible. They will determine what will be bought.
- Establish friendly relations with potential buyers even if they are not buying now. It is an inexpensive but very effective public relations effort.
- Become familiar with regulations related to government and State Economic Enterprise (SEE) procurements. Note that government agencies do not have to follow such regulations all the time.
- Find the "lion" in each organization. In each organization, one or two people will have the "final say." Make sure that you know who they are, but never ignore others who are involved.
- Become familiar with the international agreements of the developing country. Do not use political-military alliances as a part of your sales strategy.
- Offer a complete deal. Be ready to finance your own sales.
- Leverage your strengths to negotiate sales. The ability of your offer to improve the balance of payments, create employment, add value, use local resources, decrease import dependence, increase the international options of the country in terms of both buying and selling in the future, and improve the flexibility of operations are examples of some desirable strengths that can be leveraged.

---

guarantee period in addition to an adequate level of after-sales service for its customers. Exhibit 4.3 provides some guidelines for marketing to emerging economies.

Recognize that these suggestions require the seller to assemble a team that includes both managerial and technical experts. An unfortunate mistake made by many companies is sending a sales representative and expecting him or her to close deals alone. This usually results in the loss of markets. Appropriate marketing strategies promise considerable rewards from emerging markets, given the competitive nature of global markets.

Exhibit 4.4   Motives for Global Sourcing

Competitive firm-specific advantages

Proactive motives
- To exploit technological superiority (unique or differential products)
- To enhance technological capabilities
- To assure organizational flexibility
- To gain a foothold in a promising new market
- To assure delivery and quality improvements

Reactive motives
- To protect proprietary technology leakage
- To cope with intensifying global competition more effectively
- To lock out competitors from a selected competitive base
- To take advantage of more efficient logistics/delivery systems

Comparative location-specific advantages

Proactive motives
- To take advantage of foreign government incentives
- To exploit currency fluctuations

Reactive motives
- To diversify supply sources to spread risks
- To exploit cost advantages such as cheaper labor, materials, and components
- To satisfy local government requirements such as local content, counter-trade, and offset
- To overcome protectionist barriers
- To guard against currency fluctuations

Finally, each emerging economy is unique, though there are some common features. Hence, each country's potential must be viewed within the context of its own special characteristics.

Emerging Markets as Sourcing Locations

Many Western firms import or source products from emerging economies and are familiar with the process of doing business there. We repeatedly stress throughout the book that a clear understanding of the foreign market and culture provides an invaluable advantage to companies seeking to do business in emerging markets. Many firms internationalize, not because they see emerging economies as markets for their products or services but because they have other motives to source from abroad, as explained by Exhibits 4.4 and 4.5 (Cavusgil, Yaprak, & Yeoh, 1993, pp. 143-155).

Exhibit 4.5   Internationalization of Procurement Process

Phase I: Domestic Purchasing Only (Reactive)
The firm engages in no direct foreign purchasing activities because it either does not perceive the need or lacks the expertise to pursue foreign countries.

Phase II: Foreign Buying Based on Need (Reactive)
A firm progresses to Phase II because it is confronted with a requirement for which no suitable supplier exists or because competitors are gaining an advantage from foreign sourcing. The domestic supply base for a firm in Phase II is inadequate to satisfy customer requirements.

Phase III: Foreign Buying as Part of Procurement Strategy (Proactive)
This phase represents a realization that a focused international procurement strategy results in significant performance gains.

Phase IV: Integration of Global Procurement Strategy (Proactive)
The final phase of procurement internationalization process occurs when a firm realizes greater benefit through global integration and coordination of procurement requirements.

SOURCE: Reprinted with permission from the publisher, the Institute for Supply Management™ (formerly NAPM), "The Global Sourcing: A Development Approach" by Robert M. Monczka and Robert J. Trent, *The international Journal of Purchasing and Materials Management, Spring 1991, 27,* (2) pp. 1-8.

The firm involved in sourcing from emerging economies can consider the same countries as potential markets, and vice versa. The strategy is to exploit economies of scale and scope to the fullest extent and gain a competitive advantage to beat the competition, domestically or globally. Exhibit 4.6 provides som`e examples of these benefits.

Exhibit 4.6   Framework for Sourcing in Emerging Markets

Study the foreign country market environment (political, social, economic, competitive, etc.) thoroughly through market research and competitive intelligence information from existing company-owned offices or associate offices in that region and identify *sourcing niches*.[a] In some cases, sources in developing countries may provide access to better technology to the buying firm.

Decide on mode of sourcing: working with qualified suppliers, joint ventures or 100% equity investment (Herbig & O'Hara, 1993, pp. 39-43).

Examples

- Sourcing by McCormick's Flavor Division for spices from India, where they are mass grown and offer price advantages ("McCormick & Co.," 1993, p. 14).
- Souring by American chemical companies for chemicals from countries with less stringent environmental regulations and requirements ("Purchasing in the CPI," 1993, p. 24).
- Sourcing by G-III Apparel Group for apparel from countries such as Hong Kong, Korea, and China, where labor costs are low ("G-III Apparel," 1993, p. 10).
- Sourcing by General Motors for forgings from India, which is a low-cost, high-quality producer for the product ("GM Likely," 1993, p. 16).

Identify a cross-functional and cross-cultural team as the buying team. Try to involve an expatriate from the foreign country working for the buying company in the cross-functional and cross-cultural buying team.

Train the buying team in international business negotiations.

Examples

- High-context cultures such as Japanese, Arabian, and other Asian cultures create problems when indicators such as "maybe," "perhaps," or "I'll consider it" may in reality mean "impossible" (Copeland & Griggs, 1985).
- High-diversity content in foreign culture can make communication and negotiation an even greater challenge.

Exploit synergies of making the foreign market and source the same, achieving economies of scope.

Try to tap into the export subsidies provided by governments of developing countries when signing an agreement with a foreign supplier.[b]

International trade pressures have led to total government commitment to exports in some developing countries, leading to heavy subsidies for all export-related activities to local businesses.

Exhibit 4.6   *Continued*

Examples

- General Electric has entered the software export business in India, after identifying the enormous growth and profitability of the software export industry there. Investment needed by General Electric in this case was minimum because it has a large local presence in India.

Integrate the global source (organizationally and informationally) in the company value chain and maintain global databases to make purchasing information available to every office in the world.

Examples

- Siemens AG of Germany maintains a procurement office in Singapore for all its electronic parts and makes purchasing information available to all its offices around the world through global databases.

a. A *sourcing niche* can be defined as a group of products or services which, when sourced from developing countries (or globally), provides a competitive advantage to the buying firm.

b. International trade pressures have led to total government commitment to exports in some developing countries, leading to heavy subsidies for all export-related activities to local businesses.

5

Entry Strategies for Emerging Markets

To enter a foreign market, a firm needs a strategy. This chapter describes various strategies a manager can consider to gain foreign market entry. Dissimilarities in the economic environment infrastructure, the level of technology, and the political, legal, and cultural environment create obstacles to successful entry into emerging markets. Western companies have to deal with these dissimilarities at different levels: the *global level,* in which firms should investigate international (multilateral) agreements, communication, and relationships; the *macrolevel,* in which bilateral agreements and relationships between the two countries could support business operations in a certain market; and the *microlevel,* in which a company needs to take concrete steps for realization of a successful market entry (Ghauri & Holstius, 1996). Selecting an entry strategy may depend on various factors, such as the promise and size of the market, the business environment in the market, managerial understanding of the market, internationalization objectives, the product-market fit, the level of asset commitment for the target market, and the nature of competition in the target market.

Eight principal strategies, grouped into three categories, may be considered by firms venturing into international business:[1] (a) export entry modes, including indirect and direct exporting, (b) contractual entry modes, including licensing, franchising, technology transfer, countertrade, counterpurchase, buyback, offset, clearing, management contracts, contract manufacturing or subcontracting, turnkey projects, and infrastructural projects, and (c) investment entry modes, including marketing subsidiary (which includes company-owned sales, service, and distribution network), joint ventures, and foreign direct investment (which includes mergers, acquisitions, and holding companies).

For investment entry, the firm has to be clear about its objectives, or why it wants to go to a particular market. The literature suggests that firms normally follow one of the following three strategies while investing in a market: (a) market seeking, in which a firm is attracted to a market due to its size and potential, (b) efficiency seeking, in which a firm wants to enter a market because the market has special capabilities in a certain industry, and (c) resource seeking, in which a firm invests in a market to obtain access to a crucial resource (Buckley & Ghauri, 1999).

The Western firm that wants to internationalize should align its capabilities to meet the needs of internationalization and then decide on the most appropriate foreign market entry strategy. The firm's journey to internationalization does not have to follow the nine strategies in an evolutionary, step-by-step manner, which means that a firm with no experience in international business does not have to start by exporting, then get into licensing, followed by a joint venture. Though internationalization of firms in the past has been evolutionary, more often than not a firm in these days can internationalize by choosing any one or more of the strategies directly (see Exhibit 5.1).

Export Entry Modes

Indirect Exporting

When a firm becomes involved in international business for the first time, many anxieties exist concerning the firm's ability to compete in foreign markets. Indirect channels can be an appropriate form of participation in international business for minimizing risks and overcoming these fears. By using indirect channels, a firm can start exporting with no incremental investment in capital, few risks, and low start-up costs. Such participation can be considered part of a developmental process that takes the firm toward more and more international sophistication and commitment.

The *indirect exporting* approach, that is, exporting through domestic intermediaries, places the burden of responsibility for sales contacts, negotiations, and product delivery on the intermediary within the firm's home market. Indirect channels are less expensive in the early stages of exporting because the cost of foreign market penetration is born directly by the intermediary. However, consider the "opportunity cost." Because the intermediary has control over final pricing, a loss of profits may result. Also, the firm's reputation in the marketplace is reflected in the reputation of the intermediary.

Exhibit 5.1   Is Internationalization Evolutionary?

Until the end of 1980s, many managers and academicians believed that internationalization was an evolutionary process (i.e., a firm goes through a series
of steps such as indirect or direct exporting, licensing, technology transfer, and
direct investment), thus completing its internationalization process. Recent
evidence, however, as demonstrated by small, high-value-added exporters,
calls for "leapfrogging" in internationalization. Exploiting their unique advantages, these firms can break out of the evolutionary pattern of internationalization and make bolder moves.

Rapid internationalization is feasible and desirable for a number of reasons:
- The means of internationalization knowledge, tools, facilitating institutions,
  and so on have become readily accessible to all firms. Lack of knowledge
  about best export practices is less of a hindrance to firms today.
- Managers can gain valuable experience through "inward" internationalization; involvement in outsourcing, transfers of technology from foreign companies, countertrade, management of a diverse work force, and similar
  activities.
- Successful international business today has become synonymous with
  successful partnerships with foreign businesses: distributors, trading companies, subcontractors, and so on. Inexperienced managers have a solid
  chance at succeeding in international business if they take time to build
  mutually beneficial, long-term alliances with foreign partners.

Export management companies (EMCs) or export trading companies
(ETCs) are independent firms contracted by manufacturers to develop
export sales, handle shipping and delivery, arrange for payment, and sell
products along with other allied but noncompetitive product lines. The
principal advantage of using an indirect export channel is to have access to
foreign markets by "plugging in" to the EMC's foreign market network.
This advantage can be strengthened by carefully selecting the EMC or ETC
and then supporting it. Support involves working with the EMC or ETC in
formulating a marketing plan for the firm's product line; contributing
product information, advertising, and technical assistance; and backing up
its export operations with prompt servicing of orders. There are however,
differences between EMCs and ETCs, as explained in Exhibit 5.2.

The primary disadvantage of relying on export intermediaries is the
firm's loss of control over foreign sales. This loss can be moderated by
specifying in the contract that manufacturer's approval is required in key
decisions and by working intimately with the EMC or ETC. Indirect
exporting requires little, if any, foreign market knowledge on the part of

---

Exhibit 5.2   What Is the Difference Between Export Management Companies and Export Trading Companies?

Export management companies (EMCs) are normally supply-driven; that is, the EMC represents one or more manufacturers or suppliers and manages sales, advertising, and promotion in foreign markets. Export trading companies (ETCs) are demand-driven; that is, the ETC identifies demand or needs in foreign markets prior to approaching manufacturers or suppliers. Essentially, both EMCs and ETCs play similar roles as intermediaries in international business.

---

the manufacturer, and for the same reason, it isolates the manufacturer from foreign markets.

Direct Exporting

Direct exporting, that is, exporting through overseas intermediaries, offers several advantages to the manufacturer:

- Partial or full control over the foreign marketing plan
- Concentrated effort toward marketing the manufacturer's product line
- Quicker information feedback from the target market
- Better protection of trademarks, patents, and goodwill

Direct exporting requires manufacturer familiarity with the procedures of export shipping and international payments. There is a dual problem of developing distribution channel strategies and finding, motivating, and supporting overseas distributors in direct exporting. Start-up costs are higher due to greater information requirements and higher risks. In direct exporting, a manager must not ignore the costs associated with international travel, communications, and personnel familiar with international business.

Direct exporting offers potentially greater profits and challenges. As is the case of indirect exporting, there are many available options. The basic criterion is control: the amount of authority you choose to delegate to the foreign partner, which is partially dictated by the basic characteristics and technical sophistication of the product and the need for after-sale service. This situation has a set of criteria different from that of the manufacturer who is exporting a highly technical product requiring after-sale servicing. The 10 most common mistakes made by exporters are explained in Exhibit 5.3.

Exhibit 5.3   The 10 Most Common Mistakes of Potential Exporters

1. Failure to obtain qualified export counseling and to develop a master international marketing plan before starting an export business.
2. Insufficient commitment by top management to overcome the initial difficulties and financial requirements of exporting.
3. Insufficient care in selecting foreign distributors.
4. Chasing orders from around the world instead of establishing a basis for profitable operations and orderly growth.
5. Neglecting exports when the domestic market booms.
6. Failure to treat international distributors on an equal basis with domestic counterparts.
7. Unwillingness to modify products to meet regulations or cultural preferences of other countries.
8. Failure to print services, sales, and warranty messages in locally understood languages.
9. Failure to consider use of export management company.
10. Failure to consider licensing or joint-venture agreements.

Contractual Entry Modes

Licensing

The *contractual entry mode* entails a variety of contractual agreements between the domestic firm (licenser) and foreign company (licensee) whereby the domestic firm makes intangible assets, such as patents, trade secrets, knowledge, trademarks, and company name, available to a foreign firm in return for royalties and/or other forms of payments.

When a firm licenses to an independent foreign firm, the main purpose is to penetrate a foreign market. Licensing offers both advantages and disadvantages to the Western firm. Some advantages are as follows:

- Licensing is a quick and easy mode to enter foreign markets and requires little capital.
- Royalties received are guaranteed and periodic, whereas exports and direct investment imply fluctuating income and higher risks.
- Western firms can benefit from product development abroad, without research expense, through technical feedback arrangements.
- Licensing is especially attractive as a low-commitment entry mode, that is, when a small firm is unable or unwilling to commit resources (managerial, technical, or financial) to a foreign market.

- In some countries, licensing may be the only way to tap into the market.
- High transportation costs can be overcome by licensing.

Some disadvantages are as follows:

- Unless the licenser possesses distinctive technology, trademark, or a company name that is attractive to potential foreign users, licensing is not the best entry mode to use.
- The licenser lacks control over the marketing plan and production processes in the target market. Today's licensees may become tomorrow's competitors.
- Though royalties are guaranteed and periodic, the absolute size of licensing income can be very small compared with exporting to or investing in the target market.
- A licensing agreement usually gives exclusive rights of the technology and trademark to the licensee's country. The licenser cannot use an alternative entry mode until the agreement expires.

Franchising

Franchising is a form of licensing in which a company licenses a business system as well as other property rights to an independent company or person. The franchisee operates under the franchiser's trade name and follows policies and procedures laid down by the franchiser. In return, the franchiser receives fees, running royalties, and other compensation from the franchisee. This type of entry mode has its advantages and disadvantages. The principal advantages are as follows:

- Rapid expansion into a foreign market with low capital outlays.
- Marketing is standardized, and there is a distinctive image.
- The franchisee is highly motivated.
- Political risks are low.

The key disadvantages are as follows:

- Lack of full control over the franchisee's operations.
- Limitations on the franchiser's profit.
- Restrictions imposed by governments on the terms of franchise agreements.

Franchising is particularly attractive when a company has a product that cannot be exported to a foreign target country, does not wish to invest in that country, and has a production process that is easily transferable to an independent party.

Franchising will not work unless the franchiser continuously supports the franchisee. Such support includes supplying equipment, tools, training, and finance and general management assistance. The steps to establish franchising systems abroad resemble those of traditional licensing (for an example, see Exhibit 5.4):

Exhibit 5.4   Benetton's Strategy

Benetton has achieved its retail distribution through an unusual arrangement with *agents,* first in Italy and other European countries, and now in emerging economies. According to one of the company's marketing executives, the term *franchising* in describing Benetton is a misnomer. Agents of the company are assigned vast territories, largely through verbal agreements, in which they try to develop Benetton retail outlets. They find smaller investors and store operators exhibiting a "Benetton mentality" to form individual partnerships. An individual agent might supervise and hold an interest in a number of stores. In 1982, Benetton conducted business with 35 agents. Store owners are not required to pay Benetton fees or royalties for using its name. They are required to carry only Benetton merchandise, maintain a minimum sales level (equivalent to orders for about 3,500 garments per year), adhere to suggested markups of about 80% above cost, and pay for their orders within 90 days.

- Assessing sales potential in the target market
- Finding suitable franchising candidates
- Negotiating the franchise agreement
- Building a working partnership with the franchisee

Technology Transfer

The international *transfer of technology* is made through various situation-oriented, nonexclusive vehicles. Technology and services expertise can be exchanged through standard export arrangements or project work, licensing agreements, joint ventures, and direct investments. Three fundamental considerations must be combined to determine the financial, legal, and technological character of any transfer transaction:

- The seller's business plan, financial considerations, and company goals
- The nature of technology/service
- The objective, business situation, and financial and legal environment of the recipient

The nature of technology/service is the core consideration of technology transfers. Price, method of transfer, terms of exchange, and buyer-seller relationships all revolve around this center. The price of a technology/service is usually based on the cost of its development.

A company with a unique product or service can sell that product or service at whatever price the market will bear. A service centered on common knowledge will not be able to charge the same price. A technology/service may be based on a patent, trademark right, company know-how, and trade secrets. Even if a Western firm is employing a standard manufacturing process, a potential customer may approach the firm to purchase trademark rights that are essential to the success of the end product.

Countertrade

Countertrade is an ancient form of trading that has emerged anew at different times in world commerce. It refers to a transaction characterized by a linkage between exporters and importers of goods or services in addition to or in place of financial settlements. In ancient times, countertrade took place in the form of barter, so that goods of approximately the same value were exchanged without any money involved. Naturally, these transactions took place at a time when money as a common medium of exchange was not available.

This kind of trade is experiencing a resurgence. Countertrade has been used in circumstances in which it was more efficient to exchange goods directly than to use money as an intermediary. The situations leading to this can be a lack of money or a lack of appropriate exchange rates. In the past, countertrade or barter was confined to former Eastern Bloc countries because their currencies were not acceptable elsewhere or because they did not have access to foreign exchange. However, recently the use of countertrade has steadily increased. In the 1980s, countertrade was used by more than 27 countries and was commonly referred to only in the context of East-West trade (Bussard, 1984). By the 1990s, 90 countries were conducting countertrade transactions. One primary reason for this development is that the world debt crisis has made ordinary trade financing very risky. Many developing countries still cannot obtain individual trade credits to pay for desired imports. Heavily indebted countries resort to countertrade to maintain some trickle of product inflow. Some countries pursue bilateralism: They want to sell goods to those countries from which they import (e.g., the former Soviet Union's trade with India).

In the 1980s, countertrade transactions were mainly a vehicle for financing trade turnovers with developing countries. In the 1990s, the practice emerged as a vehicle for financing capital projects and production-sharing ventures, for ensuring the repatriation of profits from investments in countries beset by external debt and hard-currency shortages, and for competitive bidding on major nonmilitary government procurement (Verzariu, 1992, pp. 2-6).

Countertrade is considered an excellent tool to gain entry into a new market in cases in which producers feel that marketing is not their strength or the products face strong international competition. A firm can establish long-term relationships because the parties are tied down by an agreement. This kind of stability is very valuable because it reduces demand variations and allows for better planning and efficiency.

Counterpurchase

Under traditional barter trade, goods are exchanged with goods (e.g., cars for toys, sugar for bananas, or machinery for agricultural products). However, a sophisticated version of countertrade known as *counterpurchase* is now emerging. In such an agreement, parties sign two separate contracts specifying the goods and services exchanged (e.g., Pepsi Cola for vodka). If the exchange is not of equal value, partial payment is made in cash.

Buyback

In another form of countertrade, the Western company agrees to supply technology and equipment and receives payment in the form of goods produced by the same plant until final payment is made for the technology. This is known as a *buyback agreement.*

Offset

Offset is often found in defense-related sectors and in sales of high-priced items, such as aircraft. A developing country purchasing aircraft from France requires that certain portions of the aircraft be produced and assembled in the purchasing country. Such conditions are very commonly placed on defense and other large-scale contracts and can take many forms, such as coproduction, licensing, subcontracting, and joint ventures.

Clearing

Clearing involves establishment of clearing accounts to hold deposits and to effect withdrawals for trade. Countries buy and sell different goods and services with the goal of restoring a balanced account in the long term. This practice was common among the former Eastern Bloc countries.

Several studies reveal that a shift is occurring from using countertrade reactively to using it proactively, as a new tool for financing and marketing internationally. Another conclusion is that the countertrade is here to stay for the foreseeable future and that Western companies should be prepared to participate in this nontraditional form of trade.

The increasing importance of countertrade has resulted in the emergence of new specialists, countertrade brokers, who offer to handle such transactions.

There are a number of trading houses working internationally, frequently acting as third-party intermediaries. Due to their widespread contacts around the world, they can dispose of unwanted countertrade goods much more easily than any individual company can. Brokers are more capable of evaluating the risks of such transactions, and companies can benefit from their advice while entering into countertrade.

Management Contracts

An international *management contract* gives a Western company the right to manage the day-to-day operations of an enterprise in a foreign market. However, management control is limited to ongoing operations. Management contracts are used mainly to supplement an actual or intended joint-venture agreement or a turnkey project.

From an entry strategy perspective, management contracts are unsatisfactory because they do not allow a company to build a permanent market position for its products. Other disadvantages include time-consuming negotiations and the commitment of scarce management talent.

Management contracts are, however, considered a feasible alternative to foreign investments. Transnational firms are not philanthropic organizations, nor do they necessarily have any interest in the political or economic goals of local leaders of emerging economies. They are profit-seeking organizations, and their decisions are based on the firms' goals. All alternative commercially justified routes are feasible.

Contract Manufacturing or Subcontracting

Contract manufacturing is a cross between licensing and investment participation. In contract manufacturing, a host company secures a product or manufacturing process from a Western manufacturer and produces under contract for the Western firm. The production can then be exported or marketed locally.

Contract manufacturing requires a small commitment and financial and management resources. It allows for quick entry into the target country and avoids local ownership problems. It is attractive especially when the target market is too small to justify investment entry and export entry is too costly. However, it may be difficult or impossible to find a suitable local manufacturer. If a manufacturer is found, substantial technical assistance may be required to improve quality and production levels. There is a risk that the firm may be creating a future competitor.

Turnkey Projects

Turnkey projects involve a contract for constructing operating facilities, such as a power plant, a paper-and-pulp plant, and so forth, which are to be transferred to the foreign owner when the project is ready to commence operations. The contractor is obliged to provide services such as management and worker training after the construction is complete, to prepare the owner to operate the facilities.

The size and comprehensive nature of these projects set this type of business apart from most other forms of participation. The majority of these projects are "mega" projects involving hundreds of millions of dollars. Due to the huge financial commitments involved, this kind of business activity is limited to a handful of large firms.

More and more frequently, machinery, equipment, technology, and know-how to handle the same technology are sold as a package in the form of complete industrial plants and factories. Sales to emerging markets with limited local construction and engineering capabilities are very often of this form.

Developing countries prefer turnkey projects to direct investment and joint ventures with Western firms for several reasons. Feelings of distrust and dissatisfaction with Western firms have made economic nationalism a major issue during the past few decades. These feelings continue to worsen for some of the following reasons:

- Most developing countries are greatly concerned about becoming self-sufficient in the industrial sector.
- Superior know-how and muscle of multinational corporations (MNCs) discourages the development of local industries in the developing countries.
- MNCs have been accused of being responsible for political disturbances in certain countries.
- The results of "technical assistance" by Western firms have been disappointing in many cases, and poverty and underdevelopment still prevail in many developing countries.
- There can be advantages in buying an integrated package. It is frequently better for the buyer to deal with just one responsible seller, rather than different sellers who can blame each other if difficulties arise. Apart from the fact that in some cases, this is the only way to enter a particular market/country, there may be other advantages for Western firms:

    They do not face the constant threat of nationalization or of increasing restriction by host governments.

    They do not incur any commercial risk while entering a new market.

    They can use turnkey projects as a strategy to charge premium prices for their components.

They can improve their competitive position relative to their rivals who sell components. Once they have entered the market through a turnkey project, they can sell the spare parts and components.

Infrastructural Projects

Many Western managers have a misconception that markets for *infrastructural projects* in emerging markets are unorganized and chaotic. On the contrary, the buying process is usually more formalized. The fact that emerging markets are more concentrated and the government is an integral part of most business operations provides opportunities for the international marketer. The significant trend in emerging economies to invest in infrastructural projects involves billions of dollars, and hence buying is visible and formalized.

Most buying is performed by organizations, either privately owned or government operated. Markets are basically sellers' markets. Buying organizations follow a formal approach in their purchases, which are based on a feasibility plan that contains a strong macroeconomic orientation for development.

Investment Entry Modes

Marketing Subsidiary

Some firms prefer to have only a marketing and distribution network in foreign countries to exploit the potential of spin-off sales (generated by spare parts, etc.) and to create a mechanism to offer good after-sales service facilities. This can usually be done in the case of technology-intensive products, in which after-sales service may be a key criterion in purchasing decisions. The same facilities used for marketing and so forth can be used as powerful information-providing assets so that the firm can keep "learning" about the foreign market. As mentioned earlier, if there is a clear business logic in sourcing from the countries in which a firm-owned marketing network already exists, the firm must look for sourcing niches to gain a competitive advantage.

Joint Ventures

Joint ventures are a special type of ownership sharing in which equity is owned by two or more companies. Joint ventures are a common form of participation for firms moving beyond the exporting stage to more regular overseas involvement in which local participation may be deemed desirable. Depending on the equity share of the Western company, they may be classified as a majority, minority, or fifty-fifty venture. Joint ventures, in many cases, may be the only feasible form of investment participation in countries in which sole ventures are either prohibited or discouraged.

Joint ventures provide a mutually beneficial alternative for foreign and Western businesses to join forces. For both parties, ventures are a means to share both capital and risk and make use of each other's strengths. Problems may arise in these ventures when more than one party is involved in the decision-making process. Joint ventures can be managed successfully with the patience and flexibility of both partners. Usually, however, one of the partners must play the dominant role to steer the business to success.

The most critical decision in a joint venture involves the choice of a local partner. For that reason, joint ventures are often compared to marriages. Likewise, joint ventures frequently end in divorce when one or both partners conclude that they could benefit more by severing the relationship.

Each partner enters a joint venture to gain the skills and resources possessed by the other partner. The contribution of the Western company to a joint venture depends on both its own capabilities and those of the local partner, as well as the joint venture's purpose and scope. Usually, the key contribution of the Western partner consists of technology and products, whereas that of the local partner pertains to the knowledge and skills necessary to manage the operation.

Foreign Direct Investment

Basically, *foreign direct investment (FDI)* involves the transfer of an entire enterprise to a target market, which enables a company to benefit from its competitive advantages in that market.

Local production may lower costs, compared with export entry, because of savings in transportation and customs duties and/or lower manufacturing costs resulting from less expensive local inputs of labor, raw material, and energy. Such an investment may enable manufacturers to obtain a higher or more uniform quality of supply in the host country.

Direct investment can create marketing advantages, such as easier adaptation of products to local preferences and purchasing power. Resources devoted to marketing usually increase because in this case, the manufacturer has more to lose from market failure than from direct exporting or licensing. However, FDI requires substantially more capital, management, and other company resources, which means bearing more risks—especially political risks. Whenever possible, a company should gain experience in a

Exhibit 5.5   Timex Corporation

From 1950 to 1970, Timex Corporation expanded to a dominant position in the worldwide wristwatch industry with an inexpensive pin-lever watch developed for mass production and assembly. The company's sales at first were limited to jewelry stores. Timex then introduced its products in various retail outlets such as drugstores, hardware stores, and large merchants to break that tradition. Timex built a worldwide network of more then fifteen manufacturing and assembly plants to fabricate piece parts at a lower cost and to support world-wide sales. The lightweight watch movement, cases, and straps were shipped by air freight for subassembly and final assembly which optimized the advantages of import duties and tariff regulations.

target country first (through exports) before opting for direct investment. Such an investment project must be analyzed in the context of its political, legal, economic, social, and cultural environments. Many features of a target country's investment climate need to be assessed by managers.

An FDI may be made by acquiring an existing operation or by constructing new facilities. Timex Corporation, for example, applies the latter strategy to produce its popular brand of wristwatches. A potential investor may look for acquisitions if it is difficult to transfer resources or acquire resources locally. By doing this, the investor may have a faster start in developing the foreign target market because an enterprise with existing products and markets will already be operating. In contrast, it can take 3 to 5 years for an investor to achieve the same degree of development if starting from the beginning. An acquisition promises a shorter payback period by creating immediate income for the investor (see Exhibit 5.5).

A possible advantage is that new product lines can be acquired. However, this can turn into a disadvantage if the investor has no experience in the new product lines. Thus, although acquisition may have the aforementioned advantages, a potential investor will not necessarily be able to gain them.

Frequently, foreign investments are made in situations in which there is little or no competition, and hence it may be difficult to locate a company to buy. The process of fitting the acquired company into current operations and policies can constrain performance and earnings. Substantial problems may be created for the investor. For example, personnel and labor relations may be difficult to change, "bad will" rather than goodwill may be accrued to existing brands, and facilities may be inefficient and poorly located in relation to future potential markets.

International business executives are also cautioned about the difficulties of transferring locally earned funds to the home country—the problem of blocked currency. In the 1980s, H.B. Fuller Co., a U.S. company doing business in Nicaragua, experienced difficulties buying raw materials because Nicaragua's central bank was cutting off its supply of hard currency. The same situation was faced by several foreign companies in Argentina and during the last years of President Suharto, in Indonesia.

Usually, companies prefer to own 100% of their foreign operations to secure control and prevent the dilution of profits. However, sharing ownership is widespread because the emerging economies want local participation, and rapid foreign expansion has necessitated bringing in outside resources.

Once a company has decided to enter a market with a wholly owned subsidiary, it has two choices to enter a particular market: (a) a greenfield investment or (b) a takeover of an existing company. In the case of a *greenfield investment, a* company might end up with a relatively cheaper entry because it invests only as much as needed. It can later expand successively as the demand increases. It will not inherit any problems, which might be the case if it takes over an existing company. Quite often, the firms with problems are the ones up for sale. A greenfield investment is always welcome by the local government because it creates new job opportunities and is considered to help in infrastructure development. In this case, a company is also free to choose a location that provides the most benefits. Moreover, the company can bring in the most modern technologies.

In the case of a *takeover,* a company can gain speed and have a rapid entry because the business already exists and has a certain position in the local market. It need not go through start-up problems and problems of getting bureaucratic permits and fulfilling local rules and regulations with which it is not familiar. As it buys a whole existing company, it can get the whole package at a reasonable price. In this package, there may be some very useful and some less useful parts. But that can be consolidated at a later stage. In many such cases, a takeover is welcomed by local industry and the market because it does not disturb the competitive structure at the outset. There are, however, some problems attached to takeovers, such as the difficulty of evaluating a takeover victim. Once a company is taken over, it demands a lot of effort to integrate the new company into the company culture and style. Moreover, searching for a takeover victim costs money and time.

Note

1. The group classification of foreign entry modes has been adapted from Franklin Root, "Chapter 1: Designing Entry Strategies for International Markets," 1987, p. 6, in *Entry Strategies for International Markets*, Lexington, MA: D.C. Heath and Company.

6

Developing and Managing
Relationships in Emerging Markets

Western managers are already aware of the importance of establishing, developing, and nurturing productive business relationships. But when applying these aspects to doing business in emerging markets, managers may not realize to what extent cultural differences will affect their ability to manage relationships. Managers must also be aware that their counterparts are engaged in other business relationships as well and that business in those connected relationships may have an impact on their own business relationships (Ghauri, 1999). Not all business relationships are of equal importance or create the same impact on the focal relationship between a customer and a supplier. Exhibit 6.1 describes a few key business relationships that may have more than a marginal impact on buyers and sellers.

Generally, the stronger the impact of a business relationship on the focal relationship, the more the firm will try to control the relationship. Because many of these relationships exist beyond the boundaries of the firm, control cannot be expected to be very strong. Nevertheless, the importance of managing these business relationships leads us to the strategies a manager can use to make these relationships beneficial to the firm.

As mentioned earlier, in an international setting, it becomes extremely important to manage business relationships with cross-cultural differences in mind. A Western manager should try to master the ability to communicate well both verbally and nonverbally; be capable and willing to take action with insufficient, unreliable, and often conflicting information; inspire trust

Exhibit 6.1   Facilitative Relationships in Emerging Markets

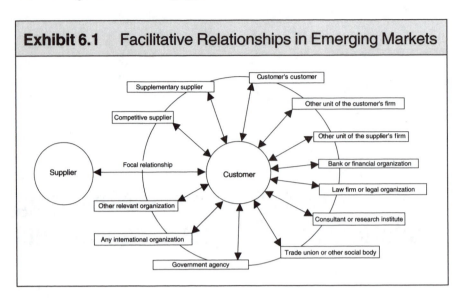

and confidence; and be able to view problem solving as a social process involving consensus and interpersonal influence rather than correct answers (Ghauri & Usunier, 1996; Harrison & Hopkins, 1967). Adjustment to a foreign country depends on being able to understand the behavior of foreigners, which in turn is predicated on being nonjudgmental (Mendenhall & Oddou, 1985). A few predictors for the success of a Western manager operating in a foreign country are as follows (Ronen, 1990):

- Relational characteristics such as tolerance for ambiguity, behavioral flexibility, nonjudgmental attitude, interpersonal skills, cultural empathy, and enthusiasm
- Motivational characteristics such as interest in overseas experience, interest in the specific host country culture, and willingness to acquire new patterns of behavior and attitudes

Types of Relationships in Emerging Markets

Managing Relationships With a Foreign Government

Managing relations with a foreign government is an extremely important task for Western businesses because a small change in a foreign government's trade policy can create a tremendous impact on the firm's business. A good example is Coca-Cola in India. In 1977, the Janata Party came into power in India, and the new government demanded that Coca-Cola reveal its secret formula for the soft drink if it wanted to do business in India.

Rather than comply with this unreasonable demand, Coca-Cola chose to leave India in 1977, not to return until 1992, when government policy became more reliable and attractive to foreign investment.

It is extremely important for Western managers to find a fit between what their company has to offer (capital, infrastructure development, technology, new jobs, etc.) and what a foreign government needs for its economic, political, and development programs. Many times, the priorities of the Western firm and the foreign government may not match, and the manager will have to use one of the following strategies to manage relations with the foreign government (Austin, 1990; Ghauri & Holstius, 1996):

- *Alter:* The company can bargain to get the government to alter the policy, the instrument, or the action of concern.
- *Avoid:* The company can make strategic moves to bypass the risk or impact of the government's action.
- *Accede:* The company can adjust its operations to comply with a government requirement.
- *Ally:* The company can insulate itself from risks by creating strategic alliances.

The matrix appearing in Exhibit 6.2 captures the above four strategies.

Depending on the relative importance of the issue to the firm and the relative power of the firm, one of the four approaches in Exhibit 6.2 can be used. If the issue is very important to the firm and the firm has the type of power needed to alter the foreign government's action, it should choose the *alter* strategy. The firm should choose the *accede* strategy when the issue is of little importance and the firm has low power. The firm should choose the *avoid* strategy to avoid confrontation with the foreign government when dealing with issues that are of low importance to the firm, high importance to the foreign government, and the firm is in the position of high power. The firm may choose the *ally* strategy when the issue is highly important to the firm but the firm is in a low power position.

While preparing for negotiations with foreign government officers, the Western manager must remember that all four strategies require some give-and-take. Minimizing conflict and building a common ground for negotiations remain the two most important first steps toward successful business in emerging markets.

Managing Relationships With Expatriates

Many Western firms ignore the need to manage relationships with their expatriates working in emerging economies. Merely providing a good monetary incentive system to motivate expatriates may not be enough; poor relations with the parent company or headquarters may directly result in

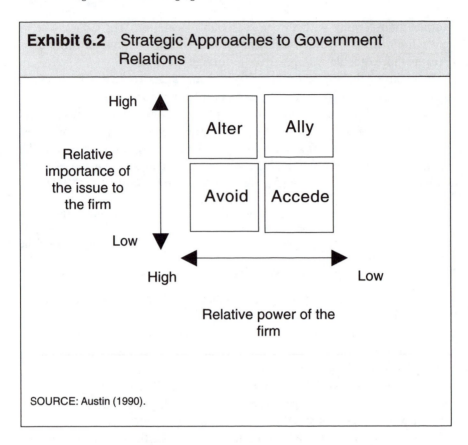

Exhibit 6.2   Strategic Approaches to Government Relations

SOURCE: Austin (1990).

poor performance by the expatriate. Many international management specialists complain that too many executives go to foreign countries ill prepared, because companies often fail to develop human resource policies to match their global strategies (Toannou, 1994). There are four general beliefs about the way international managers adjust to conditions abroad (Dunbar & Katcher, 1990):

1. The "our person in Havana" myth describes the well-connected company employee abroad who experiences little difficulty in adjusting or performing in a foreign country. Companies that view foreign assignment this way do relatively little for their staff.

2. The "lost employee" myth holds that the person who is out of sight is also out of mind. Such employees are isolated from the domestic realities of the firm and are uncertain as to when or whether they are to repatriate—or whether there will be a position for them on their return.

Exhibit 6.3   What Are the Goals of a Cross-Cultural Training Program?

Source of information: The trainee needs observation and interview skills.

Learning settings: The trainee needs to attend to all aspects of the environment, including each human encounter, as a source of information.

Problem solving: The trainee needs to independently define problems and gather information in real time.

Role of emotions and value: Because problems are usually value- and emotion-laden, the trainee needs to recognize the relevant values, perceptions, attitudes, and emotions and their implications for action.

Criteria for successful learning: The trainee needs to assess effectiveness in terms of the attitudes of the parties in the work setting and the duration of relationships.

---

3. The "ugly American myth" describes the expatriate who is unfamiliar with the cultural realities of the host country. They are not just unhappy living abroad, they are a liability to their firms.

4. The "cultural relativist" finds relocation challenging, both personally and professionally. These people are good at working with others, and companies assume that they will adapt to their foreign nation easily.

Western companies who do not wish to see their expatriates in any of the above four situations will have to develop a systematic strategy for relocating employees in emerging economies. A strategy to manage relationships with expatriates may include training programs, as illustrated in Exhibit 6.3 and in the following examples:

- Cultural training for the expatriates and their families.
- Training in international business negotiations.
- A tracking mechanism to follow (and suitably reward) the contributions made by the expatriate to the firm's business while abroad.
- A communication mechanism between the expatriate and headquarters of the firm. It is wise to keep the expatriate informed of any organizational or strategy changes that the firm may make during his or her absence.
- Incorporating the complex information gathered by the expatriate in future decision making at headquarters.
- A mechanism to tap into contacts and leads developed by the expatriate during a foreign assignment.

Exhibit 6.4   Priorities Given by Various Cultures to Different Values

When designing a cross-cultural training program, the firm must take into account the differences in priorities given by various cultures to values such as independence, competition, individual success, group harmony, cooperation, seniority, age, privacy, formality, material possessions, and spiritual enlighten-ment, as demonstrated by the following examples:

American	**Japanese**	**Arabian**
Independence	Group harmony	Family security
Competition	Cooperation	Compromise
Individual success	Group achievement	Reputation

SOURCE: Elashmawi, F. (February, 1991). Multicultural Management: New Skills for Global Success, *Tokyo Business Today* (pp. 54-56).

- Reintegration and repatriation training of expatriates into the domestic company at suitable positions after their return.

In international management, expatriate failure is considered one of the major problems. The cost of expatriate failure to the parent firm can be as high as 3 times the expatriate's annual domestic salary plus the cost of relo-cation, which can be around $250,000 to $1 million. The research shows that about 70% of all Americans sent abroad to developing nations return home early. One researcher concludes that the reasons for these failures, in order of importance, are as follows (Hill, 2001):

1. Inability of the spouse to adjust
2. Inability of the manager to adjust
3. Other family problems
4. Manager's personal or emotional maturity
5. Inability to cope with larger overseas responsibilities

It is important to note that the inability of the spouse to adjust is considered the number one problem. The selection and training of an expatriate is thus a critical issue in the success of international operations. Moreover, the manager as well as the spouse and the family should be included in any training program designed by Western firms. Any training for expatriate mangers must include cultural and practical training because different cultures prioritize different values (see Exhibit 6.4).

Managing Relationships With the Foreign Partner

A Western firm may decide to enter a foreign market in a joint venture with a foreign partner, appoint a foreign distributor, or use a foreign company for sourcing. For our discussion in this section, we refer to all the above-mentioned foreign counterparts as partners. We recommend that the Western firm try to build relationships at both the formal and informal levels with the foreign partner's company. In many cases, it is important for the Western firm to identify the "lion" in the organization—the person who holds the ultimate decision-making authority. However, the best strategy would be to have cross-functional teams from various organizational levels building relationships with each other. This assures that if the principal contact of the foreign firm leaves for some reason, the business relationship between the two firms continues to survive. There are various benefits of maintaining and developing good relationships with your foreign partner:

- If your foreign partner is better than you are in managing a specific business process, he or she may agree to get into a mutual benchmarking initiative.
- Your foreign partner can provide you with invaluable leads and contacts voluntarily if you establish trust and confidence.
- Training your foreign partner in quality management or statistical process control becomes easier with a strong relationship. This is especially true for supply chain management in emerging economies.
- Working toward common goals in the long term becomes easier if a sound working relationship is built with a foreign partner.
- Conflict resolution becomes faster with a good relationship with the foreign partner.

Managing Relationships With Foreign Communities

It is always a good corporate communications strategy to invest time and resources in building a good image in the foreign communities in which a firm operates. Participation in community activities by a firm improves its image, and this in turn attracts a better and more experienced workforce. Also, a community presence for the firm minimizes the negative stereotyping of "foreign multinational imperialism," thus increasing customer confidence in the firm's products and services. Crisis management for the firm is a lot easier when the firm has a positive relationship with community leaders and has demonstrated that it is a good "corporate citizen."

A strategy to manage relationships with foreign communities may include the following:

- Sponsoring sports, cultural events, and festivals in the community
- Reaching out a helping hand in times of natural disasters and other crises
- Institutionalizing good human resource policies in the organization

- Helping maintain a clean environment
- Maintaining complete regard and respect for the cultural norms and traditions of the community

Managing Relationships With the Foreign Customer

A firm striving for excellence never loses sight of its customers and their needs. A firm must consider all its customers as equal. To be successful internationally in the long run, the firm must keep its eyes and ears open to see or listen to any complaint or feedback a customer may provide from any part of the world. A strategy to manage relationships with foreign customers should include the following:

- Providing the customer with the promised levels of price, quality, delivery, and reliability and letting the customer know that the firm is in the country to do business in the long term and will not leave after extracting short-term profits.
- Communicating that customer views and feedback about the firm's products are extremely important and that they are taken seriously by the firm. (Having a "1-800" telephone number, available in the United States, may be a good idea to maintain an open communication channel with the customer.)
- Maintaining respect for the cultural differences in taste or choice that the customer may have about specific features of the product and removing the features that may be culturally undesirable. For example, when McDonald's entered India in 1993, it had to abide by the religious preferences of Indians and not make burgers using beef.

Forming Partnerships or Alliances in Emerging Economies

The formation of global business alliances and partnerships has been increasing in the last two decades. Sheth and Parvatiyar (1992) of Emory University have identified *purpose* and *parties* as two dimensions to describe the formation of alliances. Each isomorphically represents uncertainty and trust, respectively. Based on this dichotomy of purpose and parties, a typology of business alliances has been created:

- *Cartel:* If a business alliance is formed for operations efficiency among competitors, it is called a cartel.
- *Cooperative:* If a business alliance is formed among noncompetitors (suppliers, customers, and noncompetitive businesses), it is called a cooperative.
- *Competitive:* If a business alliance is formed for a strategic purpose among competitors, it is called a competitive alliance.
- *Collaborative:* If a business alliance is formed among noncompetitors for a strategic purpose, it is called a collaborative alliance.

The current trend in management is to form virtual organizations, made up of various firms performing activities related to their core competencies, interacting together to gain maximum benefits of business opportunities that arise in a very short time. In fact, in the future, there will be groups of companies in alliances competing with each other. The competing groups will be only as strong as the alliances between them, so individual relationships will have to be managed carefully (Gomes-Casseres, 1994).

The following sections describe what to look for in a candidate who is a potential foreign partner, foreign distributor, or freight forwarder.[1]

Selecting a Foreign Partner for a Collaboration/Joint Venture

The selection of the "right" partner for your business is extremely critical for any collaborative venture to be successful. Inaccurate or incomplete assessment of the prospective partners may lead to a "wrong" choice, which can result in serious problems in the future. Conflicts between partners can be avoided to a great extent if they are anticipated before the venture is established. At a minimum, the partners should be able to provide complementary capabilities that in both the short and the long term are necessary to enable the venture to be competitive.

The partner chosen for the venture can influence the overall mix of available skills and resources, the operating policies and procedures, and the viability of the venture. Hence, even if one or a few viable partner prospects exist, screening these companies for suitability as collaborative venture partners is still a critical task.

Partner-Related Criteria

These criteria refer to qualifications of the partner, both tangible and intangible, that are not specific to the type of operation but affect the risk(s) faced. More specifically, they include what we might call the "personality traits" of the partner, such as business philosophy, reliability, motivation, commitment, intellectual property protection approach, and some general characteristics, such as experience, reputation, and political connections.

Partner Characteristics. Several background characteristics of a prospective partner are perceived by managers as important factors for evaluating the potential contribution of the partner to the venture. Examples of these characteristics include reputation, experience, country of origin, complementariness of resources to the venture, and political connections.

Property Rights Protection. Technological know-how or other intellectual properties may constitute an important competitive advantage. Hence, companies with valuable intellectual property that enter cooperative ventures face dissemination risk. This refers to the risk that a firm's specific advantages in intellectual property will be expropriated or exploited by the venture partner(s). Thus, the partner's approach to and mechanisms of enforcement for property rights protection are particularly important if one brings valuable intellectual property into the venture.

Compatibility of Business Philosophies. One of the main reasons for failure in collaborative ventures is disagreement over operating strategies, policies, and methods. Such conflicts can be resolved to the extent that the business philosophies of the partners are compatible. The venture will be doomed to fail unless the partners have compatible business philosophies.

Commitment. Commitment of the partner to the venture is extremely important for its viability and success. The more committed the partners are, the more quality time and resources they are likely to put into the venture. Committed partners will make more of an effort and try harder to make the venture a success.

Motivation. The major benefits of entering international collaborative ventures are risk sharing, complementary resources, market access, economies of scale, and competitive leverage. One or more of these benefits may be the source of motivation for the partner to enter the venture.

In international cooperative ventures, a major motivational factor for a company is to have access to the key resources and skills needed for undertaking a business. Ideally, these resources and skills are complementary to the company's own resources and skills. Hence, a partner will be more highly motivated if the resources and skills one brings to the venture will be complementary to those of the partner.

Cooperative ventures may result in substantial cost savings and greater efficiency through the sharing of resources, the concentration of partners' efforts in areas of expertise, and scale efficiencies. Potential synergies may be created through sharing manufacturing facilities, technology, and other physical assets; marketing synergies may be created through sharing brand names, products, support services, distribution channels, sales forces, and other marketing facilities. Some other key strategic benefits may include market access, risk reduction, blocking competition, and economies of learning.

Reliability. A prospective partner's reliability refers to "the intentions and ability to accomplish what was promised." This is an important variable because it shows how much you can trust and count on the partner. One of the questions managers may ask themselves in evaluating a potential partner is "Is this partner concerned with obtaining gains only for itself?" If the answer is "yes," that partner may be inclined not to deal fairly. Partner characteristics such as reasonableness, honesty, and trustworthiness do not generally become evident until you have some business experience with the partner. Other things being equal, you should choose a firm that you know well from previous positive business dealings to be your partner.

Task-Related Criteria

Task-related selection criteria refer to those variables, both tangible and intangible, human and nonhuman, that are relevant for the venture's viability in terms of its operational requirements. Hence, these variables are specific to operational resources and skills related to the venture (i.e., financial, marketing, organizational, production and R&D resources, and customer service).

Financial Resources. The current availability and future outlook of the financial resources that the partner can provide to the venture are important considerations. The partner should have a sound and healthy financial status to be able to provide its share of the venture's funding. Partners that are not able to provide their share of funding will slow venture growth and development and put additional financial burdens on the other partner(s).

Financial ratios (e.g., profit margin on sales, return on total assets, and return on company equity) show the relationship of figures found in financial statements. By comparing the potential partner's ratios with those of its principal competitors in the same industry, it is possible to identify the relative strengths of the partner. The analysis of ratios includes assessment of absolute values and trends. Ratio analysis has limitations, but if used with care and judgment, it can be helpful.

The credit rating is an overall measure of how well a company manages its financial resources. You may refer to Dunn & Bradstreet International and the U.S. Department of Commerce World Traders Data Reports (WTDR), which provide ratings for overall soundness of companies. For example, WTDR gives information such as financial and trade references for specific foreign firms on request, at a nominal cost.

It is extremely important that the partner for a cooperative venture have a prospective future in terms of growth and profitability. Any sign that the partner might have financial problems in the future is a warning for any company that considers working with that partner. If the partner has a healthy outlook for continuous growth and profitability, then most likely it will not have a hard time generating the financial resources necessary for the continuity and success of the cooperative venture.

R&D and Technical Resources. An organization's leverage vis-à-vis other firms is often enhanced if it possesses superior technology as well as good R&D and technical resources. These are particularly important if the venture is primarily based on R&D (e.g., joint R&D). Moreover, firms often expect a potential partner to have a minimum level of R&D and technological resources and capabilities. In cooperative ventures involving technology transfer or sharing, the transfer of technology is a major component of the venture. To identify how easy (or difficult) the transfer of technology will be, an assessment of the level of the technical resources of the partner is required. The higher the level of R&D and technical resources, the easier the transfer of technology will be.

In evaluating the partner's performance in new-product development and process enhancement, it is advisable to check their records of new-product developments, available facilities, and new-product organization and coordination. The quality of the R&D and technical personnel is far more important than how many of them there are. Checking the educational qualifications of the scientists (as well as the total number of scientists) working for the partner or checking outside evaluations, such as those provided by Dunn & Bradstreet, may be helpful in this regard. Checking into the patents owned by the potential partner may also be helpful.

Marketing Resources. Market access along with capabilities in marketing, promotion and sales, and distribution are viewed as important critical success factors, particularly within the context of a local or regional target market. If the role of your partner is to bring key marketing resources to the venture, then a careful assessment is essential. In particular, it is important to determine their strengths vis-à-vis their competitors.

It is very important to ascertain whether the potential partner has coverage of and access to key customers and distribution channels in the target market(s). The partner's relations with the master distributors and their affiliates in the market are very important to facilitate access to the channels. For example, consider the drug and pharmaceutical industry in Canada. In that case, there are four different types of decision makers in the channel: certification boards (to obtain licenses for the products), hospitals, distributors (to stock and sell the products), and end consumers. Familiarity with these decision makers in the target market is very important to facilitate access to and distribution in the target market.

Marketing of the products will be done much more efficiently and effectively if the partner has a sound, established, and well-structured marketing organization. In evaluating the sales force, your partner's experience in the market and with the products, past performance in the market, reputation among customers, and knowledge of the market and the customers are important factors to consider. If the image of the potential partner is well established and its trademarks and brand names are successful in the target market, this will imply that the partner has been a good marketer of its offerings.

Production Resources. In some collaborative ventures, particularly those involving manufacturing, the production resources (both tangible and intangible) of a prospective partner may be important factors for selecting the company as a partner. For instance, the partner may provide a good location for plants and fixed assets of the venture or may have a highly productive and efficient workforce. The current condition of the partner's production plants and fixed assets must be assessed by you as adequate to produce quality output efficiently. The relevant question you must ask yourself is this: How do the production facilities and assets of your potential partner look to a casual observer? In many instances, formation of a cooperative venture may be stimulated due to the availability of "good" production facilities and assets. The more competitive, well maintained, and available these facilities and assets are, the more they represent an opportunity to invest at an advantage.

Particularly for manufacturing-related ventures, characteristics of the partner's production workforce will be an important criterion in assessing the partner's production resources. These characteristics may include factors such as education level, turnover, absenteeism, trainability, and flexibility.

Any incentives that the partner is able to secure from the government for local production are part of its production resources. The more the partner is able to obtain incentives from the government of the country in which the production is going to take place, the more attractive that partner will be to work with.

Organizational Resources. The existing managerial skills and resources of a prospective partner may have an impact on the selection of that partner. Some of these managers may become operating managers, directors, or important officers of the collaborative venture. Hence, it is important that the partner have competent, experienced people to assign to the venture, as well as an effectively run organization.

The analysis of your partner's organization provides an overall measure of (a) its approach to business transactions, (b) its measures of performance, (c) its levels of planning and control, and (d) its management and selection of personnel. In some of these areas, disagreement between the partners can lead to serious difficulties in daily decisions and management of the venture.

The way your partner establishes courses of action and goals can provide information as to whether both companies have compatible approaches to managing and conducting business. For example, you may check the reporting system in the partner's organization.

It is important that you understand the planning and control system in the partner's organization. The more similar its planning and control system is to yours, the easier it will be for you to understand it.

Senior personnel turnover refers to the number of times senior employees are replaced in a year. This number suggests the level of employment stability and thus the likelihood of continuing with the company goals, objectives, and policies set by senior people. It also represents an indicator of the overall efficiency of the firm. The higher the turnover, the lower the efficiency.

Customer Service. Customer service, including after-sales service, warranties, and reverse distribution, is another critical factor, especially for prolonged success in the market. Good customer service will increase the likelihood of repurchase by customers, which is necessary for continued presence and success in the market. Customer services can become a competitive weapon under certain circumstances and for some industries. If the characteristics of the products or technology require considerable support from the partner, then a good assessment of the level of customer service provided by your partner is very important.

The partner must have capable personnel to perform the customer service function, including after-sales service on request by customers. The amount of geographical market coverage the partner has is an important factor in assessing its customer service. In emerging economies, assessment of geographical coverage includes the extent of paved roads and the condition of the service fleet.

Selecting a Foreign Distributor

There are five major dimensions that influence the selection of a foreign distributor (see Exhibit 6.5): (a) level of commitment, (b) financial and general company strengths, (c) marketing skills, (d) product-related factors, and (e) facilitating factors. Although the final three factors should be

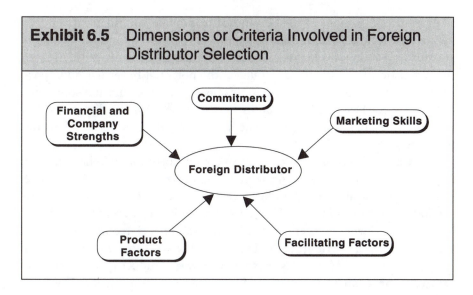

Exhibit 6.5   Dimensions or Criteria Involved in Foreign Distributor Selection

weighted less than the distributor's level of commitment and financial and company strengths, they are important because they relate to the distributor's specific marketing capabilities, product, and target market knowledge.

Commitment

Commitment is the most important factor in the evaluation of a foreign distributor. A highly committed distributor will take your product to heart and will also make it a personal objective to make the sale of your product a success in that particular country.

Be careful in choosing distributors whose product mix exhibits extreme volatility over time. You should instead consider distributors who have stable product portfolios. This stability suggests that the distributor has long-term commitments to its product lines; that is, it has grown by focusing its efforts on a few product lines at a time. Be wary if a large percentage of its sales are from a single supplier. This often means that the distributor is already committed to the product lines of this supplier and may not give you the necessary attention that your product deserves.

Although the distributor may be willing to maintain a satisfactory level of inventory, you should also determine his ability to do so. You should check to see whether the distributor has warehouse space available to carry the required level of inventory. It is also advisable to check to see whether the distributor has access to contingency space that would enable quick access to additional space when needed.

Assess the capability of the distributor to provide you financial support for advertising and promotional activities. The distributor may provide support for translation, trade fairs, and so on. Some products, because of their characteristics, are difficult to sell unless the potential buyer has an opportunity to examine them in person. In this instance, trade fairs and shows are most useful for bringing buyers and sellers together. Ask the distributor for a list of trade fairs in which he or she has participated, as well as plans for the coming year.

One way of determining the extent of commitment that will be extended to your product is to check on the quality and size of the sales force to be dedicated to your product. Another factor you need to consider is the training and compensation levels of the personnel to be dedicated to your product. If some form of sales and technical training is required for your product, choose a distributor who is willing to commit to a joint effort with you in the training of its sales personnel. If your product is of a technical nature, training can be expensive and it is better to seek a distributor who is willing to share these costs with you.

It is important for potential distributors to have a clear understanding of your objectives and expectations from the outset. One of these objectives should be the target sales volume of the distributor for your product. One way to evaluate the level of commitment is to ask the distributor whether minimum sales-level provisions are acceptable in the contract.

Financial and Company Strengths

The financial standing of the distributor is the second-most-important criteria. First, it shows the ability of the distributor to make money as well as being in "business." Second, it indicates the ability of the distributor to perform some marketing functions, such as extension of credit to customers and risk absorption. Therefore, seek distributors who are well capitalized. Their financial statements should clearly indicate their earning potential and ability to invest in the venture. Immediate investments may be necessary for certain up-front expenditures, such as hiring additional salespersons. In addition, carefully choose distributors who have the working capital to handle rapid sales increases when the need arises.

The capability of the distributor to borrow money and obtain credit indicates a strong financial position. A distributor who has the support of the local financial community is usually one whose business performance suggests strong sales and profits. The basic issue that this question addresses is whether the distributor is capable of securing any additional funding that is needed immediately or that may be needed in the future as the business takes off. There are also three other important criteria that determine the amount of capital needed: (a) the region/country that you are trying to enter, (b) the industry you are in, and (c) the number of associated lines the distributor is already carrying.

One way to evaluate the size of the distributor is by assessing whether the distributor has a critical mass of organizational capabilities to support your product in the local market. If the distributor is too small, it may not be able to provide sufficient organizational support for your product or push your product through the market channels. The distributor needs to have a critical mass of capabilities in financing, logistics, sales support, administration, and order-handling process.

The way the distributorship is managed is a critical factor to consider. The quality of the senior management can be assessed through objective measures as evidenced by its experience level, strong performance measures, or through objective evaluation methods, such as the motivation level of its employees and the care and attention given to the distributor's workplace. Determine whether the distributor has competent people who will carry out the mission. You can ask for the curricula vitae of the top management team to get a better sense of their qualifications and the length of time they have been with the distributor. Moreover, try to get a sense of the managers' share in ownership of the company, as well as bonus and compensation plans.

Seek distributors who are knowledgeable about your product and your customer segments. If you want quick entry into the foreign marketplace, the distributor may lack the necessary skills to help you achieve this goal. Check to see how long the distributor has been working in your market segment and how successful it has been (e.g., their share in your market segment). You may also ask the distributor for a list of references to check.

Although the quality and level of technical support is less important for consumer and other nondurable products, this factor is *critical* for industrial and consumer durables. If you are an exporter of either type of product, it is important for you to consider distributors who can provide an acceptable level of technical support in your product line. The issues that you need to consider are the technical expertise for the product, sales force support, and conformance with the required quality and level of technical support.

To help facilitate your assessment of the distributor, obtain verification about the distributor's reputation and effective performance. It is wise to talk with customers such as retailers and other end users who have dealt directly with the distributor. They are a good source of information concerning the work ethics of the distributor, its financial standing in the marketplace, and its general reputation in the business community. You should also seek additional information through the Department of Commerce officers in that country. Additionally, check with the bank(s) of the distributor, a good source of information about the distributor's credit and financial standing. Also, consult previous and current suppliers who have been represented by the distributor, because they are the best sources of information about the distributor's overall capability.

Trade associations and other business groups have a key role in promoting, fostering, and protecting the interests of corporations and persons engaged in business in many countries. In addition, they also facilitate coordination and cooperation among their members. Hence, distributors who are actively involved in these trade associations are likely to be highly committed and involved businesspeople. Determine which trade associations a distributor belongs to and then check with those associations to see whether the distributor is a member in good standing.

Marketing Skills

Although a high level of motivation and commitment are necessary factors to consider in the distribution evaluation, they are not sufficient. The extent of geographical coverage of the distributor and its knowledge of the target segments are also equally important. Distributors who are knowledgeable about their markets are very often also familiar with customer requirements. The quality of management, size of the distributor, and experience of its sales force also bear directly on the marketing ability of the distributor.

You should consider the distributor's number of years and level of experience with the marketing channels relevant to your product. You should also check to see whether he or she has the necessary connections with industry leaders, retailers, final customers, and consumers.

A well-articulated marketing plan is a strong indicator that the distributor has long-term goals and visions for the business. Avoid distributors who do not have the ability to chart out future strategies and implement them. Ask the distributor how marketing is planned with suppliers. In doing so, look to see whether some process is in place that has objective task-budget control.

Nearly all distributors will claim that they cover their entire national territory. Benchmarks to look for are the distributor's physical facilities, the size and training of the sales force, and the number of sales outlets. Try to determine the particular market segments the distributor services and the extent of market share in each. You should evaluate the distributor's geographic coverage in terms of principal market areas. The extent of market coverage of a distributor and how well these markets are served are often good indicators of an experienced sales force. In addition to these factors, there are more precise ways to judge the experience of the distributor's sales personnel. First, you should look at the number of customers visited by the sales force on a regular basis. Second, you should consider the average size of customers' orders.

Market share is often an indicator of marketing performance. High market share has also been shown to be correlated with high profitability. Distributors with high market shares frequently have strong marketing skills and may also have stronger financial resources vis-à-vis other distributors with smaller market shares. Distributors with more experience often tend to have higher market shares than newer distributors.

If you need to train the distributor's sales force to handle your product, an important factor to consider is the capability of the sales force to absorb training in your product line. In addition to evaluating qualitative factors, such as the level of motivation, you should also consider whether their prior experience and level of education are sufficient for the level of training needed. If the distributor's sales force has limited capabilities to absorb training, you might have to send your own sales force to the local marketplace, thereby incurring additional set-up costs.

Also, in regard to training, does the distributor have regular sales training sessions or sales meetings and/or communications among its sales people? The point of this question is to determine whether the distributor has a disciplined way of training and communicating with its sales force. The details of the actual process are not as important as its existence, acknowledgment, and regularity.

The distributor's access to local media placement and scheduling is of great importance for your advertising campaign. The distributor may also support your efforts by preparing promotional materials (e.g., brochures, handouts, etc.). Ask for samples of promotional materials previously produced.

You should consider distributors who have the capabilities to provide on-time and complete deliveries. These capabilities often reflect the quality of the distributor's logistics management. A customer-oriented distributor would attend to customer requests, complaints, and concerns as quickly as possible (i.e., within 24 hours).

Product Factors

Product-related factors include knowledge about the product, characteristics of the distributor's existing product lines, and the extent of the distributor's service and stocking facilities. Establishing a relationship with a distributor who is unfamiliar with your product may result in some marketing problems. However, training the distributor's sales force about the type of servicing and marketing that your product needs may turn an unfamiliar product around. Check the number of product lines carried by the distributor. It may be spread too thinly, concentrating only on products that provide the best compensation. Avoid distributors who are handling direct competitors' products. Instead, concentrate on distributors who handle complementary product lines and who have already achieved some degree of specialization in sales and service.

How familiar is the distributor with your product line? In this question, *product line* refers to your line of products the distributor will be handling. If the distributor has a high level of familiarity and knowledge about your product(s), this will increase his or her awareness of product applications, customer requirements, before- and after-sales service needs, as well as special inventory, packaging, delivery arrangements, and so on.

What is the quality level of the product lines currently carried by the distributor? The quality match for products is important for product-positioning reasons (e.g., a high-quality product may suffer from a bad distributor reputation). At the same time, you have to find a match between the quality of your product and the quality of the product lines carried by the distributor. This can affect the types of retailers who will want to sell your product. It is important to realize that quality is very hard to assess; however, a few guidelines can help you make a better a assessment. If the distributor is a manufacturer, you may use ISO 9000 quality standards. Has the distributor received any quality awards from customers or from any national or international associations or organizations? Have any favorable articles been written about the distributor? Does the distributor have a good brand name in the sector? You may also ask for literature about the products the distributor is currently handling.

If your product needs special handling, you may have to invest in the construction of minor facilities to accommodate your product. Unless these investment costs can be shared between you and the distributor, it is not wise to invest in assets that may lock you into a particular country.

Violation of intellectual property rights is an increasing problem in many countries that do not provide stringent intellectual property protection laws or impose strict sanctions against violators. Consider distributors who are willing to invest money in ensuring this protection. Note, however, that in certain countries, the distributor's hands may be tied and he or she may be unable to bring about effective enforcement. These are the four issues you need to check into: (a) the existence of an intellectual property protection

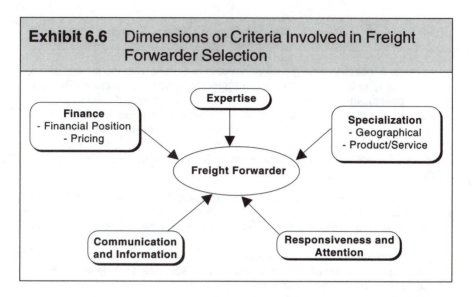

Exhibit 6.6   Dimensions or Criteria Involved in Freight Forwarder Selection

law, (b) the efficacy of the law, (c) the enforcement of the law, and (d) the ability of the distributor to protect your intellectual property regardless of regulations and enforcement (check with other suppliers on this).

Facilitating Factors

This last factor does not have a major influence in the decision-making process, but it is helpful in facilitating a smoother relationship between you and the foreign distributor. This is particularly so in certain countries. Things to consider include the distributor's English-speaking and writing skills, prior experience with Western exporters, and local government contacts and overall reputation.

Selecting a Freight Forwarder

Working in the complex world of international business can be confusing and time-consuming. Changes in the world markets, legislation, and customs laws may affect your business. Hence, evaluation and selection of the most appropriate freight forwarder is of utmost importance. Freight forwarders can be evaluated on the dimensions of expertise, specialization, responsiveness and attention, efficiency and reliability, communication and information capabilities, and finance (see Exhibit 6.6). The objective is to select the freight forwarder that will best fit your needs for customs

---

Exhibit 6.7   What Makes a Good Cross-Border Partner?

The key to success in emerging economies is not capital and technology alone, but the ability to build, develop, and nurture sustainable relationships with foreign suppliers and partners. When it comes to international alliances, North American businesses have a reputation for valuing technology over relationships; acting superior and all-knowing; preferring total unilateral control; believing few differences exist between countries and companies; and acting in their short-term interest. To be successful with a foreign partner, the following characteristics are needed:

- The good partner recognizes that relationship-building and local ties are keys to success.
- The good partner brings and transfers strengths while respecting the other partner's strengths.
- The good partner shares control.
- Good partners identify areas of conflict in advance and develop mutual understanding to resolve conflicts.
- The good partner recognizes differences.
- The good partner clearly signals commitment.

SOURCE: Kanter, R. M., & Yatsko, P. (Summer, 1994). Ice Dancing, *Global Competitor* (pp. 27-30).

---

brokerage, international freight forwarding, warehousing, cargo insurance, customs consulting, commercial insurance, and government (domestic and international) or customs rules and regulations. Hence, there is no "good" or "bad" forwarder. There is only the one that fits your needs the best!

Expertise

International transportation can be a very complex business. Shipments of single, identical contents to the same overseas destination can be routinely handled in-house. However, in-house shipping decisions can be costly. The expertise and experience of forwarders in various markets with different types of products, shipping methods, and terms constitute the most important factor in evaluating and selecting a freight forwarder. The expertise of the forwarder can be critical even in "routine" shipments that require special export documentation, customs clearance, and tracking. The forwarder must be knowledgeable of customs requirements and must be able to track your business continuously.

In shopping for a forwarder, the forwarder's knowledge of the destination country is crucial because the forwarder's expertise in import rules and regulations and customs clearance in the destination country is what differentiates a suitable forwarder from an unsuitable one. Such knowledge aids the preparation of accurate and timely carrier and commercial documents and eliminates costly delays.

One of the major reasons for going through a forwarder instead of forwarding your own freight is the expertise in specific shipping methods and terms. A forwarder's expertise in United States or your home country's export rules and regulations is also crucial for smooth and successful business. A freight forwarder's ability to quote itemized freight and common carrier costs and port charges is important in reflecting its cost structure. When evaluating these quotes, keep in mind that forwarders can obtain preferential volume rates for freight and insurance. A forwarder can save clients money by recommending terms of sale most beneficial to the exporter. Warehousing facilities may be needed from time to time, depending on the type of product exported. A forwarder need not have its own warehousing facilities but should be able to arrange for them if needed.

The expertise of the forwarder in handling high-security shipments, such as gold, antiques, and defense materials, is critical, especially if your product is such an item. High-security shipments require expertise not only in protecting the goods but also in additional measures that may be needed to protect against technology leakages.

The number of customers a forwarder has and the duration of the business relationships are good indicators of a forwarder's expertise and experience. Unless the forwarder is newly established, knowledge can be expected to increase with the number of customers, because the more customers, the more different situations the forwarder has experienced.

Specialization

Many freight forwarders specialize in very specific areas, such as fine art, agricultural products, or hazardous products, whereas others will handle almost anything. Consider the nature of your own product. If it requires specialized handling, equipment, or expertise, a specialized forwarder becomes important. Another source of specialization is geographic. Regionally and/or country-specific specialized forwarders have valuable international shipping and handling expertise.

Communication and Information

In an era in which national markets are becoming increasingly interrelated and interdependent, an extensive communication and information network is highly desirable. Communication between all parties involved in the forwarding process, particularly between exporter and forwarder, is crucial for a smooth business. A forwarder must understand the exporter's needs, and the exporter must direct the forwarder to respond to the client's needs. In today's dynamic global environment, information is becoming a significant strategic tool. Forwarders are adopting new technologies to respond to the information needs of their clients. Automation and computerization are efficient methods used in tracking and tracing shipments. They also enable a forwarder to uncover and solve problems at any point of a shipment.

International forwarding must be seen as an uninterrupted whole. "Instant worldwide tracking" is a critical service, especially for companies new in exporting or exporting to some destinations for the first time. When complications or delays occur, being able to track the goods can help you explain the situation to third parties. Tracking would also make you more in charge of the forwarding process and enable you to make quick and informed decisions when unexpected situations occur. Electronic data interchange (EDI) is the computer-to-computer exchange of business documents sent over communication lines using recognized data standards. A forwarder's ability to receive a shipper's instructions in EDI and transmit them to the carriers for booking and bill-of-lading information in EDI would not only accelerate communication but also save money and time and reduce error.

Responsiveness and Attention

A freight forwarder's responsiveness and attention to your business is very critical in determining the success of your business. Responsiveness and attention can be particularly important if your export business is small in volume and infrequent. Performance in this dimension can be enhanced by assigning a highly competent person to handle your transactions, securing high-quality continuous trade services, transportation services, value-added services, competent decision making in case of emergency or crisis, timely responses to your inquiries, and customization of forwarding services to your particular needs.

The amount of time it takes for the freight forwarder to respond to your quotation inquiries is an indicator of his or her responsiveness. A responsive freight forwarder should not take more than 48 hours to respond to your questions. The time interval may depend on the type of your inquiry, but a 24- to 48-hour response time is acceptable for most situations. Also, recognize that quotations are valid for a 30-day period for most forwarders.

Efficiency and Reliability

Efficiency and reliability are important considerations for any exporter or importer active in international trade. An *efficient* freight forwarder is one that clears merchandise quickly and obtains the stamped customs documents rapidly. *Reliability* refers to the intentions and ability of the forwarder to accomplish what it has promised. This variable is important because it will directly affect the success of your shipment.

Transporting merchandise internationally involves far greater risks than does domestic transit. Worldwide catastrophic losses directly affect a shipper's profitability. Using the services of a freight forwarder can decrease such risks considerably. To choose an experienced specialist, make sure the forwarder has a good risk history in handling the goods of other clients. However, also consider that these percentages may vary greatly from country to country. In some countries, unfavorable infrastructures may make these percentages too optimistic.

One of the most important services provided by forwarders is customs clearance. With their networks of connections and liaison persons, forwarders are able to clear goods from customs more efficiently. Hence, a forwarder's history of relations with customs officials in your port of destination are important determinants of efficiency and reliability.

Finance

Finance-related selection criteria refer to the financial stability of the forwarder and the prices it quotes relative to other forwarders. Financial stability is a very important criterion in choosing the "right" forwarder. In the United States, financial requirements are not regulated by the government. Consequently, an exporter may prepay for a shipment in the United States only to have it arrive at its destination with charges due. In this case, if the forwarder has declared bankruptcy, the exporter is responsible for paying the shipping charges a second time.

The freight forwarder's bank is perhaps the best single source for information on the financial position of the forwarder. The best way to approach the forwarder in obtaining information regarding financial matters could be the *exchange* of financial information. Do not forget that *your financial position* is of interest to the forwarder as well. Clients of the freight forwarder are another source of information regarding the forwarder's financial position. In most cases, freight forwarders are chosen on a word-of-mouth basis.

International freight forwarders deal with several third parties in forwarding goods. They rely on the services supplied by customs brokers, port operators, carriers, and so on. These third parties can provide information on the financial position of the forwarder, particularly on its ability to make timely payments.

Some freight forwarders assume total financial responsibility for your benefit with the carrier or other service providers. Forwarders charge from 2% to 5% in advance for this additional service. In this case, based on the agreement with the forwarder, you must pay the freight costs in a very short period. This is an important factor in maintaining a healthy, continuous relationship between the freight forwarder and the client. Some freight forwarders function merely as liaisons between carriers and exporters without assuming any financial responsibility.

Note

1. The authors wish to thank the Decision Support Services Division of the International Business Center, Michigan State University, East Lansing, MI, for allowing us to use their research for partner selection, distributor selection, and freight forwarder selection. This research is the outcome of a 5-year team effort working with various organizations (exporters, freight forwarders, distributors, bankers, semigovernmental and governmental trade agencies, and others) in the area of exporting. Decision Support Software Tools based on expert systems logic have been developed by the same team and are available at nominal prices. Please contact the International Business Center, Michigan State University, East Lansing, MI.

Negotiation Process and Strategies for Emerging Markets

The Nature of the Business Negotiation

Business negotiations—especially cross-cultural business negotiations—are often a frustrating and stressful process. Negotiating involves perceiving and interpreting a wide range of factors on the basis of a limited amount of information. And by their nature, *international* business negotiations are even more complex in that they involve more unknowns and often much higher stakes. If you become perplexed by these difficulties, the sheer fear of negotiating a bad deal for yourself or for your company may cloud your perceptions, negatively affecting the negotiating process itself.

Yet negotiating is a basic human activity. Every day, we enter into a series of negotiations, both big and small. We negotiate where we should eat our lunch, what time our proposals are due, and when we will arrive at home. Negotiations are a process of managing our relationships and resolving our differences. Often, they are activities undertaken and completed without much thought or difficulty. What makes these everyday negotiations different from resolving international business agreements?

Obviously, international business negotiations occur between two different business organizations in two or more different countries. Less obviously, however, are the deeper implications of the word *different*. Negotiations are inherently a perceptual and interpretive process, and thus, they are dictated by what we perceive and interpret as being different or the same.

First, when we negotiate with our coworkers regarding what time our proposal will be ready to be discussed, we are generally perceiving the negotiations to be occurring within a single organization and among people with similar goals. Here, we enter into this process with the expectation of success: A mutually agreeable solution can and will be found. Because we all are working for the same organization, we assume that everyone is working toward the same goals and will be willing to make reasonable concessions toward this end.

However, when dealing with negotiations in which we perceive ourselves to be different from the other negotiating party, the whole process of negotiating becomes suspect. Negotiating with strangers is not the same as negotiating with friends. Within the realm of business, businesspeople tend to view things in terms of competition ("What are our competitors doing?"): competitive standing, competitive intelligence, and so on. We believe that the other party might be looking out only for themselves, and thus we adjust our bargaining position accordingly. We pad our proposals with stipulations we plan to concede later, mask our true intentions, and generally take a more hard-line stance toward making concessions.

Second, because these agreements are international, we are also working with differences across a much larger realm of assumptions. Our everyday negotiations have the advantage of sharing many things in common. Despite differences in our positions, we are still working within the same culture. We have similar expectations for protocol, use the same language, and understand each other's idioms. Furthermore, we both draw on a common history and more likely than not, will use similar tactics and logic to resolve our differences.

In international negotiations, we lack these shared experiences and expectations. The Eastern mind may approach problems with a mind-set that is entirely different from the Western mind and arrive at a completely different set of conclusions. Business protocol in Arab countries often differs greatly from what we may expect, and business organizations in Eastern Europe may be completely different from the way we might want things run. Failing to meet each other's expectations often leads to unintended insults or simply a lack of communication.

For example, many countries differ in their perceptions of time. In some countries, promptness is always to be expected. Eight o'clock in the morning means being at the designated place exactly on time and ready to conduct business. Being 15 minutes late might be considered an insult or, at the least, sloppy business practice. In other countries, however, 8:00 a.m. might be more negotiable—might perhaps mean closer to 9:00 a.m. or even involve a last-minute change of location or cancellation. In these countries, such changes happen all the time and would not normally be interpreted negatively.

Countries and cultures also differ in level of formality and familiarity. On arriving in a host country for a round of negotiations, some hosts may insist on dining before discussing business. Discussing business during such a meal may be considered rude or in poor taste. In other countries, negotiations might start right away and delays might be seen as a tactic to avoid or stall negotiations.

The primary obstacle to successful international negotiations is overcoming perceptions of difference and making the negotiations a cooperative effort. "Win-lose" bargaining styles, in which gains must be offset by an opposing party's loss, are generally considered outdated. Opportunist and competitive perspectives for negotiating limit the benefits both parties can achieve by working together, especially considering the advantages and opportunities of international cooperation. Although you should always be wary of being taken advantage of, we suggest that you adopt a "win-win" technique, often referred to as *integrative negotiating*. This technique approaches coming to an agreement as a problem to be solved. Both parties work together to find a solution that leaves both parties better off. The benefits of this type of negotiations have been studied by many authors (e.g., Fisher & Ury, 1991; Ghauri, 1986; Ghauri & Usunier, 1999; Lewicki, Letterer, Minton, & Sanders, 1994; Pruitt & Rubin, 1986; Walton & McKersie, 1965).

Win-win negotiating can be characterized as follows:

- Having more open information flow between parties. Both parties sincerely disclose their objectives and try to find where their goals overlap.
- Recognizing that the parties have common as well as conflicting interests that will affect an agreement. Both parties agree to achieve common and complementary objectives as much as possible.
- Sincerely and truly trying to understand the other party's point of view.

Preparing for Success

With an amazing number of differences between cultures, it is easy to think that international business executives would be well served by a comprehensive resource describing the necessary etiquette and protocol for each country. Indeed, there are many good resources that provide this information. However, although this kind of knowledge is often very helpful, there is a distinct danger in relying on a "dictionary" of culture. People appreciate the efforts of a visitor to learn more about them, but most people distinctly dislike being defined or stereotyped by a "typical" behavior pattern.

You are still dealing with individuals. Moreover, the goal of this kind of cultural research should be to facilitate your understanding of your negotiation partner and not to mimic or simply role-play his or her expectations.

An open mind, friendly attitude, and a general sensitivity for cultural differences will go a long way toward facilitating negotiations. Knowing a culture's customs is less a quantitative or qualitative strategy for negotiating than it is a gesture of good will. Your partner probably recognizes your cultural differences and will allow you a few well-meant mistakes. The effect of shaking hands versus bowing, for example, is probably negligible.

With this in mind, the best strategy for successful negotiating is good preparation. Knowing as much as you can about your partner's position and your own will help reduce anxiety, as well as provide you with more insight toward achieving your goals. As with all negotiations, stress and pressure are the real enemies to making a good deal. Stress makes us tired, and when we are tired, we make more mistakes. It is important to analyze every offer for what it is worth, rather than accept or reject it because we feel the need for some kind of conclusion.

Self-Knowledge

The axiom "Know thyself" cannot be overemphasized. This means knowing not only your bargaining position but also the cultural biases you are bringing to the table. Recognizing your own expectations regarding protocol and business behavior will help you recognize cultural differences and avoid miscommunication. For example, American business style tends to be direct and to the point (see Exhibit 7.1). Recognizing this, you will know that you can expect a less direct negotiating style in some parts of Asia and make a conscious effort to adapt your style and expectations. You might reword your criticisms of your partner's offer to avoid offending them inadvertently, or simply pick up on subtleties that they might have implied but did not state directly.

Understand Your Partner

An acute knowledge of your negotiating partner is also very important. This includes information about the company as well as political, social, and cultural factors. These things make up the background against which negotiations are played out. A more complete understanding of the environment in which your partner operates will help you understand their position and lend you insight into how they will approach negotiations. For example, many Western executives are frustrated by their inability to extract firm

Exhibit 7.1   Cultural Baggage: The American Style of Negotiating

John L. Graham and Roy A. Herberger contend that America's frontier history has led to a "John Wayne" style of negotiating. Raised on a culture that values action and independence, the American negotiator tends to "shoot first" and "ask questions later." Although this makes for an entertaining movie, Americans may be shooting themselves in the foot when it comes to an international business showdown. Be aware of these tendencies and understand the advantages and disadvantages that come with them.

- "I can do it alone." Many U.S. executives seem to believe they can handle any negotiating situation by themselves, and they are outnumbered in most negotiating situations. Negotiating involves doing several things at once, including speaking, listening, thinking up arguments, making explanations, and formulating questions. There is safety in numbers.
- "Just call me John." Americans value informality and equality in human relations. They try to make people feel comfortable by playing down status distinctions. This may make us feel comfortable but may alienate or annoy people from less egalitarian cultures.
- "Pardon my French." Americans aren't very talented at speaking foreign languages.
- "Check with the home office." American negotiators often get upset when halfway through a negotiation, the other side says, "I'll have to check with the home office." The implication is that the decision makers are not present.
- "Get to the point." Americans don't like to beat around the bush and want to get to the heart of the matter quickly.
- "Lay your cards on the table." Americans expect honest information at the bargaining table.
- "Don't just sit there, speak up." Americans don't deal well with silence during negotiations.
- "Don't take 'no' for an answer." Persistence is highly valued by Americans and is part of the deeply ingrained competitive spirit that manifests itself in every aspect of American life.
- "One thing at a time." Americans usually attack a complex negotiation task sequentially; that is, they separate the issues and settle them one at a time.
- "A deal is a deal." When Americans make an agreement and give their word, they expect to honor the agreement no matter what the circumstances.
- "I am what I am." Few Americans take pride in changing their minds, even in difficult circumstances.

SOURCE: Graham, J. L., & Herberger, R. A., Jr. Negotiators abroad—don't shoot from the hip, *Harvard Business Review,* July-August, 1983.

commitments from their foreign partners. Westerners are accustomed to making binding, long-term deals. However, in some Latin American countries in which political and economic conditions fluctuate rapidly, local companies may find themselves unwilling or unable to commit beyond a few months.

Knowing the political climate of a country is extremely important, not only because it will affect the stability of your investment but also because it shows how a foreign partner might approach a binding agreement. In countries without a strong legal system, a company may see a written agreement as an indication of intention. Trying to hold a company to an agreement in a country with a weak legal system may be difficult or impossible. Moreover, in many countries in which businesses cannot rely on legal recourse, business culture may insist on more rapport-building efforts to establish a relationship. Finally, it is always wise to understand the possible political impediments to doing business with a foreign company. Businesses often must operate under a variety of restrictions and regulatory procedures that may affect what a business will seek in negotiations.

A familiarity with social and cultural conventions of a given country will prevent you from inadvertently offending your partner during negotiations and will also facilitate the methods and strategies you might employ. An international business executive quickly learns that business in one country is simply not like business in another country, as illustrated in Exhibit 7.2. Despite the universality of basic business motives and methods, culture plays a large role in how people perceive and evaluate things.

Culture and belief systems affect how we perceive, judge, think, and decide about the world. Normally, culture plays only a very subtle influence in our daily communications because we are surrounded by people of the same culture. However, when we are placed within the proximity of another culture, negotiating these differences becomes a very dynamic process. Human beings tend to project cognitive similarity onto other people. This means that we assume that other people will think the way we do, which is not always the case.

For example, given the emphasis on teamwork and social harmony in Japan, the role of the individual is often downplayed. In cultures like this, direct confrontation will probably be avoided and found distasteful or uncomfortable. Rather than give a direct "no" to a proposal, a Japanese negotiator might sidestep giving an answer, stall, or simply fall silent. In contrast, Americans are very often outgoing and direct. Not hearing a definite "no" might be interpreted as a "yes" or perhaps not be acknowledged as an impasse.

Different countries' speech patterns also differ in their treatment of silence. American executives are often uncomfortable with silence and will

Exhibit 7.2   Classifying Cultures for International Business Executives

The following is a model developed by Richard Gesteland for classifying cultures. It is not completely definitive but provides a useful perspective for understanding cultural differences. Keep in mind that cultures vary along each of these dichotomies and need not be completely consistent.

Deal-Focused vs. Relationship-Focused

In short, deal-focused cultures are task oriented, while relationship-focused cultures are people oriented. The United States is relatively more deal-focused than other cultures. U.S. executives often do business with people they do not know, and they often forego pleasantries to move directly to discussing business. In contrast, in more relationship-focused cultures, business executives often depend on introductions to other business associates by mutual contacts. They do not conduct business with strangers and spend more time developing relationships before feeling comfortable discussing business.

Formal vs. Informal

The United States has a relatively informal and egalitarian business culture. Although many Americans intend for their informalness to put others at ease, it may make many people from more formal cultures uncomfortable. Formal cultures rely on status to indicate how one should treat another. In such countries, people in lesser positions of power are at a disadvantage in negotiating with more senior members of the other party. Young people and women may also experience barriers. Respect is extremely important in formal cultures. When in doubt, it is always better to err on the side of overformality.

Rigid Time vs. Fluid Time

Perceptions and treatment of time differ across the world. Cultures with rigid time structures and strict expectations for punctuality are called *monochronic cultures. Polychronic cultures,* in contrast, treat time more fluidly. In a polychronic culture, associates might show up late for appointments, reschedule at the last minute, or even cancel once you have arrived. More monochronic cultures might expect you to arrive either a little bit early or exactly on time—but never even a few minutes late.

Expressive vs. Reserved

Cultures vary in the amount of expression they allow or expect from themselves and others. In some cultures, it may be perfectly normal to shout, gesticulate wildly, and otherwise express a lot of emotion. Expressive cultures also tend to overlap their speech more. But in more reserved cultures, simply raising your voice above a whisper might indicate anger, and speaking over someone is a rude interruption. In expressive cultures, strong emotions might be considered a sign of vitality, confidence, and power. In reserved cultures, however, outward displays of emotion are perceived as a lack of control or finesse.

SOURCE: Gesteland, R. R. (1996). *Cross-Cultural Business Behavior.* Denmark: Copenhangen Business School Press.

seek to fill in the void with more dialogue. Often, this leads to a quick concession that might have been unneeded or another attempt at a persuasive appeal. Long pauses in American culture are signs of an impasse but may simply be careful consideration in other cultures. Brazilian negotiators may deal with silence even less successfully than U.S. negotiators. Whereas U.S. conversational style is relatively orderly and efficient, Brazilians often speak simultaneously, fighting for the floor. U.S. executives might perceive Brazilians as poor listeners when the real problem is a clash of styles.

Finally, American businesspeople must realize that foreign executives may emphasize different goals in negotiations than Americans do. Many developing countries have placed a particular emphasis on supporting their long-term growth and development. Many of these countries have a long history with colonialism or other actions of Western powers that may affect their attitudes toward the West. They may be especially suspicious of Western companies that might take advantage of them and leave. Although this may not be true, you may have to spend considerable time establishing a relationship based on goodwill.

For example, China has been particularly shrewd when dealing with the West, often to the frustration of its would-be partners. As one of the world's oldest civilizations, China has a long history of repelling invaders and resisting foreign influences. In the past, its relations with the West have been particularly strained by imperialism, as well as by more recent rifts in ideology.

Now, recognizing its importance as the world's largest untapped market, China can be expected to drive a hard bargain in exchange for opening its doors. The Chinese have worked very hard to increase competition among the people searching for access and have played them against each other to negotiate some very favorable deals for themselves. Combined with considerable cultural barriers, Western business executives face tough negotiations when dealing with this country.

Create Alternatives

Creating alternatives ahead of time is one way of remaining flexible. Your ability to appear willing to do business and work toward a mutually acceptable agreement will be easier if you know your position ahead of time, have a good idea of the other party's position, and can readily present alternative solutions to expected impasses. Anticipate things now because it will be harder to come up with solutions under pressure. Keep asking yourself, "What should we do if they won't accept this?"

Western negotiators often believe they have only three options: persuasion, threat, or concession. In fact, there are many alternative solutions to a problem. A problem-solving attitude is important; it is not only a question of win or lose. Different issues can be combined to produce numerous alternatives. If the customer demands a 5% concession on the price, the other party can ask the customer to pay cash instead of the 1-year credit proposed. Negotiators can also ask customers to pay interest on the demanded loan. In one case, a buyer demanded a 5% concession on the contract price after everything else had been agreed on. The seller instead proposed that he was willing to give a 10% rebate on all the spare parts to be bought by the buyer during the next 3 years. This offer was accepted gladly by the buyer.

Building Bridges: The Negotiating Process

As mentioned earlier, negotiating is a process of managing relationships. Many American businesspeople expect contracts and other agreements to be negotiated within the range of a few days. Although this may be common in the United States, in many other cultures, businesspeople may expect to take their associates out for dinner and participate in other rapport-building activities before entering into an agreement. Personal relationships with partners and clients are relied on more heavily in other parts of the world, and the more experience you gain doing business abroad, the more skills you will acquire for negotiations (see Exhibit 7.3).

Communication Types

Communicating with other people can be a very complex task. It can be both verbal and nonverbal, subtle or straightforward. In addition, within the process of communication, there are many subtasks or stages that occur as participants attempt to understand each other. Communication can be broken down into four categories based on purpose: phatic, informational, persuasive, and cathartic.

Phatic communication consists of preliminary discussions intended to build binding relationships. Often overlooked, it is particularly important because we communicate better with people with whom we have created a personal bond. Greetings and small talk, for example, are important examples of phatic communication. It helps put us at ease with each other and allows us to connect with each other on a more personal level.

Phatic communication in different cultures varies in formality, length, and subject matter. What is appropriate in one culture may not always be appropriate in another. For example, in the United States, businesspeople tend to think being informal is a friendly form of confidence. In other

Exhibit 7.3   The Skilled Negotiator: Face-to-Face Behavior

A study of actual negotiations measured several behavioral differences during actual negotiations between skilled negotiators and average negotiators. Keep in mind that these measurements do not necessarily suggest a strategy but rather indicate how much a negotiator avoided common pitfalls or relied on other interpersonal skills to move negotiations along successfully.

- **Irritators.** Certain words and phrases that are commonly used during negotiation have neglible value in persuading the other party but do cause irritation, for example, using the term *generous offer* to describe your own proposal.

Number of irritators used per hour of face-to-face speaking time

Average negotiatiors	10.8
Skilled negotiators	2.3

- **Counterproposals.** During negotiations, one party frequently puts forward a proposal, and the other party immediately responds with counterproposals.

Frequency of counterproposals per hour of face-to-face speaking time

Average negotiatiors	3.1
Skilled negotiators	1.7

- **Argument Dilution.** We often tend to think having more reasons for something is more persuasive than having only one reason.

Average number of reasons given by the negotiatior to support each argument/ case advanced

Average negotiatiors	3.0
Skilled negotiators	1.8

Reviewing the Negotiation. Good negotiators set aside time to review the negotiation process afterward and recapitulate what they have learned.

Fraction of negotiators who set aside time to review negotiations

Average negotiatiors	Less than 1/2
Skilled negotiators	More than 2/3

SOURCE: Harris, P. R., & Moran, R. T. (1996). *Managing Cultural Differences* (4th ed., pp. 49-50). Texas: Gulf Publishing.

countries, however, a lack of formality and use of titles might be considered rude or make others feel uncomfortable. Americans also have a reputation for expedience. They want to arrive on the scene, begin negotiations right away, and then leave. Often, they do not realize that the round of golf their host wants them to play is actually part of the phatic round of negotiations. Until a relationship is developed, many cultures will not discuss matters of substance. A good negotiator must learn to take cues from his or her host and adapt accordingly.

Informational communication is speech intended to both request and receive information. Although this seems fairly straightforward, informational messages must still be applied within the appropriate context to be understood. Idioms, catchphrases, and adages, often used in the business world to elucidate meaning, can sometimes confuse issues even more. Even simple phrases or references can be misunderstood. For example, in the United States, an octopus is said to have several "arms." In Japan, however, it is said to have several "legs." "Next Sunday," if you are talking to a Swede, does not mean the coming Sunday, but the Sunday afterward. In India, "next Sunday" means the coming Sunday. Likewise, "nice weather" in Europe usually means sunshine, but in African and many Asian countries, "nice weather" means cloudy or rainy weather.

The third category, *persuasive* communication, includes all activities meant to persuade another person. It is most effective when the other person is a willing and able listener. This, of course, is the trick. The right kind of phatic and informational communication will play a large part in making someone receptive to your ideas. It also helps you to understand how the other person perceives and evaluates new information. Obviously, different individuals and cultures approach things differently.

Finally, *cathartic* communication provides a release of emotions. Both positive and negative emotions provide important feedback for communication, allowing you to adjust your negotiating strategy for your success and failures. For this type of communication to be effective, the other person must be willing and able to accept the conduct of the person seeking cathartic release.

By understanding your partner's communication in terms of these four communication types, you will be able to better understand what your partner is saying and how it fits in with what he or she means. Effective negotiations rely on the negotiator's ability to accurately interpret the other side and respond with an appropriate message.

Verbal Versus Nonverbal Communication

Approximately 70% of all communication occurs on a nonverbal level. Much of our meaning is conveyed in the tone of our voice, how quickly or slowly we speak, and our posture and body language. Paying attention to nonverbal cues can be a particularly helpful tool for international negotiators because many of these habits are unconscious behavior. Whereas our verbal language is carefully formulated ahead of time, our nonverbal language is generally more spontaneous and possibly more sincere or insightful. For example, sometimes people lean forward when they like what you

Exhibit 7.4   Nonverbal Signals in Business Negotiations

Hands

- An increase in hand signals, especially touching the nose or covering the mouth, suggests that a person is lying.
- A dramatic decrease in the usage of hand signals used to emphasize verbal statements also suggests that a person is not giving the correct information.
- Aggressive gestures with the hands from a person seeking cooperation suggest a contradictory message.
- Crossing arms or closing both hands together on the belly suggest non-cooperative behavior.

Body

- Increase in body shifting movements from one sitting position to another suggests that the person is lying. If he or she is on the listening end, it suggests that he or she is not comfortable with your statement.
- Body posture always gives a message. Leaning forward suggests an attentive and receptive position, whereas sagging or leaning backwards suggests boredom or a nonreceptive position.
- Foot tapping and other lower body movements suggest impatience and uneasiness.
- Looking at a wristwatch or ceiling suggests rejection of an idea or disapproval.

Face

- Facial cues are quite difficult to decode because people can control their facial behavior more easily.
- Eyebrow movements give good indication of rejective or receptive behavior. Experts can even see the shrinking or expanding of pupils accordingly.
- Sweating or licking of dry lips suggest stress, fear, or excitement.
- Coughing or swallowing of saliva suggests nervousness or a rejection of the idea presented.

SOURCE: Adapted from Hendon, D. W., et al. (1996). *Cross-Cultural Business Negotiations*. Westport, CT: Quorum Books; and Ghauri, P. N., & Usunier, J. C. (1996). *International Business Negotiations*. Oxford, UK: Pergamon Press.

are saying, or lean back and cross their arms when they don't. Excessive blinking may be related to feelings of guilt or fear. Other signals include blushing, strained laughter, or silence. Although body language is often ambiguous, it is often valuable just to note at what point of your communication your message receives a reaction (see Exhibit 7.4).

Conversely, being aware of your own nonverbal patterns may help you suppress information you might not want to give away. Sometimes rephrasing a proposal or a different approach to a problem can help tighten the presentation of your message. Acting confident physically may also help you feel emotionally confident as well.

Keep in mind that body language still varies a lot with culture. For example, U.S. business executives often require more personal space than their Latin American or Arab counterparts. Asian associates may stand even farther apart. In the United States, we consider a lot of eye contact to be a sign of honesty and sincerity. In Southeast Asia, however, direct eye contact should be avoided until a firm relationship has been established. Laughter in the West may be a sign of good humor. In Asia, it often indicates embarrassment and humility. Physical space, eye contact, and personal contact vary with how comfortable one feels with another.

Each culture also has a number of signals that are distasteful to them, although they may seem innocuous to outsiders. In Malaysia, for example, you should never touch the top of anyone's head. Malays believe this is where their souls reside. In Arab countries, it is almost impossible to sit with your legs crossed without offending someone. Showing the sole of your shoe (or pointing it at someone) is considered an insult. And in Muslim countries, one should refrain from using one's left hand—it is reserved for personal hygiene and thus is considered dirty.

Conservative behavior is almost always a wise choice, at least until one has a good idea of what is going on. American culture is relatively informal compared with much of the world, so being more formal than you think necessary is better than taking undue liberties. Until you get a feel for what is expected of you, remain perceptive and refrain from holding judgment on things you do not yet understand.

It's All in the Tongue

If you plan to be doing a lot of business in a particular country, consider learning the language. Although English is rapidly becoming the business language of choice, you may be putting yourself at a disadvantage if you don't speak your partner's language. Interpreters are often cumbersome to work with and may not be completely reliable. Speaking for yourself is always a good choice.

The dominant position of the British and U.S. economies has made English a popular language with foreign executives. Many countries require their students to have at least some competency in this important language. Conversely, although foreign language training is very popular in the United States, few people reach an adequate level of fluency. If your partners understand English but you don't understand their language, you're giving them an edge.

Sometimes, foreign executives with a high level of English proficiency will still use a translator. This allows them to help verify the accuracy of what they hear. It also gives them twice the amount of time to analyze the information while they are waiting to hear the translation. More important, while the translator is giving the English version of their message, they can focus on watching your reactions.

Bargaining in English also creates a substantial loophole for foreign executives. Although negotiating in English may seem like an advantage to us because we are more comfortable quickly formulating arguments, it can also backfire on us. The other side can always say that they did not understand our complex arguments, or use selective understanding to misinterpret what you have said. They may also dissolve previous commitments by claiming a misunderstanding between what they said and what they meant. When facing a group of foreign executives, we also have a tendency to think that one who speaks English the best is the most intelligent and influential person in the party. We then aim most of our persuasive efforts at this person. If that person is not the brightest or most influential person in the party, our efforts are somewhat misguided.

Finally, learning the language is an excellent offer of goodwill. People appreciate the effort and feel more comfortable when speaking in their own language. Also, native idioms and constructions can provide a lot of insight on how people in a different culture may think.

Safety in Numbers

Traditional thinking in the United States breeds independence. It is something we admire and demand of ourselves. But thinking that one can always "do it alone" in international negotiations can be an expensive mistake.

Western executives are almost always outnumbered in international negotiations. As a result, they may be at a disadvantage. Negotiating involves doing several activities at one time, including formulating arguments, thinking up questions, issuing explanations, and, of course, listening. No matter how well you think you can do these activities, chances are you can't do them as well as several people working together. Japanese negotiation teams sometimes include one member whose sole purpose is to concentrate on listening.

Including more members on your team might raise the costs of your mission a bit more, but it could pay off in the long run. It is difficult for a single individual to have all the technical expertise and knowledge, in addition to good negotiating skills, to evaluate proposals. Having the extra personnel there will allow you to operate more effectively. Not only will you be better prepared and have greater expertise available to you, but you will also be able to pay more attention to nonverbal cues. Assembling your negotiations team will be a vital part of your preparations. You want to be able to have the input of all departments that might be seriously affected by an agreement. However, having to satisfy too many people might make finding a mutual agreement less likely. And if the place of negotiations is somewhere like Hawaii, Las Vegas, or Bali, management should be careful of volunteers who might not add to the team's usefulness. International business negotiators can do more harm than good if they lack integrated knowledge of the firm and how different parts of the firm will be affected by the deal.

Team members should have a clear idea of the role they are expected to play. For example, you may want to assign roles for spokespersons, technical experts, note takers, observers, and so on. All team members should understand the tactics and strategies you plan to employ. There should also be some organization of how the team will handle first offers, concessions, caucuses, and other issues that may arise. It is important that the team can work together well. You don't want to have part of your team fighting itself at a crucial point in negotiations.

It may also be worth it to seriously consider hiring outside help. An outside consultant is particularly helpful when a firm is entering a new market in which it has no previous experience. Consultants need not act as a firm's negotiators, but they may be able to offer assistance and advice in formulating strategies or providing information regarding environmental factors. A lawyer with expertise in that particular market can often provide a lot of help. Most international deals involve local contract law. A lawyer will help your firm understand what it is getting into.

Finally, when considering who should be on your negotiating team, you should always factor in who the other team will bring. Status plays an important role in doing business abroad. If the other side brings an important key player, such as a vice president or president of the firm, you should always have a suitable counterpart for that person. In China and other countries in which the Chinese community is very strong, CEOs are almost always present in the final round of negotiations. The CEO of family-run businesses is almost always played by the family's father.

Strategies for the Global Negotiator

Skilled negotiators offer many different strategies toward dealing with international negotiations, all of which may be practiced with varying degrees of success. A win-win approach stresses meeting the needs of both parties but does not exclude a firm negotiation stance. A wise negotiator can manage being shrewd, reasonable, and willing to adapt to each situation.

Firms in some countries may take a particularly hard-line stance toward negotiations. Others may be more willing to work cooperatively. No matter what their attitude is, it is important to remember that you are never obligated to reach an agreement. If the other party senses your need to conclude the session with a deal, a common tactic is simply to wear you down. The greatest power you have in any negotiation is your ability to walk away.

Stick to the Issues

Although this may seem like obvious advice, it is important for the negotiator to stick to the salient issues at hand and not let differences between cultures unduly interfere with making an agreement. This means that culture is nonnegotiable. Culture makes up a large part of our personal identity, and this is not easily changeable. Nor does anyone have the right to ask. Simply accept the other party as they are or don't do business with them at all. But don't enter into business with another party that you do not respect and then expect them to change. Not only is it unreasonable, it is not realistic.

Remember, a large part of negotiating is persuading. And for all intents and purposes, when your goal is to persuade someone, the person to be persuaded is always "right." No matter how much sense your proposal makes to yourself, if the person rejects it, you have failed to achieve your objective. It is no use blaming the counterpart for not understanding; in fact, this should be avoided, as indicated by Exhibit 7.5.

Build Up Relative Power

Negotiators can determine who has the relative power advantage by gathering information about the other party, considering each party's position, and developing different alternatives. They can try to build their own relative power by developing arguments against the elements of power and improving their own position. In the negotiation process, this kind of power may be exercised by mentioning the weak points of the other party: "What happened to the project you sold in Poland? We heard that they had lots of problems with your machines, and there was some dispute about guarantees. . . ."

Another good example would be addressing uncertainty regarding infrastructure and exchange rates in an emerging market. You may want to include stipulations for adjustments in the event of exchange-rate variations. In this kind of negotiation, the party with greater information automatically acquires more power.

Exhibit 7.5 Potential Irritators: Words and Phrases to Avoid

Be careful of subtle overtones you might be conveying in your language. Some words and phrases might set the other negotiating party against you, rather than persuade them to your way of thinking. The following is a list of possible irritators:

"You always/never . . ."

These are pretty strong words that are rarely true. While you may just be venting your frustration, people don't react well to being told that their behavior is predictable.

"What you need to understand . . ." or "Be reasonable . . ."

Statements like these have a tone of superiority. You are implying that they don't understand or they aren't being reasonable. Most people think that they do understand and that they are reasonable. Telling them otherwise won't make you any friends.

"Calm down!"

This statement is more likely to infuriate the other party than to have any calming effect. No one likes being told what to do and certainly not how to feel.

"Obviously . . ."

Be careful that you are not implying that your partner is incapable of seeing the obvious. Things that are obvious probably do not need to be pointed out to them.

"You can't tell me . . ."

You are undercutting their position. They can and will tell you anything they want. Why would you say this unless you are looking for a direct confrontation?

"Most people would . . ."

You are devaluating the person's identity with this statement. Some people consider *not* being like "most people" a virtue. Others might resent the implication that there is something wrong with them because they don't agree with you.

SOURCE: Acuff, F. (1993). *How to Negotiate Anything in the World.*

The negotiator may have to work as a detective to ascertain the buyers' needs, their strong and weak points, and the strong and weak points of competitors. An experienced negotiator can build up information for gaining relative power by being active in the negotiation process. This can be done by asking the other party questions. It can also be done by giving conditional answers, such as "*If* you agree to pay cash, *then* we can consider looking at our price" or "*What if* we agree to pay cash? *Perhaps then* you can lower the price by 5%."

Don't Reduce Your Own Bargaining Position

Be reasonable, but don't be afraid of setting a high initial demand. There is no sense in reducing your options, and sometimes you will be surprised by what you can achieve. High initial demands teach others how to treat you and also give you some room to make concessions. You can always lower your offerings later, but at the right time.

Some amount of haggling is expected in these situations, and you want to have some room to maneuver. Furthermore, there is an emotional imperative to "extract" concessions out of you. By starting out high and then gradually lowering your demands, you are fulfilling the other party's need to engineer a bargain. Giving in immediately, on the other hand, may arouse suspicion or perhaps be interpreted as a weakness in your position.

Timing is a key factor in negotiations. Where and when you make your concessions will give the other party valuable information about your negotiating style, your resolve, and so on. You should make your concessions a very strategic event. Some key points to remember are as follows:

- Expect to make some concessions.
- Save concessions until the end.
- High initial demands leave room to bargain; also, emotional imperative for the hard sell does not always work.
- Emphasize relationships.

What Makes a Good Negotiator?

A number of studies identify characteristics of a good negotiator. Ikle (1964) defines a good negotiator: Have a "quick mind but unlimited patience, know how to dissemble without being a liar, inspire trust without trusting others, be modest but assertive, charm others without succumbing to their charm, and possess plenty of money" (p. 253).

Empathy and respect for different perspectives are of utmost importance. It is not necessary to adapt or change yourself to local environments. It is more important to be aware of these differences and to show them due respect and acceptance. Asians and Arabs attribute great importance to social contacts and informal relations. A marketer's personality and social behavior are as important as social contacts and informal relations in many emerging countries. His or her decision in favor of a deal is often based on the salesperson's personality and not on the quality of the deal.

Negotiators can often be grouped into different categories depending on their behavior, such as "bullies," "avoiders," or "acceptors." Bullies want to threaten, push, demand, or attack. Avoiders like to avoid conflicting situations and would rather hide than make a wrong decision or be held responsible. They will normally refer to their superiors for a final decision: "I have to call my head office. . . ." Acceptors always give a very positive answer and would say "yes" to almost anything, which makes it difficult to realize which "yes" is "yes" and which "yes" is "maybe" and whether what is being promised can be delivered. The best way to handle these behavior types is to first identify them and then confront them by drawing a limit, helping them feel safe, and asking them how and when they would be able to do what they are promising.

It is essential to know the negotiator's precise authority. In Eastern Europe and China, one team may negotiate one day followed by a fresh team the next day. When this process is repeated a number of times, it becomes very difficult for the Western firm to establish who is the negotiating party and who has the final authority.

One of the characteristics of a good negotiator is the ability to discover the timetable of the other party and allow plenty of time for the negotiation process. It is usually not feasible to expect to fly to a distant country, wrap things up, and be home again in a week. Nor is it reasonable to coerce a party that is not ready to reach a decision. Negotiations with emerging-market customers take a long time! Patience and time are the greatest assets a negotiator can have while negotiating with customers from these markets. Some negotiators take their time, discussing all issues and justifying their roles through tough negotiations. Negotiators must be in a position to change their strategies and arguments, because the process of negotiation is highly dynamic. They must be flexible. The other party will often ask questions, probing the seller's weaknesses, just to provoke and obtain more concessions. It is important to keep calm and find out first if the questions asked are relevant and justified. Negotiators can use this in their favor when questions are not justified and the buyer had incorrect information. A good negotiator is not just a person who can conclude an apparently good contract for the company or one who can arrive at a contract in a short time. A good negotiator is one whose agreements lead to successful implementation, as further explained in Exhibit 7.6.

A Framework for International Business Negotiations

An overall framework for business negotiations has three groups of variables: background factors, process, and atmosphere (see Exhibit 7.7). Because the negotiation process is inherently dynamic, a certain perception of the parties or a particular development in the process may influence a change in the background factors.

Exhibit 7.6   The Skills of a Good Negotiator

Dozens of books have been written about negotiation, many with which I disagree. I don't believe in negotiating through intimidation, fear, bluffing, or dishonest tactics. A good negotiation concludes as a good deal for everyone. . . . Negotiation starts with what you want to accomplish. Then the realities and, sometimes, the complexities enter the picture. Sometimes many points of view and many elements have to be considered, but the deal itself must always be kept in view. . . . Your first step should be to rid yourself of an adversarial position. The reality is that you have a mutual problem, which you are going to solve to your mutual advantage. The intention must be to structure a deal that resolves the problem and gives each of you what you want. It's not always possible, of course. When it can't be done, you are better off making no deal than making a bad deal. A bad deal usually brings a future filled with enormous problems. Negotiating demands a recognition of reality on many levels. Only amateurs try to accomplish something that isn't real or possible; it is an attempt that inevitably leads to failure. Amateurs tend to dream; professionals consider the realities of a deal.

SOURCE: Nadel, J. (1987). *Cracking the Global Market* (pp. 89-116). New York: Amacom.

Background Factors

This group of variables serves as a background to the process. They influence the process of negotiation and atmosphere. The effect of different variables on the process and its different stages varies in intensity. One of these variables may influence one stage positively and another negatively. A positive influence means that the process saves time and continues smoothly, whereas a negative influence causes delays and hindrances. Background factors include objectives, environment, market position, third parties, and negotiators.

Objectives are defined as the end state each party desires to achieve. They are often classified as common, conflicting, or complementary. For example, parties have a *common* interest: Both want a successful transaction to take place. At the same time, their interests may *conflict* because profit to one may be cost to the other. In terms of *complementary* interests, buyers in international deals are concerned with acquiring appropriate technology to build an infrastructure. Sellers want to enter a particular market and expect to do future business with it and the surrounding countries' markets. Common and complementary objectives affect the negotiation

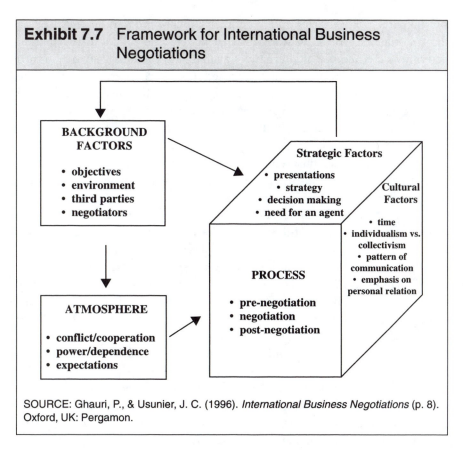

Exhibit 7.7 Framework for International Business Negotiations

SOURCE: Ghauri, P., & Usunier, J. C. (1996). *International Business Negotiations* (p. 8). Oxford, UK: Pergamon.

process directly and positively, whereas conflicting objectives have negative effects. These effects in turn influence the atmosphere and the outcome. The opportunity for an agreement decreases as conflicting objectives dominate in a relationship; it increases as common and complementary objectives dominate.

The *environment* refers to the political, social, and cultural milieu of the parties. Variation in parties with respect to environment often hinders the negotiation process. There are greater chances of interaction interferences when unfamiliar parties, having different behaviors, interact with one another. Some of the characteristics directly influence the process, whereas others directly influence the atmosphere. Political and social aspects influence the process, and cultural aspects plus the behavior of the parties influence the atmosphere.

The party's *market position* is another background variable influencing the negotiation process. The number of buyers and sellers in the market determines the number of alternatives available to each party, which in turn affects the amount of pressure imposed by its counterpart within the market. The process and bargaining position of the buyer or seller can be affected if either one has monopolistic power in the marketplace; for example, if there is a large number of sellers and only one buyer, the latter can dominate.

Most international business deals involve *third parties,* that is, parties other than the seller and buyer, such as governments, agents, consultants, and subcontractors. These parties may influence the negotiation process because they have different objectives. Often, governments of emerging economies are involved and influence the buyers toward complementary objectives, such as infrastructure, employment opportunities, foreign exchange considerations, and any other prospective relationship between the two countries. The sellers' agents play an important role, because they can help bridge differences and smooth the background for negotiations. Financiers may also be involved as third parties, for example, the World Bank. These financiers influence the negotiation process by demanding different types of guarantees and documents that may delay the process of negotiation.

Negotiators influence the negotiation process with their own experience and negotiation skills. Negotiators operate within two limits. First, they act to increase common interests and to expand cooperation among the parties; and second, they act to maximize their own interests and to ensure an agreement that is valuable for themselves. The personality of the negotiators may also play a role, particularly when information about the other party is lacking and there is greater stress. Negotiators from the seller's side can handle the situation effectively, due to experience and personality. A "good" personality is defined as an individual with the ability to make others understand a position, to approach strangers with ease and confidence, and to appreciate the other person's position. However, skills of negotiators are related to different objectives and motivations pertaining to different people and professions. Negotiators with technical backgrounds may place more emphasis on technical issues, whereas those with business backgrounds might consider other issues to be more important.

Atmosphere

The relationship developed during the negotiation process between the parties is characterized by an atmosphere that is of basic importance to the process as a whole. The atmosphere and the process affect each other through interaction at each stage. *Atmosphere* is defined as the perceived milieu around the interaction, how the parties perceive each other's behavior, and the properties of the process. It enhances the dynamics of the process. Some atmosphere characteristics are dominant at one stage, others at another stage. The offer stage is dominated by cooperation rather than conflict as parties look for technical solutions for buyers. Dominance of various atmosphere characteristics changes from process to process. These characteristics are conflict/cooperation, power/dependence, distance, and expectations.

The existence of both *conflict* and *cooperation* is a fundamental characteristic of the negotiation process. On one hand, parties have some common interests in finding a solution to the problem that fits both the supplier's ability and the user's need. On the other hand, a conflict of interest may arise because cost to one may be income to the other. The magnitude of conflict or cooperation in the atmosphere depends on the objectives of the parties in the negotiation. Some relationships are more complementary than others and consequently, less conflicting. The degree of conflict or cooperation during different stages of the negotiation process is often a function of what issues are dealt with, whereas the degree of conflict or cooperation in the atmosphere is a function of how the parties handle various problems. Conflict is sometimes perceived without the existence of real conflict, due to a misunderstanding of each other's behavior. The more unfamiliar the parties are with one another, the higher the risk for such perceived conflicts.

Distance between parties refers to each party's ability to understand the other's capabilities and needs. It is dependent on differences between the parties and on their business experiences with other countries. Firms that have previously done business with each other are expected to be closer than those that have not. One of the functions of the negotiation process is to reduce or overcome the distance between parties. This is particularly important when doing business in emerging markets in which parties are normally unfamiliar with each other. Physical distance as well as psychic or mental distance influence the process of negotiations.

The *power/dependence* relation is another basic characteristic of all negotiation processes. It is closely linked to the objective power relation, which is influenced by the value of the relationship to the parties and their available alternatives. Background factors (e.g., the market position) can influence the power/dependence relation. The ability to control a relationship is linked to the perceived power of two parties, their relative expertise, and access to information. This power is a property of the relationship and not an attribute of the actor. In fact, it is closely related to dependence. Therefore, the power relationship is in balance if both parties have equal power. The power relationship is unbalanced if one of the parties has more power or if one party is dependent on the other.

The last aspect of atmosphere concerns two types of *expectations*. First, there are long-term expectations, regarding the possibilities and values of future deals. The stronger these expectations are, the more inclined the negotiators are to agree on the present deal. Second, there are short-term expectations, concerning prospects for the present deal. Long-term expectations are related to primary objectives. The parties' decision to enter negotiations and to continue after each stage implies expectations of a better outcome from participating than from not participating. This compels the parties to proceed from one stage to the next. Expectations develop and change in different stages of the process and can also be related to expectations in organizational problem solving.

The Negotiation Process

The process of international business negotiation presented here is divided into five different stages. A *stage of the process* refers to a specific time and includes all actions and communications by any party pertaining to negotiations made during that period. Parties communicate with each other to exchange information within each stage. A particular stage ends when parties decide to proceed further into the next stage or to abandon the communication if they see no point in further negotiations. In the offer stage, parties attempt to understand each other's needs and demands and decide either to proceed with the following stage (informal meetings) or not to proceed further due to incompatibility of each other's demands, whereupon the negotiations end without agreement.

Process development depends on three dimensions: time, issues, and contacts. The more time a process/stage takes, the more conflict and distance is perceived by the parties. As discussed earlier, some issues, such as technical details, create a positive atmosphere, whereas others, such as price and terms of payment, create a negative atmosphere. Contacts, as well as time and the issues, are crucial aspects in understanding the negotiation process. This factor refers to the people who meet during each stage of the process, whether on a technical or commercial basis. Technical people tend to stress technical details and specifications; commercial people tend to stress price, terms of payment, and guarantees.

Stage 1: Offer

The offer stage begins with the first contact between parties concerning a particular venture and ends when the vendor submits a final offer. During this stage, some negotiations take place, and counteroffers are made, often resulting in a revision of the vendor's offer. The dynamism of the process can be observed at this early stage, when parties begin to understand one another's needs. It is important that vendors realize that in submitting an offer, they are committing themselves to their part of the deal. It may be necessary to make concessions on many issues.

To gain greater power, parties should gather as much relevant information as possible on each other, the operating environment, and the involvement of other third parties, influencers, competitors, and the infrastructure. Parties need to be aware that their relative power relationship can be altered at any time by events such as repositioning of competitors or changes in exchange rates. We have defined this negotiation process as being problem solving in nature, so the main issue here is to define the problem to be solved. It is important to define the problem jointly because it will not only reflect each party's expectations but is also necessary to acquire commitment from both parties. The parties should thus truly and openly discuss each other's objectives and expectations to achieve positive problem solving.

Stage 2: Informal Meetings

Parties meet to discuss the offer and to get acquainted. After the buyer receives the offer, informal meetings take place as the parties examine each other's positions. Whether the parties continue to the next stage of the negotiation process will depend on the perceived level of cooperation or conflict, power or dependence, and the degree of distance. The process often ends in failure if excessive conflict or distance is sensed or if a successful future relationship seems doubtful. In this stage, the parties should truly see how they are going to solve the problem, whether it is realistic to achieve the objectives of both sides, and identify the obstacles that have to be overcome to achieve the objectives.

The selling firm must realize that the government buyer in emerging countries has objectives different from those of a private business firm. Objectives such as job opportunities, an increase in the capacity of the industry, balance of payments, or other matters of policy will be dominant if the buyer is a government organization. This was the situation that existed in the negotiation process for a paper-and-pulp plant in which the buyer was a large, state-owned company. The right to reject the seller's subcontractors was reserved in this deal. The aim was to accept the offer that used local subcontractors, thereby solving regional unemployment problems.

Informal meetings are often more important than formal negotiations in many emerging markets. Social, informal relationships developed between negotiators at this stage can be of great help. Trust and confidence gained

---

Exhibit 7.8   Resolving Conflict

Consider the story of two men quarreling in a library. One wants the window open and the other wants it closed. They bicker back and forth about how much to leave it open: a crack, halfway, three quarters of the way. No solution satisfied them both. Enter the librarian. She asks one why he wants the window open. "To get some fresh air." She asks the other why he wants it closed. "To avoid the draft." After thinking a minute, she opens wide a window in the next room, bringing in fresh air without a draft.

SOURCE: Fisher, R., Ury, W., & Patten, B. (1991). *Getting to Yes: Negotiating Agreement Without Giving In* (2nd. ed.) (p. 40). New York: Penguin Books.

---

from these relationships not only increase the chances for agreement but also decrease the psychic distance between parties. One method of establishing such contacts is to invite individuals from the buyer's side to visit the seller's office/factory in an attempt to develop trust. The prime objective here is to discover each other's priorities. It is important to understand what the other party wants, why they want it, and their underlying interests and objectives, because this information helps the parties find solutions that are acceptable to both sides. Exhibit 7.8 presents a good example of resolving conflict with a solution that is acceptable to both parties.

Stage 3: Strategy Formulation

Parties begin to formulate their strategy for face-to-face negotiation if Stage 2 has ended in success and they decide to continue the process. By *strategy,* we mean a complete plan regarding problems, the solutions available, and preferred choices relative to the other party's choices and preferences. At this stage, parties try to build up their relative power. The buyer compares the offers submitted by different vendors, makes checklists, and assigns pro and con arguments or competitive advantages to all competing vendors. The seller decides on possible points of concession and their extent. A volatile environment can severely upset established relative power positions. It is essential that negotiators continue to monitor changes in the environment to protect their power position in this stage.

It is often assumed that information exchanged in the offer and during informal negotiations suffices for face-to-face interaction, but this is not the case. Remittance of funds, taxes, and import duties and issuance of work permits are just some examples of the rules and regulations of the particular country that must be researched at this stage. An understanding of the infrastructure of the country and the company is also critical at this point. In some countries, especially when the public sector is the buyer, purchasing organizations issue a *letter of award* (also called *letter of intent* or *acceptance*) after offers have been received. This document states that the order for the project has been awarded to "Company ABC," and that company is called for formal negotiations. The vendors from Western countries often perceive this letter of award as a grant of contract. This is an incorrect assumption, because other competitors might also have received a similar letter. The letter merely indicates the buyer's intention to negotiate further after receiving the final offer.

There are several dimensions of strategies in business negotiations, such as tough, intermediate, or soft. In using a *tough* strategy, a party starts rather high and remains firm on its stand and would expect the other party to make first concessions. In using a *soft* strategy, a party offers first concession in the hope that the other party reciprocates. In using an *intermediate* strategy, a party should not start high, and as soon as an offer is made that is within its expectations, it should accept it. Other dimensions of strategy are voluntariness, structure, informational locus, and opportunism (Lewicki et al., 1994, pp. 110-111).

In a *voluntary* strategy, we have to make a choice of what to pursue, how to pursue it, and whether to have a strategy at all. In government projects, for example, the strategies can be more or less structured. A *highly structured* strategy would provide control, sense of direction, and guidelines. The *informational locus* dimension refers to the fact that strategy is based on incomplete or unreliable information and can be changed or adjusted as the information, for example on the other party, emerges as negotiation proceeds. Here, the negotiators should try to adapt their strategies as early as possible to achieve better results. *Opportunism* refers to the fact that not having a strategy is itself a strategy. When done intentionally, it is referred to as *adaptive, emergent,* and *opportunistic,* and it enables the negotiators to exploit opportunities as they recognize them.

Whatever the dimensions, at the outset, parties to international business negotiations should have an initial strategy, which is dependent on the information attained up until then and on the expectations. The negotiators should list the problems and issues, especially the conflicting issues, and form strategies and choices for all possible solutions they or the other party could suggest. These solutions should be ranked, for example, as *preferred, desired, expected,* and *not acceptable.* If not acceptable, then a solution should be developed that is acceptable to the other party. It is thus important to have several solutions for each problem or issue.

Stage 4: Face-to-Face Negotiation

The parties should be aware that each side views the situation, or the matter under discussion, in its own way. Not only do they have a different perception of the process, they also have different expectations for the outcome. It is therefore important to start face-to-face negotiations with an open mind. At this stage, the parties should evaluate the alternatives presented and select those that are compatible with their own expectations. The best way is to determine criteria for judging the alternatives and then rank order each alternative against these criteria. Here, the parties can even help each other in evaluating these alternatives and discuss the criteria for judgment. The main issue is to explore differences in preferences and expectations and then try to reach an agreement.

The negotiation process is controlled by the partner who arranges the agenda, because each can emphasize its own strengths and the other party's weaknesses, thus putting the other party on the defensive. However, the agenda may reveal the preparing-party's position in advance and hence permit the other side to prepare its own counterarguments on conflicting issues.

Experience suggests that it is often the partner with the greater relative power who arranges the agenda. Some negotiators prefer to start negotiations by discussing and agreeing on broad principles for the relationship. Another way to ensure success at this stage is to negotiate the contract step-by-step, discussing both conflicting issues and those of common interest. In particular, discussions on items of common interest can create an atmosphere of cooperation between parties. The choice of strategy depends on the customer or supplier with whom one is negotiating. It is helpful to anticipate the other party's strategy as early as possible and then choose a strategy to match or complement it.

In Stage 4, both parties take the initiative by asking questions about the other party: aspects of the offer, price, quality, delivery, and credit possibilities. These questions clear the negotiation range, that is, the gap between the minimum point of one party and the acceptable point of the other. The negotiator should not agree to a settlement at once if there is considerable overlap between his or her position vis-à-vis the other party. The negotiator may obtain further concessions by prolonging the negotiation process. A number of studies have revealed that negotiators who submit a "final offer" up front can be at a disadvantage. In view of the diverse cultural and business traditions prevailing in different countries, international negotiations inherently involve a discussion of environmental differences. It is very difficult for parties to comprehend or adjust to each other's cultures or traditions, but it is important for them to be aware of these differences. In many emerging markets, social contacts developed between parties are far more significant than the technical and economic specifications. Negotiators from these countries take their time and are very careful not to offend or use strong words, and the other party is expected to follow suit.

Negotiation with the public sector in emerging economies often involves negotiating with civil servants and politicians. These negotiators are bound by rules, regulations, and government policy. Vendors must take these rules and regulations into account. A balance between firmness and credibility is essential in all types of negotiation. It is important to give and take signals of preparedness to move from the initial stage without making concessions. Negotiators who have had prior dealings with each other can easily send and receive signals, but it is very difficult for those meeting for the first time. The timing of a move is crucial, but the attitude and behavior of both parties can also be decisive factors. A positive atmosphere may be developed by a negotiator who is firm and at the same time exhibits a courteous, problem-solving attitude.

Negotiators from Western countries frequently adopt a tough attitude in negotiation that is perceived as a "big brother" stance and is very offensive to the other party. Negotiators often send conditional signals such as "We cannot accept your offer as it stands" or "We appreciate that your equipment is quite suitable for us, but not at the price you mentioned." The seller might say, "I understand, but you know that this is the lowest price I can offer. Otherwise, I will have to call my head office and discuss the price with them." This is a tactic used to test each other's commitment as well as the resolution of the offer. It is also common that the party perceiving greater relative power makes fewer concessions and that the weaker party yields more often to create a better atmosphere.

Maintaining flexibility between parties and issues is of great importance in regard to terms of payment, price, and delivery time. For example, price can be reduced if the party offers better terms of payment. Other elements can be traded off, but there may not be a way to evaluate them in accounting terms. For example, obtaining a reference or an entry into a huge, protected market may be strategically more important than obtaining handsome profits on the present deal. A point will be reached at which negotiators must make a final move. It is usually a poor strategy to announce that the negotiators do not have the final authority to conclude the contract. But this is quite effective when used as a tactic to check the other side's final move.

Stage 5: Implementation

At this stage, all terms have been agreed on. The contract has been drawn up and is ready to be signed. Experience has shown that writing the contract, and the language used, can be a negotiation process in itself, because meaning and values may differ between two parties. In cases involving Western firms and emerging-economy parties, the language used and the writing down of issues previously agreed on can take considerable time. This stage can lead to renewed face-to-face negotiation if there is negative feedback from background factors and atmosphere (see Exhibit 7.2).

Discussion should be summarized after negotiations to avoid unnecessary delays in the process. The terms agreed on should be read by both parties after concessions are exchanged and discussions held. This is facilitated by keeping minutes of meetings. This is helpful not only in writing and signing the contract but also in its implementation. Trouble may arise later during implementation of the contract if parties are too eager to reach an agreement and don't pay enough attention to details. The best way to solve this problem is to confirm that both sides thoroughly understand what they have agreed on before leaving the negotiating table.

What Is a Good Outcome?

A good agreement is one that leads to successful implementation. There are many examples of firms getting into trouble because they could not implement the contract conditions of a particular project. Therefore, in some cases, not reaching an agreement may be a better outcome for the firm. A good outcome benefits both parties and does not make either party feel that it has a less advantageous contract. This type of arbitration was one of the reasons for deadlock in a case between a Swedish seller and a Nigerian buyer. The buyer wanted local arbitration, but the seller wanted a Swedish or international arbitrator. The buyer commented, "Well, if they are sure that they are going to fulfil the commitments of the contract, then why are they afraid to accept arbitration in Nigeria, because in that case there will be no conflicts and no arbitration?" Sometimes negotiators want to avoid specifying some issues and want to keep them ambiguous. It is important to understand that on one hand, ambiguity can lead to reopening of the conflict later on, and on the other hand, if we want to specify such issues, it might prolong the negotiation process or prevent an agreement. Sometimes this ambiguity is unintended, and sometimes it is intentionally done to speed up the process or to give the impression that the particular issue needs to be renegotiated (Ikle, 1964, pp. 8-15).

A good deal is one that provides financial gains. But what were the objectives of the firm when it decided to enter into negotiations? Was the present deal most important, or was it future business? The outcome must be related to the firm's objectives. If objectives have been met, then it is a good outcome. A successful negotiation is not a question of "win-lose" but a problem-solving approach to a "win-win" outcome.

8

Emerging Markets of Asia

In the next couple of decades, one of the largest economic shifts in history will occur as the Asian emerging markets come on-line. Although the industrialized countries have dominated the world for the past 150 years, many of these countries may be outpaced in the next 20 to 25 years by the remarkable growth and progress of the Asian emerging economies. The four "Asian tigers"—Hong Kong, Singapore, South Korea, and Taiwan—with a combined population of only 73 million, have already been aggressively tapping Western markets for the last 30 years. Excluding Japan, whose remarkable transformation into an economic superpower is well documented, Asia still has more than 3 billion people, compared with the developed countries, which have less than 1 billion people. World Bank forecasts that over the next 10 years, developing countries will grow by more than 4% per year, compared with 2.6% for developed countries, as shown in Exhibit 8.1 (World Bank, 2001a).

A number of Asian economies have transformed their countries from agrarian societies to high-tech centers. The Asian crisis of 1996/1997, however, pushed some of these countries backward, especially Thailand and Indonesia. The Asian crisis led to increased deregulation and forced companies to be more competitive. It forced some of the region's conglomerates and leading family concerns to restructure. As a result of this consolidation, mergers and acquisition (M&A) activities reached their peak in 1999, with record M&A activity in Asia (excluding Japan) reaching an announced worth of $187 billion (Leahy, 2000).

Among these developing countries, the Asian emerging markets appear to hold the most promise. According to a 1992 study, only 3 of the world's

Exhibit 8.1   Average Annual Percentage Growth in Real GDP in Different Regions

Region	1982-1991	1991-2001
Advanced economies	3.1	2.9
Developing countries	4.3	5.6
Countries in transition (includes Central and Eastern Europe and Russia)	1.4	−2.1
Africa	2.3	2.6
Asia	6.9	7.5
Middle East and Europe	3.3	3.7
Western Hemisphere	1.8	3.4

SOURCE: International Monetary Fund (2000d).

10 largest economies were located in Asia (International Monetary Fund [IMF], 2000a). By 2020, however, Asian economies are expected to push two G-7 countries—Great Britain and Italy—out of this ranking and claim 7 of the world's largest economies (see Exhibit 8.2).

A number of major Asian countries, such as China, India, Pakistan, and Vietnam, were not affected by the Asian crisis. Most of the countries that were affected have recovered. Indonesia, however, has still not stabilized, mainly because of political disruptions. The middle class in China and India is increasing rapidly. As a result, most of the Asian markets have now entered an era of product availability and choice. In India, one of the restricted markets a decade ago, there are 50 brands of toothpaste and 250 brands of shoes. The products and strategies, however, need to be adapted to local markets, as experienced by Revlon and Coca Cola in India (Prahalad & Lieberthal, 1998).

The dominance of industrialized countries is already diminishing. Using purchasing-power parity, the developing countries already account for 44% of world output (IMF, 2000a). If these economies continue to grow at their present rate, by 2020, the purchasing share of the developed world will shrink to less than two fifths. Furthermore, in 1999, developing countries exported 27.5% of the world's manufactured goods, compared with 5% in 1970. Out of this 27.5%, approximately 45% came from Asia (U.S. Department of Commerce, National Trade Data Bank [NTDB], 2000). Of course, high growth rates such as these are difficult to sustain over prolonged periods of time. Most likely, as the Asian economies grow and

Exhibit 8.2	World's 10 Largest Economies (GDP at Purchasing-Power Parity)	
	1992	**2020**
1.	United States	China
2.	Japan	United States
3.	China	Japan
4.	Germany	India
5.	France	Indonesia
6.	India	Germany
7.	Italy	South Korea
8.	Britain	Thailand
9.	Russia	France
10.	Brazil	Taiwan

SOURCE: "2002 Vision" (1994, p. 89).

become richer, their growth rates will also slow down. Still, in comparative terms, they will soon exceed a number of today's developed economies.

Asian countries have a number of comparative advantages. For example, Chinese and Indian workers are willing to accept an average hourly wage of approximately 50¢, compared with an average hourly wage of $18 in developed countries. In the past, these low wages were also reflected in worker productivity. Today, however, the Asian labor force is well educated and skilled compared with 25 years ago (World Bank, 1993). Even the most complex technologies and machines can now be handled by this abundant workforce. According to the IMF (2000a), Asia's share of the world output in 1990 was 17%, whereas the total for all Third World countries, including Eastern Europe and the former Soviet Union, was 44%.

Investment Climate

European and Japanese firms are very active in Asia. Germany has been asserting a constant push since 1994. For example, in June 2000, Siemens launched a major investment in China; and in June 2000, Daimler Chrysler formed alliances in Korea. Investment by European firms in Asia also include BMW in the Philippines and Thailand, and Volkswagen in China. By November 1999, Siemens in China had 57 operating companies

Exhibit 8.3   Big Spenders in Asia

Company	Planned Investment by 2000	Business Area
Siemens	$3.5 billion	Energy, telecommunications, medical equipment, semiconductors, automobiles, aerospace, film, plastic, research
Daimler-Benz	$3.2 billion	
Bayer	$645 million	

SOURCE: Templeman (1995, p. 16).

(45 joint ventures), 28 regional offices, and more than 27,000 employees. This is further illustrated in Exhibit 8.3 (Miller, 1995).

The emerging economies of Asia are extremely important markets for Western firms. Around 42% of America's exports, 20% of European exports, and 48% of Japanese exports are going to developing countries (IMF, 2000a). The fast-growing economies in Asia account for the majority of these exports, and as the standard of living in Asia increases, this trend will grow. According to the Organization of Economic Cooperation and Development (OECD) estimates, if China and India grow at an average of 6% (lower than today's growth rate), by the year 2010, they will have an upper-middle class of some 700 million people, which is roughly equal to a combined total population of the European Union, the United States, and Japan (OECD, 2000).

Emerging markets are more open to imports and foreign investment than are Japan, South Korea, or other so-called Asian tigers when they were at a similar growth stage. Due to these reasons and a higher rate of return in these emerging markets, it is logical to expect that capital will move from developed economies to the Asian emerging markets. In whatever terms we evaluate—exports, capital flow, or export of technology—Asian emerging markets will provide increased market opportunities for Western technology, goods, and services. According to one estimate, U.S. exports to China and India will grow by 15% per year over the next decade (U.S. Department of Commerce, NTDB, 2000).

Japan has proven to be a big source of capital for these Asian emerging markets. To cope with a strong yen, Japanese companies are moving their most labor-intensive manufacturing to Asian countries in which lower wages, cheaper raw materials, and low-cost property are available.

Despite the crisis, Asia is now on the move. But how do the Asians do it? In a recent study, "The East Asian Miracle," the World Bank concluded that there is no magic formula but the key may be in Asian culture: People in these countries are willing to study harder, work harder, and save more than do people in other economies. Asians are highly motivated and focused on development (World Bank, 1993).

As a result, Asia is enjoying a constant flow of investment. The French Thomson Group, a consumer electronics manufacturer, now employs 3 times more people in Asia than it does in France. Fila, an Italian sportswear manufacturer, and Nike have moved almost all their production to subcontractors in Asia. Japan has also relocated much of its manufacturing to areas of cheaper production. For example, all the recorders exported by Mitsubishi are now made in Southeast Asia. Moreover, Japanese firms now account for 7% of all employment in the manufacturing sector in Thailand. According to the United Nations Conference on Trade and Development (UNCTAD), multinationals employed twice as many workers (12 million) in developing countries as they did in developed countries (Schwab & Smadja, 1994).

Asia has been absorbing most of the capital outflows from the West. Investment in these countries averages more than 30% of gross domestic product (GDP), compared with 16% in the United States (U.S. Department of Commerce, NTDB, 2000). Most estimates indicate that these countries will attract even more investment in the near future to finance infrastructure development. Asian emerging-market growth rates can be compared with those of South Korea and Taiwan, which have recently gone through the same process. If it can be assumed that the standard of living in China, India, and Malaysia will, within a couple of decades, approximate that of South Korea and Taiwan, then we can also assume that these countries will generate enormous demands for energy, automobiles, branded consumer products, electronics, and telecommunication products.

Factors Influencing Market Entry

Asian emerging economies are perhaps the most receptive to foreign firms and investment. The gaps between the West and Asian emerging markets with respect to marketing, technology, capital, management, and motivation are not as big as those between the West and Eastern and Central Europe or the West and Africa. Companies and consumers are both very familiar with Western-style marketing activities. These countries, excluding China, are technologically quite close to Western levels, and they have extensive experience with technologically advanced products. Regarding management and motivation, many of the managers and officials in these emerging markets are educated or trained in the West and understand Western attitudes toward efficiency and motivation. Moreover, other than in China, English is widely used in government and business. Although Asian emerging markets have experienced the highest growth rate in recent years, these countries have kept inflation rates under tight control. China is the only country that has had a double-digit inflation rate.

A variety of entry challenges still face Western marketers. For example, countries in Asia are quite different from each other and will pose different types of challenges to Western firms. In most of these countries, wholly owned subsidiaries are allowed, but companies must decide which type of entry is most beneficial to them. The advantages and disadvantages related to each entry mode should be properly analyzed. It is also important for companies to decide how much control they want and whether they are using resources to their best advantage. Multinationals, for example, may be able to hire top technological talent at bargain prices to speed up technology transfer and R&D capabilities (see Exhibit 8.4).

Performing a cost-benefit analysis prior to choosing a market entry strategy is relatively easy for Asian emerging markets. The role of government, other than in China, is not as dominant as it is in Eastern Europe, and most counterparts are private businesses or industrial and commercial groups. It is important, however, for Western companies to check the rules and regulations regarding import and export of their particular products or technology. The higher the need for control, the more a firm should establish a wholly owned subsidiary, especially if the technology or know-how to be transferred is of a sensitive nature and the firm is concerned about copyrights and patents.

Joint ventures are also common entry modes in these markets, especially in China and India. The Asian emerging markets have a cadre of highly qualified and devoted technologists capable of upgrading the technology they buy. We have witnessed this in Japan, South Korea, and Taiwan. Now, another group of countries—China, India, Malaysia, and Indonesia—are taking up that role. Western companies can also benefit from this development by "leapfrogging" into these markets.

Selecting the right partner/agent is an important issue. Asians have a problem saying "no," which can lead to the risk that they promise more than they can deliver. A foreign firm should systematically investigate whether a prospective agent or partner can actually fulfill the terms of an agreement. A clear policy on copyrights and patents is a must. The Western firm should have a clear policy that can easily be conveyed to the other

Exhibit 8.4   Cost/Benefit Gaps Between Workers From Different Countries

Countries	Net Earnings/Hour ($U.S.)	Working Hours/Year	Engineer's Net Earnings/ Year ($U.S.)	Bank Clerk's Net Earnings/ Year ($U.S.)
Japan (Tokyo)	19.3	1,893	51,400	54,900
United States (Chicago)	13.0	1,933	34,600	23,000
Germany (Frankfurt)	11.3	1,725	41,900	34,600
South Korea (Seoul)	5.0	2,302	20,100	22,300
Thailand (Bangkok)	2.0	2,272	17,900	12,800
India (Bombay)	0.8	1,990	2,100	1,800

SOURCE: Union Bank of Switzerland (1999).

party on these issues. We have witnessed the problems U.S. firms have had with China. This is equally important in Thailand, Malaysia, and India.

Negotiating in Asia

The cultures of Asia are as diverse as they are interrelated, and this can make negotiating in Asia a difficult process. China has a strong cultural tradition that is based on the belief that the country was a celestial empire. It once considered itself the center of the world and the home of civilization. Prevalent Confucianist beliefs value order, stability, hierarchy, relationships, family, and harmony. The cultural traditions of India are based on Hinduism and Buddhism, which also stress the importance of relationships, the family, and harmony. Between these two countries are Thailand, Malaysia, and Indonesia, which appear to incorporate a mixture of Chinese, Islamic, and Indian philosophies. South Korea, which is closer to Japan than to China and India, has yet another cultural tradition. These cultural traditions have given rise to very different negotiating behaviors.

Despite differences in religion, history, traditions, and behavior, there are some similarities in cultural behaviors. Norms about what is right and wrong, a focus on the family as the paradigm for more public conduct, respect for old age, and a hierarchical pattern of decision making are some of the common features. Based on these common values, we can present some *do's* and *don'ts* for negotiating in Asian countries:

1. A Western negotiating team must determine the seniority level of each member of the Asian country team. *Respect for superiors* in business relations, as well as in the family, is of utmost importance. When negotiating, it is important not to bypass the senior person in addressing or asking for concessions. When a question is posed by the "leader" on the Asian side, it must be answered by the "leader" on the Western side. People occupying high positions in government, such as ministers and judges, are respected even after retirement. Ex-ministers or ex-judges, unless they come from unfavored opposition political parties, are respected and may still exercise considerable power.

2. In most decisions, *harmony* is sought. Members of the negotiating team play specific roles that are parallel to those of family members. Good behavior can range from modesty to self-deprecation. This belief about roles explains why when an Asian person is praised for his achievements, he or she will often reply, "Not at all, you are so kind" or "It is all due to God's/Bhagwan's help."

3. Most Asians are *superstitious* about colors and numbers. Regarding colors, red is the color of joy and happiness, pure white is the color of sobriety or death (in China), and some colors are worn only by religious leaders. Regarding numbers, some dates are not considered positive for concluding contracts. Odd numbers are often considered positive.

4. *Use of interpersonal space* varies with the closeness of the relationship. Initial distance required for conversation may be more than in Western countries, but as a friendship is established, this will decrease. Eye contact will also increase as a relationship solidifies.

5. In Asia, *time is not money*. People take long lunches and can continue negotiating long hours. They may even take a break from the session to conduct other business and expect to resume after office hours.

6. Western negotiators should engage in friendly *small talk* and other phatic communication before sessions. Topics can include the hotel, the family, last evening, dinner (food), local history, and culture. Discussions on religion, political leaders, government rules or decisions, the status of women, or inequalities between different classes should be avoided.

7. In Asia, *body language* is an important aspect of negotiation. Certain postures show respect for older participants and superiors. Pointing the sole of your shoe to someone and standing or sitting close to one another are inappropriate. A message is conveyed not only by what is said but also by how it is said.

Exhibit 8.5   Nature of Negotiation in Asian Emerging Markets

Negotiation Factors	Comments
1. Pace of Negotiation	Slow to very slow (China)
- Value of time	Time is not money
2. Negotiation Strategy	
- Offer vs. agreement	Initial offer not too high
- Presentation of issues	In order of priority
- Presentations	Formal and orderly
- Discussions	Persuasive
- Communication	Small talk—rather indirect
- Interpreters	Not necessary, except in China
3. Emphasis on personal relationships	High
4. Influence of third parties	Rather high
5. Distance	Personal space shorter with time
6. Decision making	
- Overall	Rational but influenced by personal relationships
- Hierarchy	Strong hierarchical decision making
- Collective vs. individual	Emphasis on collective decisions
- Degree of details	Less than average
- Degree of bureaucracy	Moderate
- Need for agenda	High
7. Administrative factors	
- Need for agent or local partner	Moderate to high
8. Emotional factors	
- Degree of rationality	Moderate (visibility)
- Sensitivity	High and valued

SOURCE: Format based on Acuff (1993).

8. In Asia, the *giving and receiving of gifts* as a token of friendship and appreciation is very common. Gifts might include a nice pen, a necktie, or an ethnic decoration. In most Asian countries, the receiver of the gift does not open it in front of the guests, so as not to appear greedy and to avoid embarrassment.

9. In most Asian countries, *face saving* is very important. You must not point out someone's mistake in the presence of others. Points can be earned saving someone's face by not pointing out a fault in front of the group. Discretion of this type will be considered as a favor, which the other person will try to return. Some salient features of Asian negotiation behavior are given in Exhibit 8.5.

Selected Country Analyses

China

China is still conscious of having been the number one global power until the 18th century. The Chinese have had difficulty accepting foreign ideas, such as democracy, Western value systems, and organizational changes. In the past, international trade was not considered important for the prosperity of the country. As a result, foreigners were not usually welcome. Discrepancies in thought have existed, however, with those at the top favoring hierarchical Confucianist values and those at lower levels placing greater emphasis on Taoist individual values. Relationships and family values predominate on both levels. After enacting strict family-planning laws in the 1970s, China's rate of population growth has now become entirely manageable, at 1.3% per year. At the same time, the economic growth rate, which has averaged close to 8% since 1979, means that economic output has quadrupled in the last two decades.

In its efforts to join the World Trade Organization (WTO), China has been reshaping its economic outlook. The country has been more liberal to foreign investments, and several state-owned companies are being sold, including companies in telecommunications, banking, and the insurance industry. Huge amounts of foreign investments from Hong Kong and Taiwan have also boosted the growth of the Chinese economy. The economy grew by 8% in the first 9 months of 2000. Companies such as Microsoft are increasing their investments in China. As a result of a new breed of Chinese middle class, it is no longer difficult for foreign companies to find skilled labor in China.

After the reforms led by Deng Xiaoping, three systems emerged: (a) ideological authority based on tradition, (b) authority of ancient beliefs and values, and (c) authority of competence, that is, primacy of the "expert" over the "ideologue" (Euro-China Association for Management and Development, 1986). At present, the third value system is gaining ground, with China becoming more open to Western technology and know-how.

In October 1984, the Chinese government declared that central planning would no longer be used and that a system of interfirm contracts would be used to facilitate the distribution of raw materials. Each enterprise was made responsible for its own profits and losses. Trading companies were given more power to negotiate with foreign firms directly. New management reforms, accounting systems, fiscal rules, wage increases, and recruitment rules were introduced. During the same period, five special economic zones (SEZs) were established to encourage foreign investment. The five

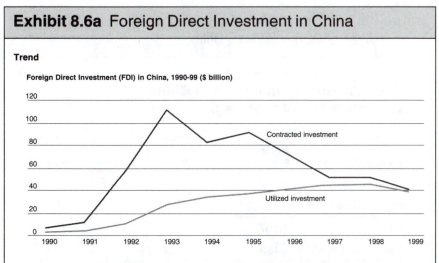

Exhibit 8.6a Foreign Direct Investment in China

Trend

Foreign Direct Investment (FDI) in China, 1990-99 ($ billion)

SOURCE: Orginally published in the November-December 2000 issue of the *China Business Review*, www.chinabusinessreview.com. Reprinted with the permission of the US-China Business Council, Washington, DC, www.uschina.org.

SEZs—Shenzhen, Zhubai, Shantou, Xiamen, and Hainan—have all the benefits of free trade areas in other countries. Facilities include the following:

- Tax exemption for 2 years
- Lower tax rate (15% on profits)
- Advantageous cost of land and general expenses
- Freedom to set the parameters of personnel management
- Inexpensive labor
- Exemption from customs on imported capital and intermediate goods
- Simpler entry and exit rules
- Easier access to the rest of the Chinese market
- Free transfer of profits after tax, in hard currency
- Possibility of credit in local currency

Foreign investment in the SEZs and elsewhere has been soaring for the last 10 years, with the majority (more than 80%) of businesses showing a profit. In 1979, a new law regulating joint ventures was introduced, and by 2000, China received more than $40 billion in foreign investments, of which $6 billion is invested in SEZs ("Analysts Predict," 2000). Exhibit 8.6 illustrates the foreign investments trends during the 1990s.

As shown in Exhibit 8.6, caution was exercised by Western businesses until 1990, a year after Tiananmen Square. After 1991, however, the annual growth in investments accelerated to more than 10% annually ("Foreign Direct Investment," 2000). In late 1993, the government

Exhibit 8.6b Foreign Direct Investment (FDI) in China, 1990–1999 ($ Billions)

Top Ten Foreign Investors in China by Source Country or Region, 1999

Country/Region	Number of Projects	Amount Contracted ($ billion)	Amount Utilized ($ billion)
Hong Kong	5,902	13.33	13.33
United States	2,028	6.02	4.22
Japan	1,167	2.59	2.97
The Virgin Islands	495	3.49	2.66
Singapore	503	2.26	2.64
Taiwan	2,499	3.37	2.60
Germany	196	0.94	1.37
South Korea	1,547	1.48	1.27
United Kingdom	230	1.09	1.04
France	110	0.47	0.88

approved additional reforms aimed at giving more play to market-oriented institutions. China's trade flows and trade partners are shown in Exhibit 8.7. We can see that China has a huge trade surplus. All the foreign direct investment (FDI) coming to China plus a consistent trade surplus has put China into a very sound economic situation.

China has been successful in avoiding short-run transition costs experienced by Eastern European countries in which unemployment and inflation rose sharply and output declined. In China, output increased at an annual rate of 40% compared with the pre-reform period ("Foreign Direct Investment," 2000). One reason for this lower transition cost is China's gradualist approach, which helped the country maintain political and social stability. Political stability is the most decisive factor in attracting FDI. Even the Tiananmen Square incident helped China in demonstrating this stability. At present, most of the senior leadership is behind the commitment to reform

Exhibit 8.7   Trade Ties of China (China's Trade, 1999, $ Billions)

Partner	Imports	Exports
United States	19.4	42.0
Europe (ex-EU)	5.7	4.9
European Union (EU)	25.4	30.2
Asia (ex-Japan)	60.2	64.6
Japan	33.7	32.3
Rest of the World	21.3	21.1
Total	165.7	195.1

SOURCE: International Monetary Fund (2000c).

state-owned enterprises (SOEs). A number of changes to the tax system were introduced in 1994, and in 1995, about 100 SOEs were subject to "modernization," which also included removal of subsidies. The firms have to arrange their own payrolls, unemployment insurance, and pension schemes.

China's advantage is not only its 1.3 billion people but also its 55 million overseas Chinese entrepreneurs. Overseas Chinese businessmen are estimated to control more than $2 trillion in liquid assets (Economist Intelligence Unit, 2000). They dominate the business sectors in countries in which they are in a minority, such as Indonesia (3% of the population) and Thailand (10% of the population) and in countries in which they are in the majority, such as Hong Kong, Taiwan, and Singapore (Economist Intelligence Unit, 2000). A major portion of FDI coming into China is coming from these overseas Chinese. Many foreign firms are also using these overseas businessmen to help them enter the Chinese market. Furthermore, the Chinese economy, which grew at a rate of more than 8% from 1995 to 1999, is stimulating the entire Pacific Rim (IMF, 2000a). The inclusion of Hong Kong into China is another factor that has encouraged foreign firms to do business with China through Hong Kong. The potential of the Chinese market in some industries is enormous. For example, Exhibit 8.8 presents prospects for the automobile industry in China.

A Word of Caution

China's image has been damaged by stories about disputes between Chinese businessmen and foreign investors. The central government feels its growing responsibility to foreign investors and is taking measures to assure

Exhibit 8.8   Prospects for the Automobile Industry in China

	1990	1992	1994	1996	1998	2000
New cars in use (thousands)	1,150	1,500	1,850	2,500	3,400	4,450
Cars in use per 100 population	10	13	15	20	27	34
Production (thousands)	38	147	315	575	825	1,100
Growth in registration (%)	21.2	32.8	8.6	19.8	15.9	11.1

Industry Forecast

	1994	1996	1998	2000
Sales:				
Passenger cars	380	575	800	1,000
Commercial vehicles	880	1,100	1,280	1,500
Total	1,260	1,675	2,080	2,500
Production:				
Passenger cars	315	575	825	1,100
Commercial vehicles	850	1,100	1,275	1,500
Total	1,165	1,675	2,100	2,600

Production & Assembly Forecast by Manufacturers

Manufacturer	1994	2000
Tianjin Auto/Daihatsu	60	175
Shanghai/Volkswagen	110	250
Dong Feng/Citroën	25	150
Guangzhou/Peugeot	30	150
First Auto Works/Volkswagen	44	230
Changan/Suzuki	18	60
Guizhou/Fuji Heavy Industries	10	35
Hainan/Mazda	3	30
Others	15	20
Total	315	1,100

SOURCE: Economist Intelligence Unit and Financial Times (1994, p. 21).

them that their interests will be protected. China scores poorly on political and policy risk. Overall, it is rated as an average country, similar to Philippines and Thailand (Economist Intelligence Unit, 2000). In the short to medium term, however, there are some hazards. Record-breaking expansion and double-digit growth rates are colliding with primitive transportation systems, inadequate electric power, and other infrastructure constraints. Free market reforms in the agricultural sector have boosted food production but have created a rural-to-urban labor migration wave of millions of peasants. Moreover, a get-rich-quick fever is creating widespread corruption that could derail the modernization train. Aware of these threats, the government is trying to limit the growth rate at or below 10% in the coming years (Economist Intelligence Unit, 2000).

One such attempt is the creation of a miniature version of Singapore in Suzhou, around 50 miles west of Shanghai (which was designed with the help of an overseas Chinese, Lee Kuan Yew, the senior leader in Singapore). The Singapore government will provide the management expertise for this zone, called the "Singapore-Suzhou Township." Here, 19 Singapore companies are helping to build a 27-square-mile site. It has also signed up more than 15 companies from Japan, the United States, and South Korea to invest a total of $900 million in factories. The biggest challenge is to assure the investors that the town will be run with honesty, efficiency, and without any corruption. To achieve this, 300 Chinese officials are to be trained in Singapore, with at least 100 more coming from Singapore to train additional people ("Foreign Direct Investment," 2000).

Negotiating

Negotiating in China begins with contacts with Chinese authorities. The Western firm must make presentations for a number of groups. In these sessions, the firm must convince the Chinese that it has the technology China needs. The process of negotiation can be divided into the following stages:

1. Lobbying: The firm must understand the objectives of the Chinese. Calculations must be made as to what the firm might gain or loose in tangible and intangible terms. Negotiators should try to identify the decision makers on the other side and develop relationships with them. The Western firm should also find out who the competitors are and convince the Chinese side of the firm's advantages over competitors. Presentation materials should be available in ample copies and should be distributed in English and in Chinese. The Western negotiators should build up trust both in the products that are the subject of trade and in the individuals who are negotiating.

2. Offer: After establishing the objectives and consequences of the deal, the firm should make an offer outlining general principles, technology, equipment, price, and the terms and conditions for the deal. At this stage, it is very useful for a Western firm to invite the Chinese team to their home country to show them their manufacturing plant and products. This invitation will help the firm gain an edge over competitors and build trust.

3. Formal negotiations: Due to increasing decentralization, it is possible for Western firms to negotiate directly with Chinese firms and organizations. The Chinese use different tactics to get the most out of their counterparts, such as flattery, embarrassment, and the use of historical facts. They also create a more competitive environment by revealing selective information on competing offers. The Chinese want the best and the latest technology, but it is very difficult to make them understand the cost of R&D. The firm should be specific about patents and copyrights. In joint ventures, the contributions of each partner should be very clearly specified.

4. Implementation: Experience shows that real problems start after formal negotiations. The Chinese normally like to agree on principles and broad terms in the formal negotiations and leave the details for the implementation stage. This tactic gives them the advantage of being flexible in their own favor. Exhibit 8.9 provides a Western view of Chinese negotiation behavior.

As a general guideline, a Western firm entering China should consider the following (Ghauri & Fang, 2001):

1. Priority sectors: In the late 1980s, a number of foreign firms were trying to enter China. Many of them were greatly disappointed. After years of negotiation, they realized, for example, that foreign exchange was not available or that the project was not considered a priority. Although decentralization of decision making has authorized firms and organizations to negotiate and act independently, it is still wise for a Western firm to determine whether the sector they are in is a priority sector.

2. Patience: Time and patience are the most important assets a Western firm can have when entering and negotiating in China. The negotiating process may not commence until Western negotiators have toured some of the country and made several presentations about their products. For Ericsson, it took more than 2 years to conclude a telecommunications contract; for Otis, it took 5 years to establish a joint venture.

3. Precision: The Chinese are very detail oriented when negotiating about technical specifications. They need these details to compare offers

Exhibit 8.9   Negotiating in China: A Swedish View

We had, in total, four rounds of negotiations within a little over a year. At the first meeting, they asked us to present our position. We did this. We regarded our opening proposal as very generous to the Chinese side, and we thought that it would satisfy them. They listened politely, and the atmosphere was in every way friendly, but we did not succeed in getting any concrete reaction from them. Every time we elaborated a little further on our position, and every time the process was repeated.

Since it did not seem possible to get any further, the meeting was concluded at that point. It was not until the next time that the actual negotiations started. It also turned out that they did not have the mandate to sign a contract in Sweden, this had to be done in Beijing. Our positions were wide apart. We even made some further concessions, but this did not satisfy them.

The negotiations continued for a third round in Beijing. It really began to seem as if the subject matter was unfamiliar ground to them, that they simply did not master the substance of our agreement. They made frequent comparisons with other more or less similar deals that they had made, and under no circumstances would they agree to anything which seemed any less favorable. At one point, when they did not grasp our solution to a specific issue, they even suggested an alternative arrangement which was actually less favorable to them than the one proposed by us.

The situation was made further complicated by an incompetent interpreter. We also often had to fight unreasonable arguments and pressure tactics. On several occasions, they raised issues which we had already agreed on, in an attempt to renegotiate them. The atmosphere at times became rather strained due to many such irritating occurrences.

One of the Chinese negotiators was a militant, quite aggressive, while the other main character had a more conciliatory approach. The militant negotiator insisted on discussing every little step in painstaking detail, which was incredible, and really a complete waste of time. The final phase, up until the signing of the contract, resembled a contest in perseverance and endurance.

SOURCE: Knutsson (1986, p. 20).

from competing foreign firms and to be convinced that they are buying the best. It is thus important for a Western firm to provide as much detail as possible to avoid delay in negotiations.

   4. *Price:* The Western firm should be very careful in calculating the price for their technology. If a foreign firm reduces its price radically, say 15% to 20%,

the Chinese negotiators become suspicious. The cost of any expatriate personnel to be stationed in China should be included in the budget.

5. *Relationship building:* The Chinese are very concerned about developing friendships with Western counterparts. Trust emerges from friendships.

India

After decades of isolation and restrictions on FDI, in 1991, India opened its economy to foreign firms and investors. The government and local businessmen were convinced that the Indian economy must be integrated into the rest of the world. The seriousness of and commitment to the reforms are apparent from the speed with which decisions were made in the first 12 months of reforms. The investments approved by the government's Foreign Investment Promotion Board included a $40-million joint venture with General Electric (GE) to manufacture refrigerators and washing machines, approved within 6 weeks of application. In the same period, the board approved investments by General Motors, BMW, Dupont, Fujitsu, IBM, Kellogg, and Coca-Cola (Rahul, 1992).

India is a country with an abundance of well-educated people. About 125,000 engineers graduate every year, twice as many as in the United States. These engineers and other graduates have turned India into a major provider of software. In 2000, the country exported computer programs worth $6.5 billion, and export estimates show that this figure will increase to $30 billion by the year 2004 (Whelan, 2000). Indian companies are also very active in e-commerce and wireless technology. Companies such as Cisco and Nortel are setting up their R&D centers in the country. Due to this boom, the middle class is increasing by 4% every year. As a result, India has a middle class of about 300 million people, more than any other country, in the world. In the year 2000, there were more than 70,000 subscribers for mobile phones every month (Whelan, 2000).

Liberalization in India provides enormous opportunities for Western firms, especially in consumer goods, to satisfy the demand of the more than 300 million members of the middle class. Unlike Eastern Europe and China, India has a relatively well-developed infrastructure, distribution channels, and a well-trained and educated workforce. Western companies are now allowed to have majority- or even wholly owned subsidiaries, the tax rate has been lowered, and licenses have been eliminated for most imports.

In 1991, India had almost no foreign exchange reserves, and the inflation rate was at 16% (Moshavi & Engardio, 1995). The former Soviet Union, which had been a major export market, had collapsed. The Gulf War had decreased overseas remittances sent to India by thousands of expatriate workers. State planning and excessive administrative control of the "license raj" had protected too many domestic-, public-, and private-sector firms, which could produce only high-cost, low-quality, and rather outdated goods.

The government reforms, including reducing aggregate demand, devaluing the Indian rupee by 22%, lowering import duties, and bringing the free market mind-set into the public and private sectors have stabilized the economy. To boost investments and business confidence, corporate taxes have been lowered, and tariffs have been lowered from 135% to as low as 25% for some imports (Ganguly, 1998; Kaushik, 1996). Two-tiered exchange rates have been abolished, and a single, market-determined exchange rate for trade transactions and inward remittances has been determined. No clearances are required to obtain foreign exchange for imported goods. In the first quarter of 2001, foreign exchange reserves accounted for $41 billion. Annual growth rate of exports for 1990 to 1999 was more than 11%, and FDI in 1999 reached $2.1 billion (Ministry of Finance, Government of India, 2001).

Despite some accusations of halfhearted reforms and setbacks in industrial growth, a mere 3% in 1993, the reforms are working and foreign investments are pouring in. The industrial-production growth rate rose in 2000 to 8%, and economic growth rose to approximately 6%. During 1998 to 1999, the government approved approximately $6 billion worth of FDI. Only 12% of this comes from the United States, from companies such as GE, Hewlett-Packard, Wrigley, Kellogg, and Ford. The rest of the investments come from Europe, Japan, and South Korea (Indian Investment Center, 2000).

A number of public-sector industries are being liberalized. Telecommunications are one such example. In a country of 1 billion people, there are only 9 million lines. The government's target for the year 2000 was 30 million lines, with an estimated cost of more than $20 billion. At present, all the global telecommunications actors are competing to get a piece of this $20-billion cake. Foreign firms are allowed to participate in new ventures in this sector. AT&T and Sprint are already doing business in India. AT&T has a joint venture with the Tata group to make transmission and switching systems. Philips India, with 9,000 employees and $325 million in sales, is trying to form joint ventures with local companies to serve the telecommunications industry (Indian Investment Center, 2000).

During 1999, India's total exports amounted to $38,463 million, of which the United States accounted for nearly 22%. Total trade (imports plus exports) between India and the United States accounted for $12.7 billion, with India having a surplus of $4.7 billion. In the same year, direct investment in India reached $2.168 million (Indian Investment Center, 2000).

It is relatively easy to identify opportunities to do business in India and to conduct feasibility studies, because it is possible to find reliable information and learn local business practices. Most of India's private businesses are members of three leading business organizations:

1. Associated Chambers of Commerce (ASSOCHAM), the oldest national chamber of commerce in India. It is nonpolitical and seeks to develop working relationships between government institutions and private businesses.

2. The Confederation of Indian Industries (CII) has more than 2,000 corporate members, whose total investment is more than $33 billion (Indian Investment Center, 2000). Membership includes public enterprises, such as the oil and gas authority and the steel authority. CII arranges seminars, fairs, and conferences and has signed a number of memoranda of understanding with foreign manufacturing associations.

3. The Federation of Indian Chamber of Commerce and Industry (FICCI) is the central organization of industry, trade, and commerce in India. FICCI members also sit on government policy-making bodies as advisers. It organizes trade fairs, conferences, and workshops for its members. It has a good relationship with foreign chambers of commerce, including that of the United States'.

All these organizations are willing to help foreign investors with information on their member organizations and industries.

The government of India has been very active in establishing business relationships with major industrial countries, including the United States, Germany, the United Kingdom, Japan, and Canada. The government has signed a number of bilateral agreements, exchanged ministerial visits, or sent combined government and business delegations to these countries (see Exhibit 8.10).

As a result of these activities, India's exports have been increasing at an annual rate of more than 10% since 1991. Textiles account for nearly 25% of Indian exports, followed by diamonds and jewelry for 20.5% (U.S. Department of Commerce, 2000d). Other exports include engineering products, chemical and related products, and marine products. Imports also show similar acceleration. The main imports are petroleum products, pearls, precious and semiprecious stones, fertilizers, and consumer products.

Western investors may develop majority-owned joint ventures or wholly owned subsidiaries after negotiations with the Foreign Investment Promotion Board. Some industries, however, are reserved for the public

Exhibit 8.10 Trade Promotion Activities by India in 1994: Selected Countries

Country	Prime Minister's Visits	Minister's Visits	Trade Missions	Bilateral Agreements
United States	2	1	1	1
United Kingdom	1	2	4	2
Germany	1	3	1	1
Japan	0	0	2	0
Canada	0	1	2	0
Italy	0	1	1	0

SOURCE: U.S. Department of Commerce (2000d).

sector: arms, ammunition and defense equipment, atomic energy, mineral oils, minerals used in atomic energy, and railways. There are no restrictions on plant location other than those directed by pollution and environmental regulations. There are no requirements to employ Indian nationals and no restrictions on foreign technicians and managers. Some benefits are available for location in export-processing zones (EPZs) and for 100% export-oriented units (EOUs), including duty-free import of goods, materials, and components; permission to sell 25% of product in the domestic market; exemption from state and central taxes; liberal loans; and government financing schemes. There are six EPZs, and EOUs can be established outside these zones.

Western firms entering the Indian market should consider the following:

1. India is a market with a well-qualified and motivated workforce. Almost everyone speaks English and can easily be trained to work for Western companies. Distribution channels are well established, and manufacturing is common throughout the country.

2. Joint ventures are the most popular entry strategies, and Western firms can raise capital on the Indian Stock Exchange. In the automobile industry, a considerable number of joint ventures involving Western firms have been established (see Exhibit 8.11).

3. There is no shortage of well-educated, Western-trained Indian managers. They are adept at handling local infrastructure problems and can negotiate with active labor unions.

Exhibit 8.11 Foreign Investments in the Automobile Industry in India

Foreign Company	Local Partner	Cost of Plant ($ Millions)	Start-Up Date
General Motors	Hindustan Motors	100	January 1996
Mercedes	Tata group	115	Mid-1995
Daewoo	DCM	900	July 1995
Investment by already-established Suzuki	Maruti	400	Mid-1996

SOURCE: Moshavi (1995b, p. 31).

4. The market for consumer products is enormous, and Western firms should not ignore rural markets (the majority of the Indian population) and a middle class of more than 300 million consumers.

5. India is attractive not only as a market but also as a sourcing country. There are great opportunities to buy or make components and parts for the local as well as the home market. A number of smaller companies are producing parts and components for Western companies in accordance with ISO 9000 quality standards. These companies include ASEA-Brown Boveri, Motorola, IBM, and a number of other computer firms. Relatively smaller firms are also manufacturing in India, such as Stork (Netherlands), Hennes & Mauritz (Sweden), and Mexx (Netherlands).

Finding a suitable partner is still the most important issue for a Western firm. The main problem is that the Indian partner may have personal ambitions and dreams that may not be consistent with the Western firm's objectives. Indians are very hospitable people and have a tendency to promise more than they can deliver. A Western firm entering the Indian market should ascertain the extent of these risks. The risk is minimal with well-established groups such as the Tatas and Birlas but can be quite high with small and medium-sized firms or entrepreneurs. This is illustrated by Coca Cola's experience in India (Exhibit 8.12).

Approximately 10 million Indians live abroad, most of whom have skills and financial resources that are now in high demand in India. These nonresident Indians (NRIs) are investing heavily in several places in India, depending on their language and ethnic links. In its cover story of July 3, 1995

Exhibit 8.12 Coca-Cola's Experience in India

The relationship between Coca-Cola and an Indian businessman, Chauhan, began in September 1993 on the initiative of Chauhan (company name *Parle*). The contract was signed 2 months later in Atlanta. Chauhan already had a considerable-sized bottling business with his own trademarks, Thums Up, Limca, Citra, Gold Spot, and Maaza. He negotiated a contract to bottle three beverages marketed by Coca-Cola, Fanta, and Sprite, as well as a contract to use concentrates made at Coca-Cola for his existing brands. Coca-Cola was to invest $20 million in a plant in Pune (near Bombay) to make these concentrates. Several contracts were signed to upgrade Parle's 56 existing plants. An annual consulting fee of $125,000 was to have been paid to Chauhan and his brother for 5 years, and a proposed $20 million investment was to have been made to establish an equal partnership and to expand the bottling plants. Chauhan would get first rights to add additional bottling plants in Pune and Bangelore.

The conflicts began at an early stage. Coca-Cola found that Chauhan's plants in Delhi and Bombay were not up to its standards. The launch of Coke was delayed in almost all cities. Coca-Cola believes that Chauhan was slow in upgrading his plants and in finding sites for new plants in Pune and Bangalore. In 1994, Coca-Cola noticed that Chauhan's plants in Delhi and Bombay were buying an "amazingly low" volume of concentrates for his brands. Coca-Cola believes that Chauhan was making concentrates on his own for his brands, which was against the agreement, because Coca-Cola's revenues are related to the volume of concentrate sold. Consequently, it withheld the consulting fee.

At this point, Chauhan agreed to pay Coca-Cola Rs45.7 million ($1.45 million U.S.), and on December 13, Coca-Cola informed Chauhan that he had violated the contract. Chauhan then launched a harsh media campaign against Coca-Cola and threatened legal action. Coca-Cola had obtained preemptive injunctions requiring Chauhan to inform them of any impending legal petitions.

Raja, the President of Coca-Cola India, has reminded the Ministry of Finance that Coca-Cola had invested approximately Rs3.4 billion, paid Rs1.5 billion in excise tax, exported Rs450 million worth of items, and in 1994, expanded the soft-drink market by 7% (against 1% growth in 1993). Experts believe the partnership between Chauhan and Coca-Cola will continue because both parties have invested a lot in the relationship. Chauhan cannot manage the increased capacity in his plants without Coca-Cola, and it will be impossible for Coca-Cola to find a new partner and to get new permission for new plants in Delhi or Bombay.

SOURCE: McDonald (1995, pp. 74-75).

Exhibit 8.13 Overseas Indians and Their Investments

Country	Number	Industry	Target Area
Britain	1.6 million	Banking and power	Punjab, Haryana, Andhra Pradesh
Persian Gulf	2.5 million	Real estate Agri-business	Kerala, Bengalore, Madras, Goa
South Africa	1 million	Textiles	Gujarat, Madras
North America United States Canada	3 million 1 million	Technology, finance, serve as executive of U.S. firms in India	Bombay, Gujarat, Bangalore, Madras
Asia Malaysia Singapore Hong Kong	1.2 million 190,000 24,000	Finance, high tech, real estate, telecommunications	Tamil Nadu, South India, Bombay, Pune, New Delhi

SOURCE: Barnathan, Moshavi, Dawley, Sunita, & Chang (1995).

(Barnathan, Moshavi, Dawley, Sunita, & Chang), *Business Week* presented the statistics on NRIs and their investments. These are found in Exhibit 8.13.

After years of building their skills and fortunes in other countries, NRIs are now returning home and share a major part of inward FDI. According to the Standard Chartered Bank in Dubai, the combined annual income of the 10 million Indians living abroad is approximately $340 billion—equivalent to the GDP of India, which has a population of more than 900 million. They are bringing capital, Western management, and marketing know-how to India. These NRI investors are at an advantage compared with foreign investors. They understand the culture and have family connections. Moreover, although equally frustrated with the slow pace of reforms and bureaucratic delays, they are very committed to India.

A Word of Caution

Indian government procurement is not transparent, and often local suppliers are favored if their prices and quality are acceptable. In some sectors, for example, defense, foreign companies are forced to act through local agents, which can be costly. Some government entities use foreign bids to pressure local suppliers to lower their bids and are allowed to resubmit tenders when a foreign supplier/contractor has underbid them. India is not a member of the Paris Convention on Intellectual Property Rights, nor does it have bilateral patent agreements. However, Indian law is based on British common law, and courts consistently uphold intellectual property protection. For patents, the situation is different. The long-established Indian Patent Act prohibits patents for inventions intended for use in food, medicine, and drugs, which means that many Western-developed medicines and drugs are widely reproduced. Policy guidelines normally limit royalty payments, including patent-licensing payments, to 8% of selling price. Royalties and lump-sum payments are taxed at a 30% rate. Although Indian courts provide adequate safeguards for enforcement of property and contractual rights, case backlogs often lead to long procedural delays. India is not a member of the International Center for Settlement of Investment Disputes.

It is, however, the political sense, not the economic, that creates some doubts about India's economic potentials. Many foreign investors believe that the Hindu nationalists that came to power in the 1996 election are openly against foreign investments and foreign influence on the Indian society. Additionally, incidents such as the Enron power project and Kentucky Fried Chicken are fuelling fears that India has chosen a path that will lead to the reversal of liberalization. However, both Enron and Kentucky Fried Chicken have since renegotiated their futures in India in mutually agreeable ways (see Exhibit 8.14), although the Enron project is now in limbo.

Indonesia

Indonesia, with its 3,000 islands, became independent from the Netherlands on December 27, 1949, although it proclaimed independence on August 17, 1945. It has a mixed economy, with some socialist institutions and central planning. In recent years, however, much of the economy has been deregulated and privatized. Indonesia has extensive natural wealth and an increasing population. GDP growth averaged 6% during the period 1985 to 1995. The agricultural sector accounts for 21% of GDP and 50% of the labor force. Industrial output accounts for 40% of GDP and is based on a number of natural resources, for example, oil, natural gas, timber, metals, and coal (U.S. Department of Commerce, 2000h). However, Indonesia is the country that suffered most from the Asian crisis, due to political disruptions.

Indonesia is a member of the Association of Southeast Asian Nations (ASEAN), together with Brunei, Malaysia, the Philippines, Singapore, Thailand, and Vietnam. The group was formed in Bangkok in 1967. With an overall population of approximately 265 million in the 1980s, the group

Exhibit 8.14 Politics and Entering the Indian Market

Enron Development Corporation's $2.8 billion deal to develop a liquefied natural gas project in Dabhol, India, was largely hailed as one of the largest foreign projects undertaken since liberalization measures began in India in 1991. The 2,015-megawatt project would not only supply the power-starved area with the electricity it needed but also bring in an estimated $300 million in local expenditures. The deal all but blew up in the American company's face when the Maharashtra state government decided to pull the plug on the project in August 1995.

During a power struggle between the ruling Congress Party and the right-wing Bharatiya Janata Party (BJP), Enron became the punching bag for Indian nationalism. The BJP and the Shiv Sena Hindu National Alliance (SSH) alleged corruption in awarding the deal to Enron and accused them of threatening Indian economic sovereignty. Using Indian nationalism as a political platform to counter the historically entrenched Congress Party, the BJP said the project was too costly, that the tariffs suggested by Enron were too high, and that the Congress Party was too tied to foreign business interests. Although the bribery charges were never substantiated, the project was canceled soon after the BJP won the elections.

This was not the first sign of controversy regarding the project. In mid-May of 1995, villagers induced by political leaders demonstrated against the forced acquisition of their lands for the project. Destroying the site, they damaged the equipment and chased off 400 armed guards and 2,000 workers.

Similarly, other foreign companies have met resistance to Western investment attempts. Kentucky Fried Chicken (KFC), which had just opened its first restaurant in Bangalore in June 1995, was forced to step up security after threats by local political groups to destroy KFC outlets. Many Indians feel the need to resist a perceived American cultural invasion and say India does not need America's greasy food. Indian environmentalists and socialists have also forced DuPont to relocate a nylon plant and are protesting against a paper plant being built by Sinar Mas, an Indonesian company.

In Enron's case, however, India's need for power eventually won out, or perhaps it was because international arbitrators may have forced the Maharashtra government to compensate Enron up to $2 billion for backing out of the deal. Just 6 months after cancelling the deal and after heavy negotiation, the government once again sanctioned the project. Enron agreed to scale down the project's costs to $1.8 billion and renegotiate its power rates.

Despite fears that the liberalization trend in India might be reversed, most experts believe these occasional backlashes against foreign companies are symptoms of societies in transition, rather than the warning signs of a future reversal. Likened to American resistance to Japanese investment in the 1980s, India is expected to outgrow this reluctance.

SOURCE: "An India That Still Says No" (1995, p. 12); Moshavi (1995a, p. 44); Nicholson (1995, p. 23).

was more concerned about the Vietnamese occupation of Cambodia than with economic integration. ASEAN'S obsession about Vietnam and its Soviet allies dates back to early threats of communism. These threats have now disappeared, but there is still not much improvement in ASEAN economic integration. For Indonesia, ASEAN trade represents approximately 15% of the country's world trade, whereas ASEAN investments in Indonesia account for less than 5% of total foreign investment. Despite its proximity, Malaysia's trade with Indonesia is one of the smallest among ASEAN countries. Indonesia has realized that it cannot rely on ASEAN countries to develop capital and must instead rely on its oil earnings to develop its economy. As a result of the Asian crisis, several economic reforms were undertaken. Indonesia has encouraged its private sector to play an active role in the economy. The private sector is dominated by the Chinese, who are still often regarded with suspicion.

Japan is Indonesia's most important customer and supplier of development loans. But Japanese generosity is becoming a mixed blessing because much of the country's debt is in yen, whereas most of its income is in U.S. dollars. Every time the yen goes up 1% against the dollar, it adds $300 million or more to Indonesia's debt.

Indonesia is one of the biggest debtors among the emerging economies. During 1998, its external debt reached 169% of present GNP, with a total of $150,875 million, compared with $69,872 in 1990 (IMF, 2000a). Indonesia, however, has an excellent record of debt management. In the last 30 years, it has not had to reschedule its debt once, and it has had adequate foreign reserves. Its current-account balance is at 2% of GDP. As a precaution, it has raised its foreign reserves in yen from 27% to 35% (IMF, 2000a). And the increasing devaluation of the Indonesian rupee has induced a new surge of Japanese investment. Foreign investments are thus soaring and are boosting manufacturing, output, and exports.

Until 1996, Indonesia enjoyed a high international profile. In November 1994, it hosted the summit meeting of the Asia-Pacific Economic Cooperation Forum (APEC), with 17 heads of state attending (including U.S. President Bill Clinton). Indonesia has also had some form of "political stability"; President Suharto was in office from 1967 to 1997. The Asian crisis also brought a political crisis for Indonesia. Although a new, elected government is in place, politically and economically, Indonesia is still somewhat unstable. Domestically, it has a huge, growing middle class that is demanding Western technology and products.

With President Suharto's 20 years of steady economic growth, averaging 6.8% annually, the country demonstrated great potential. The World Bank ranked it as one of the highest-performing Asian economies. Poverty declined from 60% in 1970 to 15% in 1995 ("Suharto's Pals," 1995). The shift in political power, although through election, has created some uncertainty for international investors. Indonesia has cut tariffs on more than 6,000 products, exceeding its commitment to the WTO. Indonesia is thus trying hard to get the confidence of foreign investors back.

In 1993, the government introduced a drastic deregulation package for foreign investors. The rules on minimum investment and location were lifted, and foreign investors were no longer required to divest their shares to Indonesians. In 1995, a new deregulation package was announced that provided a tariff reduction schedule for the next 8 years. As a result, there is a lot of activity in the private sector and in the nonpetroleum-related industries. Traditionally, Indonesian exports are dominated by petroleum-based products. According to Bangko Sentralng Pilipinas (BSP) Statistics Indonesia (2000), the share of non-oil and -gas exports reached $38.73 billion in 1999. The non-oil and -gas exports contributed 79.87% to the total export value. During the same year, the oil and gas exports increased by 24%, whereas the non-oil and -gas exports decreased by 5.48%. In 1994, after introducing new regulations on foreign investment, $23.7 billion of investments were approved, compared with $8.4 billion the year before. Foreign investments are being made in all sectors, from raw materials and manufacturing to retailing (Barnathan et al., 1995). A number of supermarkets, such as Hero and Golden Tryly, are appearing. Shopping malls have stores such as Britain's Marks & Spencer and Japan's Sogo. Government must now turn to improving the infrastructure; that is, more roads, telecommunications, ports, railways, and power stations must be constructed, and large, protected monopolies need to be dissolved (Exhibit 8.15 provides an example of state influence). Only then will the benefits of foreign investment and deregulation be realized.

Big conglomerates and protected monopolies are not the only hindrances in Indonesia's liberalization policies. The association of most larger conglomerates with the Suharto family has become a major concern for foreign investors. In July 1995, Bimantara Citra, the holding company for a wide range of Indonesian conglomerates, was listed at the Jakarta Stock Exchange to issue 20% of its stocks to the public. In 1994, Bimantara Citra had a profit of $280 million. Although its business ranges from oil and gas to hotels and financial services, 50% of its revenue comes from telecommunications (Pt. Bimantara Citra Tbk, 2001). It was the only company that was allowed to set up a commercial television network in Indonesia, and it shares the duopoly for international telephone links. Despite these positive points, there was some reluctance to invest in the stocks. The main reason, discussed in the international press, was that this is precisely the sort of

---

Exhibit 8.15 Timber Development and the Suharto Family in Indonesia

In 1994, British censors banned an advertisement by the Indonesian Wood Panel Association (IWPA, locally known as APKINDO) in which flourishing wildlife was depicted in Indonesia's rain forest. It was claimed that some of the scenes were filmed with captive animals, and not in the rain forest.

IWPA monopolizes Indonesia's $5.2-billion trade in wood products. Its 115 member companies are forced to sell to APKINDO's agents abroad. IWPA is said to be run by President Suharto's close associate, Bob Hasan. The recent deregulations and setbacks have upset some businesses. The timber industry accounts for 15% of total export earnings. IWPA is blamed for being a cartel, because no timber company gets a concession or loses one without its involvement. Even some of ruling party parliament members are demanding that IWPA be "dismantled."

Some of the companies have started business with offshore companies, for example, from Malaysia, instead of doing business with IWPA. Critics claim that APKINDO is ill prepared for competition from Malaysia and Brazil. Indonesia's export earnings from plywood dropped by 10% in 1994, to $4.1 billion. It is said that APKINDO cannot match buyers with exporters fast enough.

SOURCE: "Suharto's Pals" (1995).

---

industry that a less friendly government might open up to more rivals. Although the government has now changed, the Asian crisis has proven to have created new uncertainties for foreign firms.

This fear is also apparent in other deals. For example, in July 1995, PT Telecom, a state-owned monopoly, awarded five contracts to install and operate 2 million new phone lines. None of the five contracts went to companies associated with the Suharto family. Instead, all of them were awarded to a consortium of foreign companies in fair competition. This project is considered an economic landmark in Indonesia. This is the first time ever that a multibillion-dollar project has no direct involvement with the Suharto family. The family, however, could not be excluded without a fight. According to *Business Week* ("Suharto's Pals"), in June 1995, the Minister of Telecommunications attempted to force the consortia to merge with two companies linked to the Suharto family. Heated media attention deterred the minister from carrying out his plan. The emergence of a more transparent business environment is encouraging foreign investors to take a fresh look at Indonesia (see Exhibit 8.16).

Exhibit 8.16 The New Shape of Indonesian Telecommunications

	Foreign Partner	Local Partner	Location	Investment ($ Millions)
1	U.S. West	Tiga-A	West Java	600
2	Nippon & Telstra & Australia	PT Indosat	Central Java	528
3	France Telecom	Astra	Sumatra	552
4	Telecom Malaysia	Atlatief	Kalimantan	84
5	Singapore Telecom	Bukaka Telekomindo	Eastern Indonesia	484
	Total			**2,248**

SOURCE: "Suharto's Pals" (1995).

Malaysia

Few countries in Southeast Asia are blessed with better fortune than Malaysia. It is a major world producer of five key commodities: rubber, palm oil, tin, timber, and pepper. Moreover, it is an oil and gas exporter. Its population (19 million) is educated and enterprising. Although differences in race and religion give rise to periodic conflict, each group has prominence in the country. The Malays dominate politics, the Chinese dominate the economic system, and Indians and Westerners cooperate in small-business ventures.

Datuk Seri Dr. Mahathir, a physician, the first Malaysian prime minister without any royal connection, has provided aggressive leadership. He has ordered civil servants to clock in for work and started several campaigns to end corruption and increase efficiency. In his early years, he developed good relations with Britain. (Margaret Thatcher visited Malaysia in 1984, the first official visit of a British prime minister since its independence in 1957.) One of his main problems has been the balance of payments, especially the current account, which damaged Malaysia's excellent credit ratings in the early 1980s. The current-account deficit was at an unacceptably high level throughout the 1980s and delayed or jeopardized Malaysia's plan to enter into heavy-industry projects to process its own raw materials, including a "made in Malaysia" car. In the late 1980s, the government realized that the public sector had grown too large, and started an ambitious privatization program. The government decided to curtail its share and role in sectors such as telecommunications, the national airline, railways, and ports.

Since then, Malaysia's privatization program has been working very successfully. The shift of state-run enterprises to private hands has helped boost economic growth and has made both the manufacturing and service sectors more efficient. Many experts rate Malaysia's privatization program as one of the most successful in the world. According to Khoo Eng Choo, the managing partner of Price-Waterhouse in Kuala Lumpur, "Compared with the developing countries, privatization in Malaysia is more advanced and more widely applied. . . . To say that Malaysia is a model to developing countries is an understatement" (Jayasankaran, 1995, p. 42).

Since 1983, the government has sold all or part of 120 businesses, raising RM4.2 billion ($1.68 billion U.S.). The government has also spent enormous amounts on infrastructure projects: RM3.4 billion on the North-South highway in 1986 and RM16.3 billion on the Bakun hydroelectric dam (construction began in 1995). The revenues earned from the sale of these assets helped Malaysia solve its current-account problem and provided the funding to invest in the above-mentioned infrastructure projects. However, Malaysia's privatization drive of the past two decades has been cut as a result of the Asian crisis. In December 2000 alone, the government pledged $2.1 billion to buy back two ailing light-rail transit systems and a 29% stake in Malaysia Airlines, the loss-making national carrier. As the country recovers from the Asian crisis, the government has started to award consortiums for new infrastructure projects, such as water treatment plants and a dam on the Selangor River to supply water to the Klang Valley. Inflation is under control, there is a large trade surplus, the country has $22 billion in foreign reserves, and there was an average annual growth rate of more than 8% for the period 1990 to 1996 (Jayasankaran, 2001).

Malaysia plays a dominant role in the ASEAN group of countries and has considerable trade with China and Taiwan. In the 1960s, when China was supporting an armed Malaysian Communist Party, the relationship between the two countries was strained. In 1974, Malaysia and China established diplomatic relations, which led to increased trade between the two countries, amounting to $4.5 billion in 1999 (an increase of 16% over 1998). Malaysia's ties with Taiwan are even stronger. The value of trade between the two countries amounted to $7.3 billion in 1999 (Malaysian Central Bank, 2001).

In recent years, Japan has established a number of its manufacturing facilities in Malaysia. A number of Western firms have moved their offices and manufacturing from Singapore to Malaysia. After Japan, the United States is Malaysia's second-largest supplier of goods. Firms such as Motorola and Intel are producing computer chips for the global market. Foreign automotive companies such as Audi, Ford, and Toyota are also making large investments in Malaysia (see Exhibit 8.17).

Exhibit 8.17 Automotive Production in Malaysia

	2000	2005	% Change
Light vehicles	4,586	5,760	25.6
Vehicle sales	343,283	504,362	46.9
Light-vehicle production	382,016	584,922	53.1

SOURCE: Autopolis (2002).
NOTE: Manufacturers: Audi, BMW, PSA Peugeot-Citröen, Daihatsu, Daimler Chrysler, Ford, Honda, Inokom, Isuzu, Kia, Mahindra & Mahindra, Mazda, Nissan, Perodua, Mitsubishi, Suzuki, Toyota.

The Malaysian economy has grown at more than 8% annually for almost a decade. This rapid growth has led to rising incomes and a rising demand for both consumer and capital goods. It has also led to a tight labor market; the unemployment rate is around 3%. The country has become highly dependent on international trade. For 1999, exports approximated 124% of GDP (see Exhibit 8.18). It had an overall balance of payment surplus of $4.6 billion in 1999. Malaysian per capita income rose to $3,400 in 1999 in terms of the international exchange rate and more than $7,963 in terms of purchasing-power parity. As a result, Malaysia has been transformed from a low-income producer of natural resource commodities, such as tin, rubber, and palm oil, to a middle-level manufacturing economy. It is at present the world's third-largest producer and the largest exporter of semiconductors. For agricultural imports, Malaysia's market is worth $3 billion. Politically, Malaysia is quite stable (U.S. Department of Commerce, 2000i).

Malaysia has bilateral investment agreements with 29 countries and country groups, such as ASEAN. It has double-taxation treaties with 36 countries, and foreign and domestic investors have equal access to its 10 free trade zones (FTZs). Investors establishing operations in FTZs are allowed to sell a portion of their production on the domestic market. There are no foreign exchange restrictions and no restrictions on foreign portfolio investment. Foreign investors may borrow locally in foreign currency to finance their business activities. The local banks are sound; in 1993, the top five commercial banks held assets worth $45 billion (Malaysian Central Bank, 2001). For the most attractive sectors for foreign firms in Malaysia, see Exhibit 8.19.

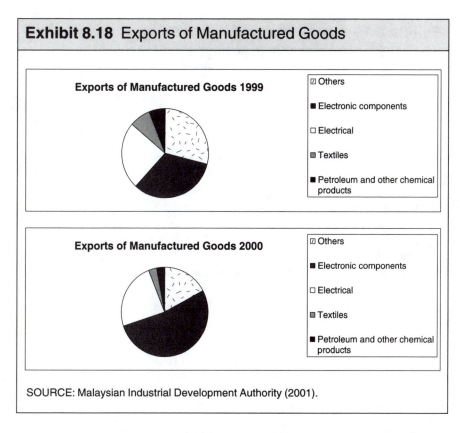

Exhibit 8.18 Exports of Manufactured Goods

SOURCE: Malaysian Industrial Development Authority (2001).

There are some rules to be followed for employment of expatriate workers. A company with a paid-up capital of at least $2 million can employ five expatriates, and permission to employ more can be obtained. These expatriate posts can be retained for 10 years. Malaysia has one of the region's strongest laws for intellectual property protection, and the country has accepted the Berne Convention, the Paris Convention, and is a member of the World Intellectual Property Organization. Cases of uncompensated expropriation or investment disputes involving foreign investors or contractors are unheard-of. It has signed the United-Nations-sponsored convention on the settlement of investment disputes. Some industries attracting considerable FDI are given in Exhibit 8.20.

Thailand

Thailand has been one of the fastest-growing and most attractive markets for Western exporters and investors for the past couple of decades.

Exhibit 8.19 Most Attractive Manufacturing Sectors for Investment in Malaysia

| | *January to February 2001* | | | *2000* | |
	Industry	Number of Projects Approved		Industry	Number of Projects Approved
1.	Paper products	9	1.	Electronics & electrical	224
2.	Electronics & electrical	34	2.	Natural gas	1
3.	Nonmetallic products	7	3.	Petroleum products	7
4.	Chemical products	13	4.	Nonmetallic products	25
5.	Wood & wood products	8	5.	Paper products	26

| | *January to February 2001* | | | *2000* | |
	Country	Number of Projects Approved		Country	Number of Projects Approved
1.	China	1	1.	United States	48
2.	United States	7	2.	Japan	117
3.	Singapore	27	3.	Netherlands	14
4.	Taiwan	10	4.	Singapore	144
5.	Korea, Rep.	5	5.	Germany	30

SOURCE: Malaysian Industrial Development Authority (2001).
* All rankings are based on investment amount in RM.

After the Asian crisis, the economy is still recovering, with a 4.9% annual growth rate. The country has a base of 60 million affluent customers, with per capita income of $1,960 (U.S. Department of Commerce, 2001e).

Thailand has been open to Western investors for many years. A number of developments in the region enhanced the attractiveness of Thailand for foreign investors: the political instability of the Philippines during the Marcos years, the higher cost of establishing manufacturing facilities in Singapore, and the decision of the British government to hand over Hong

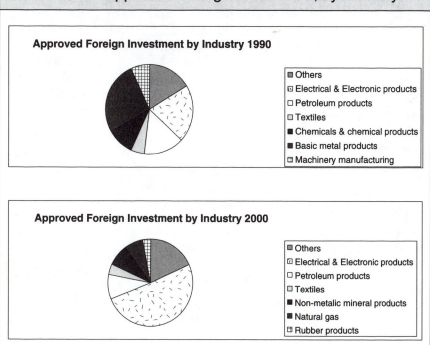

Exhibit 8.20 Approved Foreign Investment, by Industry

Approved Foreign Investment by Industry 1990

- Others
- Electrical & Electronic products
- Petroleum products
- Textiles
- Chemicals & chemical products
- Basic metal products
- Machinery manufacturing

Approved Foreign Investment by Industry 2000

- Others
- Electrical & Electronic products
- Petroleum products
- Textiles
- Non-metalic mineral products
- Natural gas
- Rubber products

SOURCE: Central Bank of Malaysia (2001).

Kong to China in 1997. Most Western firms and countries have thus been very successful in Thailand. The United States alone exported around $6 billion worth of goods to Thailand in 1999. Thailand's imports grew by 16.9% in 1999, to $47.5 billion. The main suppliers were Japan (26%), the European Union (20%), and the United States (12%) (IMF, 2001). The export and import growth in selected sectors is given in Exhibit 8.21.

Thailand's economy is in transition from one based on agriculture to one based on industry and trading. Although the majority of the people still depend on agriculture, the manufacturing, trading, and service sectors are expanding and account for two thirds of GDP. The policies of economic development are based on a competitive, free market philosophy. Thailand is an active member of the ASEAN group of countries and has implemented the first round of cuts on high-tariff goods imported from ASEAN countries. Thailand, however, has traditionally been more oriented toward Western markets, particularly the United States and the European Union

Exhibit 8.21 Export and Import Growth Rates for Selected Sectors

	Export Growth Rates (%)	
	1999	*2000*
Agriculture	− 3.6	1.4
Fishery	− 4.2	10.9
Manufacturing	9.8	21.3
Labor	3.1	8.0
High Tech	11.5	27.6
Resource	12.0	7.5
Total	**7.4**	**19.6**
	Import Growth Rates (%)	
	1999	*2000*
Capital	3.5	26.1
Raw Material	21.0	29.8
Consumer Products	13.9	20.1
Oil	36.3	59.9
Vehicles & Parts	154.3	54.7
Total	**16.9**	**31.3**

SOURCE: Bank of Thailand (2001).

(see Exhibit 8.22). Despite frequent government changes, political and economic stability are ensured through a balance between the king, the military, the bureaucrats, and the business sector. There is also close cooperation between the public and private sectors.

The public sector controls public infrastructure through 65 enterprises. The manufacturing and construction sectors have traditionally been in the hands of the private sector. In some public sectors, such as telecommunications and transportation, private-sector participation is increasing. The government offers a number of incentives for FDI. For example, the U.S./Thai Treaty of Amity allows U.S. citizens to engage in business on the same basis and rules that Thai citizens do. The legal environment is not complex, bureaucratic procedures and processes are quick and efficient, and the main hindrance is rather stiff competition from domestic and foreign firms, especially from Japan.

Rapid growth has had its drawbacks. The shortage of skilled personnel and environmental degradation have increased over the years. The low level

Exhibit 8.22 Destination of Thai Exports

Destination	Percentage Share of Total Exports	1999 (%YOY*)	2000 (%YOY)
United States	20.4	4.0	17.5
Association of Southeast Asian Nations (ASEAN)	19.1	31.3	24.6
European Union (EU)	16.1	1.2	11.9
Japan	16.0	10.3	25.5
Hong Kong	4.4	7.0	18.2
China	4.3	5.4	52.4
Taiwan	3.3	17.3	22.0
Total	**100.0**	**7.4**	**19.5**

SOURCE: Bank of Thailand (2001).
*Year on Year," as compared with last year.

of education of the country's workforce is a serious problem. In the past, when only low-wage, labor-intensive industries were expanding, a poorly educated workforce was adequate, but now such industries are being developed in China and Vietnam. If Thailand wants to attract high-technology industries, it must increase the education levels attained by its workforce (Kenan Institute Asia, 2000). The government is planning to spend about 1 trillion baht on infrastructure projects between 2000 and 2006, including electricity generation, new oil refineries, a second airport, an additional 6 million telephone lines, and new mass transportation systems, including highways and railroads ("Budget Constraints," 2000). Plans to develop a new central government administrative city, solid-waste treatment, and wastewater treatment plants are also to be implemented.

Major opportunities for foreign exporters and investors exist in the following top 10 sectors:

1. Telecommunications equipment

2. Computer software

3. Electric power systems

4. Computers and peripherals

5. Aircraft and parts

6. Food processing and packaging equipment

7. Industrial chemicals

8. Industrial process controls

9. Defense industry equipment

10. Medical equipment

In the agricultural sector, main opportunities exist in the following commodities:

1. Temperate hardwood lumber

2. Wheat

3. Soybeans

4. Cotton

5. Other foods

According to the Bank of Thailand (2000), in 1999, while the manufacturing sector grew 12.5%, the production of construction material grew 12.3%. Revenues from tourism grew to $7.3 billion. The government controls 59 state enterprises that employ 309,000 people. Despite the large number of employees, the state enterprises account for less than 1% of total employment. As a result of the Asian crisis, the current-account deficit reached more than 8% of GDP in 1999. The local currency is stable and is attached to a basket of currencies of principal trading partners. The government has simplified remittance-reporting requirements and has removed most restrictions on inward and outward currency flows. Repatriation of investment funds, profits, and repayment of loans and interest may be freely transferred, and foreign exchange is easily available from all commercial banks. In the following areas, 100% foreign ownership is permitted: transportation, accounting, legal services, advertising, and tourism (Gearing, 1999).

Entry into the Thai market is reasonably easy and quick. The Thailand Board of Investment gives permission for most foreign investments. Other institutions involved in granting permission are the Department of Commercial Registration (Ministry of Commerce), the Ministry of Industries, and the Ministry of Labor. The Board of Investment provides incentives for some 125 different types of investment. Sectors that bring in new technology, such as the manufacture of parts for engines, machinery, electricity, and electronic products, receive generous incentives, including exemption of 50% to 90% concession on import duties, permission for expatriates to work in the country, guarantees against nationalization, state competition, or monopolization, and other tax incentives. There are, however, some restrictions on these incentives: a minimum export level and a minimum Thai share holding. The 1972 Alien Business Law grants foreigners permission to engage in certain business enterprises in Thailand only if more than 50% of the capital is owned by Thai nationals. However, the Foreign Business Act of 1999 introduced some adjustments. For companies promoted by the Thailand Board of Investment, majority ownership is permitted for projects that export not less than 50% of sales. Moreover, 100% foreign ownership is permitted for the following areas (Thailand Board of Investment, 2001):

- Projects in agriculture, animal husbandry, fisheries, mining, and services with investments of more than 1 billion baht (for only the first 5 years of operation)
- Projects that export at least 80% of sales
- Projects that are located in the special "investment promotion zones"
- Manufacturing projects, regardless of location

Concerning negotiations, Thailand is a rather typical Asian country, with cultures that value strong family connections, face saving, and friendships. The Chinese community dominates a number of business sectors, similar to Indonesia and Malaysia. Thailand is committed to improving its laws on intellectual property rights. In 1992, it passed new legislation that extended patent protection to pharmaceutical products and agricultural machinery. A copyright act has been in force since 1978 but provides no explicit protection for computer software and allows several exceptions. The government has suggested the establishment of an independent intellectual property court to deal with such cases.

Foreign firms have had very few disputes with the local government or private sectors. Some copyright disputes and contract enforcement cases have been documented but were settled through the local legal system. Thailand is not a member of the International Center for Settlement of Investment Disputes, but companies may establish their arbitration agreements in the negotiation process. Both value-added tax (VAT) and other income tax rules were modified in 1991 and 1994 in favor of companies and individuals. Thailand has a double-taxation system with 26 countries, which includes most European countries but not the United States.

Thailand has 17 EPZs. Companies located in these zones may import raw materials and export finished goods without any duty. There are also 30 privately owned industrial estates, and any company located in these estates importing raw materials to be used for export products can enjoy the same rules as EPZs. Exports and investments from Thailand and Thai companies are increasing. Traditionally, these companies have been investing in the United States, Japan, and Europe, as well as in the ASEAN countries. For example, Siam Cement (a joint venture with an Italian firm) sells ceramic tiles in the United States; the Saha Union Company recently took over a thread-spinning mill in the United States; and the Charon Pokphand (CP) Group is manufacturing motorcycles in China. CP is most probably the largest single foreign investor in China. Thailand has invested huge amounts in China and Indonesia to acquire raw materials and supplies. In 1993, it established an export-import bank to finance credits for Thai exports.

Vietnam

After many years of war and instability, Vietnam is back in business. It has become a full member of the United Nations and has been accepted as a member of the ASEAN group of countries. With its population of 73 million, it is one of the major countries in Asia. Unlike many other Asian emerging markets, such as Malaysia and Thailand, it has a rather homogeneous society, with about 90% Vietnamese, 3% Chinese, and the rest a mixture of Thai, Meo, Khem, Man, and Cham. It has made significant economic progress in recent years and has moved away from a planned economy to a more market-based economic system. Prices have been decontrolled, and the Vietnamese currency has been devalued and floated at world market rates.

According to the U.S. Department of Commerce (2000j), the Vietnamese economy has made significant progress during the implementation of "The Strategy on Stabilization and Socioeconomic Development up to the Year 2000." The economy grew by an annual average of 8% from 1991 to 1998. Inflation declined from 67% in 1990 to less than 10% in 1998 and declined further to 0.1% in 1999. In the early 1990s, it was an agricultural- and resource-based economy, with almost 75% of its export earnings coming from rice and crude oil. However, this situation has changed with the rapid growth of industrial and services sectors. Heavy- and light-industrial product together accounted for more than 60% of export in 1998, whereas agricultural products were only 24% for the same year. Industry, although dominated by state-owned enterprises, is quite competitive. Unemployment, approximately 7% in urban and 70% in rural areas, is one of the major problems. Agriculture, which employs two thirds of the labor force, contributes 25% of GDP. The country has received a lot of positive attention from industrialized countries and is a major recipient of foreign aid ($2 billion in 1994), with Japan being the major contributor.

Exhibit 8.24 Joint Ventures, Vietnamese-Style

Hanel Electronic (HE) is a state-owned enterprise and is a Hanoi-based producer of consumer electronics and household appliances. HE was established in 1985 by 5 scientists and their 13 employees. In 1995, HE had 500 employees. Unlike other state organizations, it sells its products through its 11 domestic outlets. It had an annual revenue of $27 million in 1994. HE is owned by the influential People's Committee of Hanoi and has been able to cut through red tape and enter several joint ventures.

HE began one joint venture, Orion-Hanel, with the Korean company Daewoo, which owns 70% of the $170-million venture. HE began another joint venture with Daewoo (Daewoo-Hanel) worth $233 million, also a 70/30 venture. Together, the two joint ventures make all types of consumer electronics. The two partners also have another huge project, Daeha Business Center, outside Hanoi. A hotel and two high-rises with shopping malls are being constructed. The $250 million project will take up real estate as large as six football fields.

SOURCE: Schwarz (1995a, p. 60).

Japanese interest in Vietnam is based on its cheaper and younger workforce, its huge oil reserves closer to Japan, and in joining other Asian countries to create a balance against China. Most investments coming to Vietnam emanate from Taiwan, Japan, and Hong Kong. Moreover, Japan provides approximately 50% of the total foreign aid received by Vietnam (Schwarz, 1995b).

In 1995, a team of Japanese bureaucrats and academicians came to Vietnam to advise them on what type of economy and economic system they should have. The Japanese believe that America and Europe went through unplanned industrialization whereas the Asian experience is different, and Japan wants to play a role in a planned industrialization in Asia. They believe that the World Bank and the IMF might push Vietnam into the U.S. model of development based on privatization and anti-inflationary measures. They feel that privatization should occur gradually. In countries like Vietnam, where market forces are not yet in place, the government has to play a major role. Exhibit 8.24 provides an example.

Like other Asian emerging markets, Vietnam has also established five export zones, two in Ho Chi Minh City and one each in Quang Nam Danang, Can Tho, and Hai Phong. Applications for investment in these zones are handled by a special commission, which consists of representatives from the Central Bank of Vietnam, the Ministry of Finance, the

Exhibit 8.23 FDI in Vietnam: Number of Foreign Direct Investment Projects Licensed 1999 by Main Counterparts

Country	Number of Projects	Total Registered Capital ($ Millions)	Realized capital ($ Millions)	
			Total	In Vietnam
United Kingdom	4	19.1	15.7	0.0
Taiwan	91	170.8	73.7	3.8
Korea, Rep.	29	173.6	60.1	17.8
United States	17	120.2	64.7	1.3
Malaysia	7	161.9	65.3	0.4
France	13	303.4	138.5	39.6
Others	137	599.3	259.2	51.6
Total	**298**	**1,548.3**	**677.2**	**114.5**

SOURCE: "Number of Foreign Direct Investment Projects" (2002).

Since 1992, the United States has been trying to launch a new beginning in Vietnam. The 18-year trade embargo was lifted, although this action was heavily criticized by the families of U.S. soldiers still missing. In 1992, the U.S. government allowed American enterprises to open offices, but were not allowed to sign contracts (U.S. Department of Commerce, 2000j). By 1994, approximately 50 U.S. companies had already obtained licenses to operate in Vietnam and were doing business unofficially. FDI has been pouring into Vietnam since 1990 (see Exhibit 8.23).

American companies such as Caterpillar want to supply equipment for $2 billion; GE wants to help build two high-tech medical centers and electric power generation plants; Mobil corporation is teaming up with three Japanese companies to start drilling for oil; Coca-Cola has signed a joint-venture agreement for the construction of bottling plants; and U.S. airlines are adding Vietnam to their routes. The BBI Investment Group, Citibank, and Bank of America, from the United States, and six banks from France, Australia, and Thailand have opened their offices or branches in Vietnam. Airbus Industries has established a $1-million training facility for pilots and crew in Ho Chi Minh City (Transportation Research Group, 1999).

In 1994, the Japanese prime minister, Tomiichi Murayama, visited Vietnam, and in early 1995, the largest and most influential delegation ever was sent to Vietnam by Keidauren, the Japanese big-business federation.

Ministry of Internal Affairs and Trade, Customs, and People's Committees. Companies working in these zones pay only 10% tax and 15% for the service sector. Companies enjoy tax holidays on profits for the first 4 years in manufacturing and the first 2 years in the service sector. Profits are exempt from tax if they are reinvested, and no duty is paid on imported goods, raw materials, and equipment. Profits that are repatriated are liable to only 5% tax. Due to a lack of infrastructure and demand for consumer products, Vietnam is importing more than it is exporting. Almost 80% of foreign trade is with Asian countries, whereas 60% of that comes from ASEAN countries (U.S. Department of Commerce, 2000j). Consumer goods and equipment constitute the majority of imports. There are thus enormous opportunities for Western firms to enter this market.

9

Emerging Markets
of Eastern Europe

The end of the Cold War and the liberalization of Eastern Europe are
perhaps the most dynamic and exciting events of the last decades of the
20th century. With the introduction of perestroika in 1985, the fall of the
Berlin Wall in 1989, and the dismantling of the Soviet Union in the early
1990s, enormous opportunities have been created for the world economy.
Containing more than 429 million people, Eastern Europe represents a very
large market with vast amounts of resources. It is 30% more populated than
the European Union (EU) and almost double the population of the United
States. If integration efforts in Western Europe continue and begin to include
Eastern Europe, the total European market will represent more than
720 million consumers. Moreover, Eastern and Western Europe's resources
complement each other well. Eastern Europe has huge raw material reserves,
including metal ores, coal, oil, and gas (as well as agricultural production
resources), whereas Western Europe has the technology and human
resources to exploit these resources effectively (Buckley & Ghauri, 1994).

Different countries in Eastern Europe have made different commitments
to economic reforms. The German Democratic Republic (GDR) became a
part of the Federal Republic of Germany in 1990, but it shares many characteristics of Eastern European countries. The former Soviet republics have
strong regional differences in commitments to reforms. The Commonwealth of Russian States (CIS) is still struggling with political instability,
and Asian republics have varying levels of ambitions and goals depending
on their location, resources, and political leadership.

Today, most Eastern European countries are ruled by democratically elected governments and have made the conversion to free market economies an immediate goal. Most of these countries are desperately trying to attract foreign investors and establish technology transfers and trading links with the West. However, the situation in many Eastern European countries remains uncertain, complex, and difficult to predict. The transition from a centrally planned economy to a free market system involves many hardships, and the transition itself has been a slow process. Still, a few leaders are emerging: Poland, Hungary, and the Czech Republic now have free pricing, convertible currencies, and considerable amounts of foreign investment. These countries have clear goals and objectives to achieve Western-style market economies and have taken rigorous measures to reach their goals (Buckley & Ghauri, 1994; Havlik, 1991). These countries are also among the first group of countries negotiating with the EU for its expansion. They may become members of the EU as early as 2003. The importance of these markets for companies in the United States would then increase enormously.

Although most countries in Eastern Europe are committed to improving their economies, many interrelated obstacles still exist that are impeding their growth. Issues such as trade barriers, inadequate banking and loan systems, pricing mechanisms, and property and contract law need immediate attention to improve the investment climate. Privatizing state-owned businesses is also an important goal, but it involves many changes that must be spread out over time. Initial estimates about bringing Eastern Europe on-line with the global economy were generally overoptimistic. Now that more than a decade has passed, some of the major markets, such as Russia, former Yugoslavia, and Romania are struggling with establishment of a sound political and economic climate.

As a result, reactions from Western companies have been rather cautious, but investments are slowly beginning to pick up the pace. Despite some hesitation, the potential of this region is too immense to ignore, and many multinationals are beginning to cultivate these markets. McDonald's, Pepsi-Cola, Coca-Cola, Statoil, Ericsson, Ikea, Fiat, Nokia, Volkswagen, Ford, General Motors, Estée Lauder, Philip Morris, and many pharmaceutical companies have already established operations in these countries. Seventy-seven major retailers from the West are also now active in Eastern Europe (Tietz, 1994). Joint-venture operations are also on the rise. In 1989, there were 12,512 registered joint ventures between Western companies and organizations in Eastern Europe. In March 1992, this figure rose to 34,121 registered joint ventures, and in 1994, it ballooned again to 106,295 registered collaborations (Ghauri, 1995). However, most of these joint ventures are still nonoperative as the Western companies wait for economies to stabilize.

Other than in the three market leaders—Hungary, Poland, and the Czech Republic—a number of problems must be resolved before a proper market involvement can be expected from Western companies. These problems are as follows:

- The dismantling of the existing power structure left over from earlier years
- A lack of clear priorities
- Black markets and security issues
- Political instability
- Obscure legislative systems
- Unlimited demand
- Extremely high inflation
- Lack of infrastructure
- Ineffective banking and monetary systems

All these problems are critical and cannot be solved simultaneously and immediately. Companies that want to enter Eastern European markets must either wait for these problems to be solved or find a way to work around these obstacles.

Investment Climate

Consumption and demand for products and technology in Eastern Europe are simply monstrous. There is a shortage of almost everything, including communication products, consumer electronics, modern photographic equipment, books, and CDs. Demand for consumer products such as Western clothing and automobiles is also gigantic.

Strong brand awareness already exists for many Western products. Despite their scarcity and high costs, many Western branded products are well-known and in high demand. Coca-Cola, Levi's jeans, Canon cameras, branded cigarettes, Bata shoes, and McDonald's enjoy almost unlimited demand. When McDonald's inaugurated its first restaurant in Moscow in 1990, the restaurant set corporate records. On the first day, an estimated 30,000 customers were served, surpassing the previous record of 9,100 (set during the Budapest opening in 1988). McDonald's had 700 seats (indoor) available and opened in the very cold month of January. Despite the lack of advertising for the opening in Moscow, people stood in line for hours. Moreover, to avoid the black-marketing of hamburgers outside the restaurant, McDonald's had to limit the number of Big Macs per customer (see Exhibit 9.1).

Exhibit 9.1   McDonald's in Moscow

McDonald's is a good example of a company that developed its own infrastructure to manage its business in Eastern Europe. McDonald's chose the Moscow City Council as a partner (51% Moscow City Council, 49% McDonald's; as of the time of the contract, this was the maximum a foreign company could own). McDonald's considered the infrastructure, especially for supply procurement, to be a major problem. The rigid bureaucratic system gives rise to supply short-ages (due to production and distribution) and low-quality products. The com-pany had to be sure that it would be able to access sufficient raw materials, such as sugar, flour, meat, and mustard. Moreover, some of the supplies, such as iceberg lettuce, pickled cucumber, and a special type of potato were not available in Russia. To overcome these problems, McDonald's trained its suppliers and built a $40-million food-processing center close to its restaurant. To overcome the distribution problems, McDonald's provided its own trucks to carry the supplies. As a result, today McDonald's has the most successful restaurant in Russia, serving an average of 50,000 customers per day.

SOURCE: Daniels & Radebaugh (1995, pp. 117-119).

The success of McDonald's in Eastern Europe represents a remarkable achievement for the international economy. Prior to the collapse of the Soviet Union and the resulting influx of Western business interest, Eastern Europe did not trade outside of COMECON—the former alliance of economically linked communist countries. Until 1992, this region accounted for less than 10% of world imports and exports, including the trade they conducted with each other. As a result, the potential for marketing and business opportunities remains wide-open in these countries (Franklin & Moreton, 1994). But of course, the required level of development needed to capitalize on these opportunities and open up these markets will take several years and cost several billion dollars. According to one estimate by Michael Palmer, former Director General of the European Parliament, an investment package of $16.7 billion per year is needed from the advanced industrial nations if the economic reconstruction of Eastern Europe is to be completed within the next two decades (Euromonitor, 1998). The large area and population of Eastern Europe present an optimistic perception of commercial opportunities, but they also in some ways hinder the marketing activities of Western firms. In terms of area, Eastern Europe constitutes the largest group of countries in the world. However, much of this population is scattered in small cities and towns in which communication, distribution channels, and infrastructure are lacking. Moreover, the absence of a stable price mechanism in these markets makes it difficult to use the same marketing planning and strategies used in the West.

The retail sector in Eastern Europe can be divided into three major groups: (a) food retailers, (b) retailers of industrial goods, and (c) general retailers (Tietz, 1994). These groups are not well structured and have no training or skills to handle foreign products or firms. However, the number of retailers in Eastern Europe is increasing rapidly, mainly as a result of privatization and free trade regulations within each country. Most of the new foreign firms, however, are sales outlets. For example, Julius Meinl, an Austrian retailer, has returned to its prewar markets in Hungary; several Finnish retailers are now doing well in Russia; and Britain's Tesco, Holland's Ahold, and Belgium's Delhaize have bought into supermarkets in Poland, Hungary, and the Czech Republic ("All the World's," 1995, pp. 15-17). In the past, most retailers were under state or cooperative ownership. Since 1990, the ratio of privately owned retail outlets has increased considerably, but the proportion of total retail sales handled by state-owned outlets is still much higher. The retail sales space per person is 20% to 30% of that in the West, and the average size of retail stores is also smaller than those found in the West (Guy, 1998). Due to the limited infrastructure and lack of transportation facilities available to most people, households have to do their shopping in nearby stores or in city centers.

The EU is already in negotiations with Poland, Hungary, the Czech Republic, and Estonia for their entry into EU as members. This will result in stronger economies for these countries as well as for the countries that are next in line: Latvia, Lithuania, Slovakia, Romania, and Bulgaria. This will also eliminate the problems mentioned earlier in this chapter. As the scarcity of goods is diminishing, the excessive demand and inflation are now under control in many of these countries.

Factors Influencing Market Entry

Marketing Western products and technologies in Eastern Europe is not as simple as selecting a market and applying one of the existing market entry strategies. A different set of problems and situations—characterized as "gaps"—exists between Western and Eastern economies and must be addressed (see, e.g., Jain & Tucker, 1994; Kraljic, 1990, pp. 14-19):

1. *Marketing:* Goods are normally bought, not marketed. Because demand has always been greater than supply, the concept of marketing and the importance of consumers is unknown in much of Eastern Europe.

2. *Technology:* A huge gap between Western and Eastern European technologies exists in machinery, equipment, and know-how. The concepts of technical standards, plant efficiency, and operating efficiency are missing. In this respect, the mentality is different and will take some time to change.

3. *Capital:* Investment and profit-making capabilities are limited compared with those in the West. When seeking a local partner, a Western company may find that those interested in responding have nothing more to contribute than the claim that they understand the local market.

4. *Management:* There is practically no management know-how at the middle and upper levels. It is therefore very difficult for foreign firms to organize effective agents, distributors, or partnerships with local staff, and it is even more difficult to have expatriates manage the local staff. Some companies bring middle-level managers and supervisors to the West to train them.

5. *Motivation:* Motivation of the workforce was seriously damaged due to years of "equalization" in the workforce. There is little willingness to take responsibility, and the work ethic is very weak. Taking initiative and displaying drive are relatively new concepts.

Western businesses can also expect other marketing challenges in Eastern Europe. Despite the fact that most countries have democratically elected governments and have a high degree of privatization, government still plays a major role in the business sector. This role is even greater when a foreign company is involved. The most important difference between the West and Eastern Europe is the very wide generation gap in productivity and infrastructure. In the most advanced countries—Hungary, Poland, and the Czech Republic—a lot of progress has been made in maintaining property rights and removing some market imperfections.

For the rest of the Eastern Europe, three important factors will determine whether Eastern European economies will achieve some parity with the United States and Europe: (a) the ability of governments to promote and influence restructuring and to convince people that they have to suffer through a transitional period before they can see the benefits of a market economy, (b) development in the CIS and the course it will take, because it will have linkage effects to other Eastern European countries and encourage foreign investment in the entire region, and (c) the investments and capital flows that will be realized if the global economy is prepared to allocate funds for the long-term development of this region. The support expected from the European Bank for Reconstruction and Development (EBRD), the

International Monetary Fund (IMF), and the World Bank is crucial, but is not yet wholeheartedly forthcoming.

Before 1990 to 1991, the economies of Eastern Europe were overestimated, partly because there were no statistics available and partly because of political reasons. According to the Central Intelligence Agency (CIA), the GNP of the Soviet Union was about half that of the United States, which gave Western companies an exaggerated and overly optimistic picture of the Soviet economy (Ghauri, 1995). After 1990, due to the devaluation of the ruble, the estimated GNP of the former Soviet Union was about one tenth of that of the U.S., with a per capita income that was only 14% of that of the United States (Ghauri, 1995).

Several examples of successful entries exist: Siemens AG (Germany); Alcatel (France); ABB i Sverige (Sweden/Switzerland); General Electric (U.S.); McDonald's (U.S.); Coca-Cola (U.S.); PepsiCo (U.S.); Volkswagen Worldwide (Germany); Fiat (Italy); and Statoil (Norway). Coca-Cola Beverages, one of Coca-Cola's bottlers, announced that it would buy Romanian bottler Ozgorkey Coca-Cola for $24 million (Thompson Financial, 2000), and Danish brewer Carlsberg bought a 95% stake in Lithuanian brewer Svyturys for $45 million (Economist Intelligence Unit, 1999). Siemens made large investments in Eastern Europe, especially in the Czech Republic. With a total of 9,300 employees, Siemens' consolidated companies in the Czech Republic posted total sales of some $500 million. In July 2001, General Motors sealed a $340 million deal with a Russian partner, AvtoVAZ. The production will start at the end of 2002, and by 2006 the venture plans to produce 75,000 cars (Economist Intelligence Unit, 2001). Exhibit 9.2 shows successful examples of foreign entries in Hungarian markets.

With the excessive demand, Western companies entering the market at an early stage will have a greater potential to reap benefits. They should, however, be prepared for a lean period of 3 to 5 years. Investments in these markets will also have spin-off effects on a company's global marketing and positioning activities. Marketing efforts in Eastern Europe should be considered a part of a company's total international marketing and networking activities. The positive effects of international activities, the support and encouragement expected from the international community, the benefits and other incentives offered by local governments and profit opportunities—in the long run—are enough reasons for companies to consider these markets.

To be successful in these markets, companies should demonstrate long-term commitments. It is not possible to travel to these markets occasionally and expect to establish successful business operations. Marketing managers

---

Exhibit 9.2   Foreign Entries in Hungarian Markets

Hungary opened its markets to foreign multinationals first through privatization. Ameritech International and Germany's Deutsche Telekom became the biggest backers, with a combined $1.7 billion investment. General Electric invested $1 billion in Hungary. International banks and consulting companies opened their branches, and electronic companies such as Flextronics and IBM bought old defense industry factories. When the buying spree ended, 80% of Hungary's banking and telecommunications and 65% of electric utilities and insurance industries were in foreign hands. At the end of 2000, the private sector accounted for 80% of the GDP. More important, companies with foreign ownership accounted for 74% of all exports and 71% of all imports.

Foreign investment level reached $23 billion in the last decade. Sony is one of the entrants in Eastern Europe. In 1994, Sony entered Hungary by investing $500,000 in a former military electronics factory. The company now has a $21 million operation, with 1,200 employees turning out audio products for the European Union. Similarly, Samsung Electronics went into Hungary in 1991, with a production of 100,000 TVs annually, mostly for domestic market. The factory currently exports close to 2 million color TVs annually and is Samsung's third-largest TV plant worldwide.

SOURCE: Clarke (2001, p. 54).

---

should stay in-country for longer periods to understand the market and business culture. It is also advisable to acknowledge some differences in the development and commitment levels of these countries and not treat all countries in the same manner. Foreign companies must develop new and individual approaches to cultivating mutually beneficial business transactions.

Joint ventures or wholly owned subsidiaries are considered the best entry strategies into Eastern European markets. Entry can be achieved through greenfield companies, taking over a local company, or by obtaining majority ownership in a local company. The financial state of locally owned companies is such that it is quite beneficial for a foreign firm to acquire a local company. This favorable situation has arisen due to changes in price structure, exchange rate variations, interest rates, and credit possibilities. For a foreign firm, it is quite easy to gain control of an existing company or to create a mutually beneficial partnership.

Trade fairs, exhibitions, and frequent visits are the most useful tools to make customers aware of your company and products. Fiat has been successful in obtaining large contracts by using these strategies. It signed a

$1.3 billion contract for an automobile assembly plant in Poland. Fiat had no difficulty in identifying subcontractors because the publicity surrounding the contract signing yielded many inquiries by local manufacturers wishing to join Fiat in their venture.

Although joint ventures have been a particularly popular entry strategy, the evaluation of local partners may present a challenge. Contradictory objectives can exist when the local government is the local partner. Quite often, a local partner would like to contribute technology or know-how, but both may be obsolete or of no value to the new operation. These misunderstandings do create problems and are considered the most important factors for a joint-venture failure.

Foreign companies will also need assistance and expertise in handling East European bureaucracies. Companies have realized the synergistic benefits of cooperative agreements. When entering these markets, a company should consider the following approach:

1. Priorities: Learn about the priorities of the government and business sectors to determine which goods or projects at-hand might be received most favorably.

2. Regulations: What rules and regulations apply to the importation of goods? Are import licenses or other documents necessary? In the case of a joint venture, check all applicable rules and regulations. Is it permissible to have a majority-owned joint venture, property rights, and so forth?

3. Local agent/partner: Is it difficult to check the validity of the claims made by the local partner or agent? If the claims are valid, how can they be evaluated?

4. Competition: Establish who your competitors are—local government or another foreign company. Will you have the same competitive advantage in 5 years?

5. Financial implications: Determine at the earliest stage whether you must participate in counterpurchasing or bartering. Check the financial position of your counterparts to determine whether they will be able to fulfil their financial obligations.

6. Negotiations: Determine whether the objectives of both parties are complementary. If the objectives are totally different, then one should analyze the situation and determine whether this is acceptable. If so, one should also evaluate whether the desired objectives can be achieved and then commit oneself accordingly.

7. Implementation: It is very important to carry out the project wholeheartedly and think in the long term. The potentials and opportunities should be evaluated at every step of implementation and matched with the company's objectives.

When the purpose of entering an Eastern European market is to make products in Eastern Europe and sell them in the Western market, many of these countries offer the potential of creating a competitive advantage because they have a good supply of raw materials, cheap labor, government incentives, and other resources (Hertzfeld, 1991; Jain & Tucker, 1994). A fore0ign company must be aware of the pitfalls that may influence the success or failure of such a venture.

First, due to excessive demand, price mechanisms are not fully operational, which could lead to overestimated profit expectations. When the gap between supply and demand closes, market pricing will start functioning. The same is applicable to labor, raw material, and component pricing. Second, these markets are not, in the long run, typically low-labor-cost economies. Standards of living are improving rapidly, and within a couple of decades, it is anticipated that the standards will approximate those of Western Europe. Investments in plants and technology that are primarily based on low labor costs may yield diminished profits in future. Finally, sectors that may appear attractive at this time may not survive in the long run.

Despite an excessive demand at this time, some sectors may not survive in the long run. Consequently, it would no longer be beneficial to produce certain products in Eastern Europe and sell them to Western markets. A long-term analysis and strategy is therefore of great importance. Some countries offer excellent opportunities for export-oriented investments, and others do not. Factors such as local government attitude, incentives given to foreign investors, investment protection, repatriation of profits, the capability and quality of the labor force, and the general economic outlook of the country are also important.

The process of foreign market entry in Eastern Europe differs to a great extent from a traditional market entry process. In entering a foreign market, a firm must establish contacts at both macro- and microlevels because the firm must have middlemen to access government officials and departments, a very difficult process. In Eastern Europe, however, it is very easy to obtain access to the highest government officials in the early stages of the entry process. Ministry doors are wide-open. The real problems appear in the later stages of the process when gaps often occur. If we conceptualize three phases of an entry process—feasibility, project, and establishment—a foreign firm will experience the most problems in the project and establishment phases because a firm must first resolve the problems caused by the lack of infrastructure and the gaps discussed earlier (Ghauri & Holstius, 1996). Moreover, the firm needs to handle the state bureaucracies, difficulties in marketing research, and cultural differences.

Negotiating in Eastern Europe

It is not possible to provide absolute guidelines for negotiation with customers/parties from Eastern Europe, because conditions have been rather volatile and rules and regulations have been changing. Though every transaction involves a different type of negotiation process, we can extrapolate some commonalities. Price adjustments due to inflation are one such factor. Inflation has been high in almost all Eastern European countries. Even in countries such as Poland and Hungary, inflation hovered around 30% for a long time. In Russia, Eastern Europe's largest market, inflation was 15% per month at times (Ghauri, 1995). Variation in exchange rate is another factor that should be kept in mind while negotiating business deals with these countries.

A foreign firm often requires a distribution channel to sell its products within these newly available markets. A local partner is essential to represent the foreign party and to engage in marketing and customer service functions. In this relationship, a mutual dependence exists. The parties have to be engaged in a negotiation process to agree on the contribution to be made by each party. Finding the right partner and evaluating each other's contribution is thus a crucial issue in this process. Establishment of this relationship is difficult and time-consuming, but it is even more difficult to terminate or modify the relationship. The power/dependence aspect of the atmosphere is most relevant here. Power or dependence perceived by one of the parties may affect the relationship in the long term, with one party always demanding better performance by the other.

The firms entering these markets should have clear objectives, for both short- and long-term accomplishments. In most of these countries, the rules regarding foreign ownership (minority-, majority-, or wholly owned foreign operations), remittance of profits, property rights, and tax exemption are still changing. One way a firm can accommodate changes in the future is to build in renegotiation of the contract after regular intervals or after changes in relevant rules and regulations.

Sometimes, negotiations are undertaken for only a single transaction. This is particularly true in the case of project marketing. A project sales negotiation is different from a process in which a long-term relationship is

Exhibit 9.3   Nature of Negotiations in Eastern Europe

Negotiation Factors	Comments
1. Pace of Negotiation	Slow
- Value of time	Moderate and punctual
2. Negotiation Strategy	
- Offer vs. agreement	High initial demand
- Presentation of issues	Group issues may be presented
- Presentations	Quite formal
- Discussions	Argumentative
- Communication	Rather direct, little small talk
- Interpreters	Necessary
3. Emphasis on personal relationship	Very low
4. Influence of third parties	High
5. Distance	Personal space shorter
6. Decision making	
- Overall	Somewhat impulsive
- Emphasis	Logic and long-term benefit
- Hierarchy	Top-down decision making
- Collective vs. individual behavior	Emphasis on group- and teamwork
7. Administrative Factors	
- Need for agent or local partner	Average
- Degree of details	Moderate specificity
- Degree of bureaucracy	High
- Need for agenda	High
8. Emotional Aspects	
- Degree of rationality	Rather high
- Sensitivity	Low

SOURCE: Format based on Acuff (1993).

being negotiated. In project-based negotiation, a foreign firm should be very specific about what they can and cannot do. When an agent or a local third party is involved, roles should be properly defined and related to one particular deal.

So far, joint ventures have been the most popular entry mode in these markets. In this type of entry mode, selection of a partner is the most complex activity. Facilities and resources, market position, personnel, and capital to be offered by the local partners are important criteria. The distribution of tasks and responsibilities between the parties should be clearly specified. The parties should be open to each other, and the agenda for negotiations should be prepared together. Factors that influence negotiations in Eastern Europe are listed in Exhibit 9.3.

Selected Country Analyses

Russia

Russia, with a population of more than 200 million, is the most important market emerging from the former Soviet Union. The collapse of the Soviet Union heralded the downfall of the Communist Party and an increase in democratization. Members of the government, the army, regional politicians, and industrialists are all scrambling for power. Current political instability is expected to dissipate, and new democratic principles will lead Russia toward normalization. A new constitution was adopted by referendum in December 1993.

Since then, prices have been liberalized, large and medium-sized manufacturers are being privatized, lavish government subsidies to inefficient producers have been cut, and companies are paying normal or positive interest rates, that is, above the rate of inflation. All these changes are forcing massive restructuring of Russian industry. According to State Committee of the Russian Federation on Statistics (2000) data, there were 1.1 million officially registered unemployed people in 2000, the overall figure standing at 7.6 million, which is 10.47% of the economically active population. Moreover, in 1999, unemployment increased by 7.9%, whereas in 2000, it declined by 17.9%.

The major problem for Russia, however, is instability. Experts believe that if Russia could remove uncertainty, it would experience a major investment boom that could sustain rapid growth (Laynard, 1995). Industrial output has shown signs of stability, and experts predict growth will now begin at a slow rate. Russia is continuing to shift its trade away from other former Soviet republics toward the more lucrative West.

Many industries, however, are insolvent. For example, the director of a vodka distillery set up a joint stock company through which the output of the plant is sold at an artificially low price. The joint stock company then resells the vodka at the market price, and the directors pocket the difference. In another example, the books of one coal-mining operation show that its coal was sold for $3 per ton to a private firm. The mine's director owns the private firm, which then bought the coal and exported it for 10 times the purchasing price ("Russia's Bankruptcy Bears," 1994). Despite these irregularities, foreign firms have invested heavily in Russia. Most foreign products are available, from automobiles such as Ford, General Motors, Volvo, and BMW to the consumer products of Unilever, Mars, Procter & Gamble, and Chiquita Banana—and most of these products are generating enormous business.

Despite political and economic instability in Russia, foreign firms have great opportunities and first-mover advantages when entering this market. For example, according to the U.S. Department of Commerce (2000k), by the end of 1993, more than 6,500 businesses were operating with some foreign investment. By 1999, that number increased to 26,000, in which the share of foreign investments in the authorized capital reached about $14.3 billion. Although the old economy is weakening and many state-operated industries are failing, the private sector is continuing to boom. Ninety percent of all small companies are now in private hands. Eighty percent of all service companies are also privately operated. Overall, 70% of the total economy is privately owned. Employment is rising, and two thirds of jobs are in the private sector. The number of registered commercial banks is now more than 2,000, and this number continues to grow. All these factors should be encouraging to foreign investors. In 1994, foreigners were investing at a rate of $500 million per month. Moreover, many American products (such as Marlboro, Winston, and Pall Mall cigarettes) are produced under license in Russia. The oil industry is another major investment area for Western companies. For example, from 1994 to 2000, the contractual value of offshore production sharing agreements in Azerbaijan accounted for more than $50 billion. Exhibit 9.4 shows the main contracts by their signing partners and investment values.

As long as uncertainly prevails, the Russian market will be mostly for bold and preferably more-established companies. Russian consumers continue to admire Western, especially American, products and well-recognized brand names will do well. A number of smaller firms from countries such as Sweden, Finland, Norway, Italy, and the Netherlands are also successfully doing business in garments, dairy products, and other consumer goods. But due to uncertainties and trade financing, smaller firms are at a relative disadvantage. The cost of market entry, general difficulties in conducting business, severe infrastructure problems, and mounting crime and corruption inhibit the success of smaller firms (see Exhibit 9.5).

Eventually, many of these factors will improve. Investors unwilling to enter the market should continue to monitor its progress. The infrastructure is slowly improving. There are now direct flights, for example, from Frankfurt to the Urals (Yekaterinburg) and to Siberia (Novosibirsk), which have helped stimulate Western investment in these areas. The United States government has also opened a Consulate General in the Urals and in the Russian Far East. The number of American business centers in Russia is steadily growing.

A Word of Caution

Russia has a body of contradictory, overlapping, and rapidly changing laws and rules that produce ambiguity in the selection of the approach to

Exhibit 9.4   Offshore Production Sharing Agreements in Azerbaijan

Sign Year	Partners	Investment
1994	BPAmoco (34.1%), Lukoil (10.0%), Socar (10.0%), Unocal (10.0%), Statoil (8.6%), Exxon (8.0%), TPAO (6.8%), Pennzoil (4.8%), Itochu (3.9%), Ramco (2.1%), Delta (1.7%)	$10 billion; $2 billion invested by 2000
1995	LukAgip (45.0%), Pennzoil (30.0%), Lukoil (12.5%), Socar (7.5%), Agip (5.0%)	$1.5 billion; $120 million spent
1996	BPAmoco (25.5%), Statoil (25.5%), Socar (10.0%), LukAgip (10.0%), Elf (10.0%), OIEC of Iran (10.0%), TPAO (9.0%)	$4 billion
1996	BPAmoco (30.0%), Unocal (25.5%), Itochu (20.0%), Socar (20.0%), Delta Nimir Hazar (4.5%)	Initial est. $2.0 billion; $70 million spent
1997	Elf (40.0%), Socar (25.0%), OIEC of IRAN (10.0%), Total Fina (15.0%), Wintershall (10.0%)	$1.5 billion; $36.6 million invested by 2000
1997	Lukoil (60%), Socar (40.0%) (Arco pulled out of the consortium)	$2 billion; $70 million spent
1997	Socar (50.0%), Chevron (30.0%), Total (20.0%)	$3.5 billion; $10.6 million invested by 2000
1997	Mobil (50.0%), Socar (50.0%)	$2.0 billion; $5.5 million invested by 2000
1997	Exxon (50.0%), Socar (50.0%)	$2.0 billion; $22.5 million invested by 2000
1998	Socar (50.0%), Agip (25.0%), Mitsui (15.0%), TPAO (5.0%), Repsol (5.0%)	$2.5 billion
1998	Socar (50.0%), BP Amoco (25.0%), Royal Dutch Shell (12.5%), Central Fuel Company (CFC) (12.5%) (Royal Dutch Shell to buy CFC's share)	$3 billion; $7.5 million invested by 2000
1998	Socar (40.0%), BPAmoco (15.0%), Statoil (15.0%), Exxon (15%), TPAO (10.0%), Alberta Energy (5%)	$9 billion
1999	Socar (50.0%), JAOC consortium (50.0%); divided as Japex (22.5%), Inpex (12.5%), Teikoku (7.5%), Itochu (7.5%)	$2 billion; $35 million invested in 1999
1999	Socar (50%), Mobil (30%), unassigned (20%)	$2 billion
1999	Socar (50%), Exxon (30%), Conoco (20%)	$4.5 billion

SOURCE: U.S. Energy Information Administration (2000).

enter the market. Independent and/or impartial dispute resolution is quite difficult to obtain. The courts are not yet familiar with commercial and international matters. There have been some cases of disputes with Western firms. For example, in one case, an American partner ceased participation in its joint venture, citing "a pattern of harassment, physical threats, attempted extortion and misinformation by the Russian partner aimed at forcing (us) out." In this case, the Moscow city government supported

Exhibit 9.5   Design Talo in Russia

Design Talo is a small firm making wooden houses for private clients in the northern city of Kemi, in Finland. The company was a victim of the Finnish housing depression, which plummeted from 10,000 to 2,000 new houses annually. Design Talo, a company with 300 employees building 500 houses a year, was badly hit. At this point, Mr. Kurkela, the owner and manager, started looking for other markets. In 1993, he learned from a consultant company that local authorities in the Russian city of Cherepovits, 600 km north of Moscow, were looking for a company to supply municipal guest houses. He traveled with Mr. Erkki Hurtig, the consultant, to Cherepovits. In the words of Mr. Hurtig, "We took a car and drove 14 hours to Cherepovits, through the snow and cold. The radiator froze and it was a terrible journey. But we got there, met with the municipality and the building engineer, and looked at the site."

At this point, Mr. Kurkela decided to prepare a bid to build two houses. Drawing up the details, negotiating, and reaching a deal took several months. The deal included all the supplies as well as labor from Finland. Kurkela wanted payment in advance in Finnish *markka,* which was agreed to. But things went very slowly. Several faxes were sent and received, but there were no signs of payment. Finally, the Russians said that the problem was they didn't have any Finish markka, only dollars. "We laughed and said 'Just send us the dollars,'" said Mr. Hurtig. The money came and the houses were built. The local authorities were pleased, and they ordered four more houses.

Mr. Kurkela wants to expand in Russia, but it is not an easy task for a small firm. In the second contract, Mr. Kurkela managed to agree to a portion of labor coming from Russia. The material is still to be imported from Finland to ensure quality. Payment is still a problem because Finnish banks are reluctant to accept guarantees from Russian banks. Selling to private, newly rich customers is even more difficult because they are not willing to pay in advance and banks are not willing to give guarantees. Design Talo and the consultant thus have problems in expanding in Russia. As Mr. Hurtig stated, "It is too hard. What we want to do more is to sell our know-how to them, rather than carrying out the whole building project. That is what they need in Russia."

SOURCE: Robinson (1995b, p. 14).

liquidation of the venture and declared that continuous operation of the venture was illegal. According to the American partner, both the city and the Russian partner felt they could make more money without him and therefore decided to drive him out. In such cases, it is difficult to achieve justice in the local judicial system. The only way out is to sell your shares and go home. Due to such incidents, a number of companies have moved out or decreased the scope of their operations in Russia. The present government is, however, committed to tackling these problems.

Poland

Poland adopted economic reforms early in its transition, and after 10 years, the results are noticeable. The Warsaw Stock Exchange was reopened in April 1991 after being closed for almost 50 years. In the same year, a new foreign investment law was introduced to make investment conditions more attractive. A goal of the new law was to privatize 80% of the once state-run economy. To attract foreign investment, the Finance Ministry may exempt a company from income tax if the foreign partner's contribution exceeds $2 million. As a consequence of these efforts, GDP rose by 6% on average for the last decade (World Bank, 2000). Poland has also received generous help from the West to develop an efficient infrastructure. For example, the World Bank provided $200 million in credit for a program to privatize Polish commercial banks, and the EU provides continuous assistance and credits to accelerate the privatization program.

Remittance of profits in foreign currency is permitted, and private land or property can be purchased or leased on a long-term basis (up to 99 years) when permission is obtained from the Ministry of the Interior. Most investments are coming from Western Europe, especially Germany. Fiat invested $2 billion, and approximately $5 billion has been invested in the development of the oil and petroleum sector by various other countries (World Bank, 2000). Poland is thus considered to have managed the transition period quite efficiently.

Since 1991, U.S. trade with Poland has been increasing significantly, with a peak level in 1997 of $1.9 billion. Due to the crisis, the trade level decreased to $1.6 billion in 1999 and began to recover in 2000, reaching $1.8 billion (U.S. Census Bureau, 2000). Trade started with agriculture but now consists of manufactured goods, machinery, computers, telecommunication equipment, automobiles, and aircraft. U.S. firms are among the top 10 import partners for Poland, whose partner list also includes Germany, Russia, the United Kingdom, Italy, France, and the Netherlands. According to the U.S. National Trade Board, Poland has been ranked as the "number one emerging market." Poland was also the largest recipient of U.S. aid in Eastern Europe. It has received more than $4 billion since 1989 for different projects. According to the U.S. State Department, after 1999, with an aid amount of $26.3 million, it would not be necessary for Poland to receive further aid from the SEED (Support for East European Democracy) program, the biggest U.S. aid program for Central and Eastern Europe

Exhibit 9.6   The Shipbuilding Industry in Poland

When the Soviet Union was dismantled, the demand for Polish ships also collapsed. The shipyards were in a deep crisis, with ships ready but not paid for by different Soviet authorities. At that time, the Poles realized that they would never sell another ship to Russia. Not long after, however, the Szczecin shipyard was supplying ships to Russia, not to the government but to a private shipping company, FRESCO, in Russia. The 12,400-dwt container vessel was purchased by a company called Roselaw, registered in Cyprus. The owner was able to arrange a mortgage from Cyprus-based institutions, which helped Roselaw to finance a $20-million vessel from the European Bank for Reconstruction and Development (EBRD). Because the procedure at EBRD took longer than expected, a 6-month financing agreement was reached with a London-based merchant bank. As a reserve alternative, the shipyard and the Russian owner jointly arranged for a German company to buy the vessel and then rent it out to FRESCO in case EBRD refused to finance.

When completed, FRESCO decided to operate the ship between the West Coast of the United States and Australia, instead of from the Russian Far East, as had been planned earlier. As a result, the vessel will probably never touch Russia or other countries of the former Soviet Union. To make it competitive in the U.S. market, the ship has been equipped with the most modern navigation and guidance equipment. At present, the Polish shipyard is in negotiation for the supply of more ships to Russian private companies.

SOURCE: Robinson (1995a, p. 13).

(National Trade Board, 2000). Poland has supported the continuous presence of American and NATO forces in Europe, the U.S. policies on nuclear proliferation, regional cooperation, and U.S. involvement in the Gulf War.

Infrastructural development has received significant assistance from global donors and investment. The country has developed a program for construction and modernization of its motorways, to be completed in 2007, at a cost of approximately $6 billion. The World Bank has agreed to a loan of $150 million for roads and bridges, and the EBRD has given a loan of $35 million for road improvement. Railways, telecommunication, and power supplies are getting similar attention (EBRD, 2000). Poland has eight major airports that are now being modernized. Poland traditionally has a well-developed shipbuilding industry (see Exhibit 9.6).

By making its laws conform with those of the EU, Poland is making a serious effort to join the union and is among the first group of countries negotiating to do so. The new law on copyrights is one example of compliance, and the reduction in tax rates providing new tax holidays and controlling inflation is another. In 1999, the overall deficit was 1% of GDP, and the external debt accounted for $47 billion in 1998. Poland was able to offset 90% of the current-account deficit in 1998 by foreign investment, compared with 69% in 1997. The deficit balance of payments is largely due to merchandise trade, in which imports are running about 65% higher than exports (EBRD, 2000).

A tremendous unrealized demand for Western goods is creating opportunities for multinational companies and small and medium-sized firms from the West. American and European companies are competing with each other for this market, and for some sectors, such as computers and consumer electronics, there is tough competition coming from Asian firms. Due to an agreement between Poland and the EU on tariff structure, signed in 1991 and implemented in March 1992, European firms are receiving favorable treatment.

The investment climate is quite suitable for foreign investors. In fact, privatization plans rely on foreign investors. A number of smaller Western firms are involved in these investments. For example, 48 smaller U.S. firms have invested more than $1 million in these programs (U.S. Chamber of Commerce, 2000l). Capital brought into Poland by foreign investors may be withdrawn freely, and full repatriation of profits and dividends is allowed without any prior permission. The Foreign Investment Act of 1991 guarantees the availability of foreign currency for these purposes. The legal system is based on German and French laws and is quite efficient in handling commercial conflicts and disputes.

Hungary

Hungary began implementing economic reforms in 1968. Since 1989, these reforms have sought to replace the system of central allocation of resources with a market system and to create equal legal conditions for local and foreign enterprises. The aim is to increase the share of foreign enterprises in the economy as a whole. Attracting foreign capital has thus been one of the prime objectives of Hungarian reforms. The United States has invested in Hungary more than in any other country. However, if we put all European countries together and look at EU vs. U.S. investments, European investments are more than double that of U.S. investments. The largest investments are by Deutsche Telekom (Germany), General Electric, Volkswagen/Audi (Germany), General Motors, Ericsson (Sweden), and Coca-Cola.

According to the National Bank of Hungary (2001), Hungary started off in a rather difficult position. In 1990, it had accumulated a debt of $20 billion, and it had a foreign exchange reserve of only $700 million. The government was unable to stop the outflow of foreign exchange arising from private imports, and it failed to meet the conditions of the last standby credit by the IMF. After declining to a 20-year low of $987 million, or 2.2% of GDP, in 1997, the current-account deficit widened in 1998 to $2.3 billion, which is 5% of GDP. The current account closed with a deficit of $2.1 billion in 1999, which accounts for 4.3% of GDP. By 1999, Hungary had a hard-currency reserve of $11 billion. Despite this difficult start, Hungary received almost one third of all foreign direct investment (FDI) invested in Central and Eastern Europe during 1989 to 2000. Exhibit 9.7 shows the FDI during the period 1991 to 1999. At present, about 80% of the GDP originates in the private sector. Almost 75% of exports are produced fully or partially by foreign-owned companies. Furthermore, foreign owners control 90% of telecommunications, 70% of financial institutions, 66% of industry, 60% of energy production, and 50% of the trading sector (Central and Eastern Europe Business Information Center [CEEBIC], 2001).

There is stiff competition between U.S. and European companies, and local companies are not able to compete. Hungary has also signed an associate agreement with the EU and with the European Free Trade Association (EFTA). Hungary is attempting to revive trade among the former Eastern Bloc countries. The most promising sectors include telecommunications, pharmaceuticals, cosmetics, oil and gas, electric power systems, plastics, chemicals, computers, software, and food-processing machinery. In the automotive sector, a number of Western and Japanese companies are very active; Suzuki and General Motors have invested $500 million. One of the purposes of this investment is to earn foreign exchange. In 1993, more than 40% of Suzuki and General Motors cars produced in Hungary were exported (U.S. Department of Commerce, 2000m). At present, General Motors (U.S.), Ford (U.S.), Audi (Germany), and Suzuki (Japan) are all producing vehicles in Hungary. All these companies are increasing the local content to comply with the rules-of-origin of the EU in anticipation of the entrance of Hungary into the EU. Hungary is also very active in outward foreign investment, and Hungarian companies have invested in a number of EU countries and the United States.

The investment climate has been very favorable for foreign companies. Hungarian enterprises with a foreign partner pay 20% less tax on profit than locally owned companies (if the foreign capital represents more than 20% of the total capital of at least 5 million forints). Foreigners are allowed free transfer of funds in foreign exchange whether the enterprise is showing

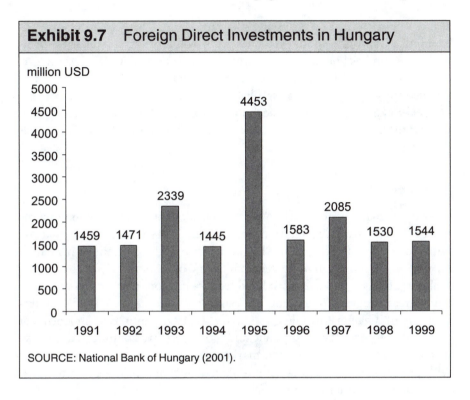

Exhibit 9.7   Foreign Direct Investments in Hungary

million USD

SOURCE: National Bank of Hungary (2001).

a profit or not. Hungary is leading most other Eastern European countries because its legal and institutional framework for foreign investments is developed, adequate, and functioning. Hungary's current-account deficit of $2.1 billion and an overall foreign debt of $28.6 billion are dangerous for such a small economy (U.S. Department of Commerce, 2000m). But despite these facts and some crisis over privatization in early years (in January 1995, the rejection of a deal to sell the state-owned hotel chain to a U.S. investor led to the abrupt resignation of Finance Minister Lazlo Bekesi), the inflow of foreign investments continues. In 1999, $1.5 billion in FDI flowed into the country, and 22,000 foreign companies had established operations in Hungary ("Second Thoughts," 1995).

Foreign investors are allowed to enter the Hungarian market in any way they deem desirable. They may either buy state companies or make portfolio investments. Foreign ownership up to 100% is permitted, with the exception of designated "strategic" holdings, some defense-related industries, and the national airline, Malev. Since July 1996, government approval is not needed for foreigners to invest in financial institutions and insurance. Foreign-owned companies that are Hungarian legal entities may acquire real estate, with the exception of agricultural land. There are also some tax exemptions and tax holidays available for some priority industries, firms with a certain level of foreign investment, and firms achieving a certain level of revenue related to their gross investment. Duty-free imports are also allowed for goods needed to establish a joint venture. Foreign investors are allowed to keep and maintain accounts in foreign currency. The companies can use these funds for traveling, advertising, and import of duty-free goods and investment goods.

The Czech Republic

Prior to the Second World War, Czechoslovakia ranked as one of the most highly industrialized nations in Europe. Until the 1960s, it was at par with Austria in GDP per capita, but at the time of dissolution, its per capita income was about 30% lower than that of Austria. Czechoslovakia, Hungary, and Poland are considered leaders in economic reform and have made great progress in creating a Western-style market economy. The dissolution of Czechoslovakia on January 1, 1993, into two independent nation-states—the Czech Republic and Slovakia—has complicated the task of moving toward a more open market economy. The republic is dealing with problems such as aging capital plants, lagging technology, and a deficiency in energy and many raw materials.

Since the dissolution of Czechoslovakia, thousands of businesses have been privatized, leased out, and even returned to their original owners. In general, the Czech Republic has been quite successful in attracting huge Western investments, such as a $3-billion investment by Volkswagen. More than 100,000 small and medium-sized trading and service firms were auctioned. There have been several well-publicized cases of both Japanese and Western manufactures switching the location of their new investments from the Iberian Peninsula and Greece to the Czech Republic (Dunning, 1994). More than half of the country's trade is with neighboring European countries, Germany, Austria, Slovakia, and Poland. The United States accounts for approximately 4% of overall Czech imports, and U.S. firms have invested more than $2 billion (U.S. Department of Commerce, 2000n). It is a commonly held opinion that the Czech Republic is the most advanced emerging market of the former Eastern Bloc. It has a stable currency, low unemployment (lower than most countries of the EU), low national debt, and huge foreign currency reserves. The main problem is that the market lacks capital and expertise in marketing and finance. However, there is a considerable flow of FDI from Europe and the United States (see Exhibit 9.8).

Exhibit 9.8   Foreign Direct Investment Inflow Into the Czech Republic: Origin of Investment

Country	1997		1998		1999		1990-1999	
	Millions, $U.S	%	Millions, $U.S.	%	Millions, $U.S.	%	Billions, $U.S.	%
Germany	391.3	30.1	537.6	21.2	781.1	16.0	5.0	26.2
Netherlands	133.8	10.3	608.4	24.0	729.4	15.0	4.6	24.0
Austria	95.0	7.3	244.7	9.6	630.9	12.9	2.3	11.8
United States	99.2	7.6	257.8	10.2	561.5	11.5	1.7	9.0
Belgium	NA	NA	NA	NA	1,235.9	25.3	1.4	7.2
United Kingdom	196.4	15.1	337.4	13.3	168.8	3.5	0.8	4.4
France	101.8	7.8	NA	NA	162.2	3.3	0.8	4.3
Switzerland	NA	NA	NA	NA	305.4	6.3	0.6	2.9
Others	283.0	21.8	553.7	21.8	301.8	6.2	1.9	10.2
Total	1,300.5	100.0	2,539.6	100.0	4,877.0	100.0	19.3	100.0

SOURCE: Czech National Bank (2000).

Foreign firms doing business in the country operate as Czech firms and are allowed to repatriate profits and withdraw their investments without any restrictions. These firms are also protected from expropriation under both international and Czech law. A bilateral tax treaty between the Czech and the U.S. government was implemented in December 1993. Development of basic infrastructure and privatization have been the priority issues for the government. Priority needs include pollution control equipment, telecommunication, medical equipment, building equipment, machine tools, electric power systems, computers and software, and food-processing and packaging equipment.

A relatively small, homogeneous population in favor of reforms and tight monetary and fiscal policies has helped the government through the transition period. According to the Czech Agency for Foreign Investment (2000), inputs from Germany and Austria comprise approximately 30% of machinery and heavy equipment and another 30% of semifinished goods. Imports from other countries include automobiles, computers, and service machines, which constitute another 20% of imports, and consumer products represent only 25% of total goods brought into the country. The products exported from the Czech Republic include steel, cement, timber, building stones,

---

Exhibit 9.9   Budweiser Beer in Czechoslovakia

Budejovicky Budvar, which makes the original Budweiser lager beer, is perhaps the most well-known Czech company. Its most famous brand, Budweiser Budvar, is exported to 30 countries. More than 50% of its production is sold outside the country. Production has risen from 490,000 hecto liters in 1991 to 755,000 hecto liters in 1994, and to 1 million hecto liters in 1995. Demand is increasing at home and abroad, resulting in a demand that cannot be satisfied.

Budvar is a small brewery, even according to Czech standards. The industry is dominated by three other breweries. A bottle of beer is cheaper than a bottle of mineral water or Coca-Cola. Budvar's biggest problem, however, is its dispute with Anheuser-Busch, the U.S. brewery that also makes Budweiser. The decades-old dispute about who has the right to use the brand name, Budweiser, is keeping Budvar from expanding into North American markets.

Budvar is still state owned and is in no hurry to privatize; the company first wants to solve the brand-name dispute with Anheuser-Busch. At present, the parties are trying to reach an agreement, but the Czech side does not seem to be in a hurry. The company is expanding in Europe and has very good prospects there.

SOURCE: Boland (1995, p. 16).

---

sand, leather, glass, and ceramics. At present, more than 70% of the total output comes from the private sector.

The Czech Republic's highest priority is full membership in the EU and the Organization of Economic Cooperation and Development (OECD), which is now in sight because it is among the first group of countries negotiating to become EU members. Legal reform includes bringing the rules and regulations of the country into compliance with OECD and EU legal norms. Foreign and domestic investors are treated equally, and both are subject to the same taxation and laws.

All sectors of the economy are open to foreign investors, with the exception of the defense industry, national and cultural monuments, salt production, and distillation of pure alcohol. In all other sectors, 100% foreign ownership is possible. The country is complying with international copyright conventions, and the government ensures that the protection of intellectual property rights will match those of the EU. Czech businesspeople are tough negotiators, as is illustrated in Exhibit 9.9.

10

Emerging Markets of Latin America, South Africa, and Turkey

Doing Business in Latin America

Traditionally, Latin American economies have a history of successful reforms followed by occasional relapses. During the last few years, most Latin American economies have tackled inflation, freed markets, and reduced state control of businesses in major enterprises. Brazil, for example, has made some remarkable gains. Stimulated by the introduction of new currency in July 1994, Brazil reduced monthly inflation from a high of 50% to 5%. On the whole, inflation in Latin America is down from rates of 400% in the 1980s to a more reasonable rate of around 10% annually (U.S. Department of Commerce, 1995b).

According to the U.S. Department of Commerce (2000e), average gross domestic product (GDP) in Latin America is also growing and has averaged around 5% in recent years. Argentina, although experiencing a serious crisis in 2001, had balanced budgets in 1993 and 1994, which was achieved through increased taxes, slashing government expenditures on subsidies, and selling state assets. By the end of 1998, the deficit was only 1.5% of GDP (U.S. Department of Commerce, 2001a). Mexico also has balanced its books and even enjoyed a budgetary surplus from 1991 to December 1994. The rate of deficit-to-GDP was 1.1% in 1998 (U.S. Department of Commerce, 2000e). Furthermore, *apertura*, or the liberalization of markets, has taken place in most of these countries. As a result of tariff cuts and the elimination of import/export licenses, intraregional trade has doubled.

Moreover, restrictions on capital flows have been removed, and financial and other restricted sectors have opened up. Foreign banks and insurance companies are now allowed to enter many Latin American markets. Mexico is an active member of the North American Free Trade Agreement (NAFTA), and its trade activities with the Mercosur Trading Area (members are Argentina, Brazil, Paraguay, and Uruguay, with associate members, Chile and Bolivia) have been a big success.

Privatization in these countries has totally changed Latin American economics. Numerous enterprises, ranging from oil companies, telecommunication, and electricity companies, have been sold to private hands. In Brazil alone, where a number of state companies still exist, 65 companies (worth $72 billion) were sold through early 2000 (U.S. Department of Commerce, 2000b). During 1989 to 1999, Argentina underwent massive privatization, selling the telephone system, electrical plants, state airlines, and the state oil company, and partial privatization of social insurance programs. As a result of this privatization process, two important effects can be noted: First, sales assets have helped these countries balance their books and stabilize their currencies. Second, privatization has infused previously state-owned enterprises with productivity and efficiency, paving the way for foreign investment.

According to the United Nations Center for Trade and Development (UNCTAD, 2000), foreign capital is now flowing into Latin America. Foreign direct investment (FDI) into Latin America and the Caribbean as a whole increased by 32% in 1999, from $73 billion to $97 billion (see Exhibit 10.1). The inflow of foreign capital has induced an increase in imports, mostly of consumer goods. It has also increased fears of regional dependence on foreign capital.

Latin America saves only 17.9% of its GDP, compared with Asia's 31.9%. Economic growth, however, is still taking place. In the period from 1990 to 1999, Chile led the region with an annual growth rate of 7.2%, followed by Argentina. However, all countries appear to be growing at a steady pace. During the same period, Latin American exports grew at an average of nearly 9% ("Another Blow," 2001; U.S. Department of Commerce, 2000a, 2000c).

Mexico's currency collapse, however, hurt the emerging markets of this region rather badly. The crisis started in December 1994, and the following $50-billion bailout in February 1995 scared many investors away from these markets for some years. The currency crisis had also left its mark on the currencies of other emerging markets in Eastern Europe and Asia. Experts believe that the Asian crisis (1996/1997) was related to the Mexican crisis. Most of these countries have, however, recovered from currency devaluation and have now stabilized their economies. However, after decades of soaring

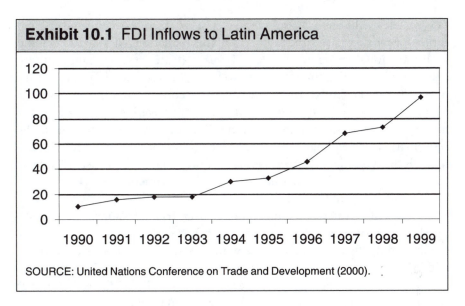

Exhibit 10.1 FDI Inflows to Latin America

SOURCE: United Nations Conference on Trade and Development (2000).

inflation and political turmoil, Latin American countries are finally showing some economic and political stability. In countries such as Brazil, the inflation rate is now stabilized around 6%, down from 78% some years ago, and the economy is growing at the rate of 4% to 5% (Whelan, 2000, p. 92).

Entry Strategies for Latin American Emerging Markets

Western companies have traditionally had a hard time in Latin American markets. Turbulent political situations have exacerbated economic conditions, such as balance of payments, interest rates, and inflation. In the past, some of the countries have been rather hostile to Western firms, especially those from the United States. Fortunately, however, this situation is totally changing. Most countries are now welcoming American investors and firms. A number of countries, such as Argentina and Brazil, are now offering incentives to Western firms, and Mexico's membership in NAFTA has made its markets more attractive.

Firms entering these emerging markets should be aware of the regional and bilateral agreements. A successful bilateral trade pact between Argentina and Brazil led to the creation of Mercosur in 1991. At present there are four members: Argentina, Brazil, Paraguay, Uruguay, and two associate members, Chile and Bolivia. Mercosur seeks to achieve free movement of goods and services, establish a common regional tariff for third-country imports, and harmonize macroeconomic trade and exchange rate policies. Although Mercosur had a slow start, its members had cut tariffs for most of each other's imports. This reduction led to a 200% jump in intraregional trade in the last 5 years (Cateora & Ghauri, 2000). Mercosur is now functioning quite well, and a number of Western firms have already benefited from the regional cooperation. Firms such as Siemens (Germany) and Greenwood (U.S.) are covering Brazil and other markets by entering through Argentina. It is thus important to choose the right market, depending on the nature and scope of your marketing ambitions. Firms targeting North American markets should consider Mexico as the point of entry. Firms wishing to cover Latin American markets should initially enter Argentina or Brazil.

Several Latin American countries have been trying to approach NAFTA for some sort of bilateral trade agreement. But within Mercosur, there is a strong feeling that any agreement with NAFTA should deal collectively with Mercosur rather than singling out individual countries. This approach appears to be favorable for Western—especially U.S.—firms because it would allow them easier access to a huge regional market.

From Mexico to Argentina, democratically elected governments are sincerely working to boost national economic development. All these governments have launched a program of privatization and introduced attractive terms and conditions for foreign firms. Many American multinationals already have offices and production facilities in these emerging markets. With the enormous demand for consumer products, the opportunities look promising. For example, Mexico and Brazil have become an emerging battleground for the automobile industry. In the United States, there is approximately one car for every 1.7 people. In Europe, there is one car for every 2.5 people. But in Mexico, there is only one car for every 12.5 people, and in Brazil there is only one car per 14 people (U.S. Department of Commerce, 1995b, 1995e). Thus, Latin America represents relatively unsaturated markets for automobiles. Furthermore, demand for automobiles seems to generally coincide with demand for other consumer goods. Chile has progressed well in the last decade. Export of agricultural products has been excellent. Chile, exporting only apples in the 1960s, became one of the world's largest fruit exporters by the year 2000. Salmon farming has reached world standards, and salmon exports to the United States have reached more than 40,000 tons annually (U.S. Department of Commerce, 2000c). All this is bringing foreign exchange and prosperity into the country, leading toward higher living standards and demand for Western products. However, there are bright prospects for Western firms in the industrial/manufacturing sector. Exhibit 10.2 presents prospects for the automobile industry in Mexico and Brazil.

Exhibit 10.2 The Automobile Industry in Latin America

Mexico Future Focus (In Thousands)

	1999	2000	2001	2002	2003
Domestic market					
Made in Mexico	476	553	606	261	721
Imported	236	253	273	302	335
Export vehicles					
Automobiles	723	806	847	891	950
Trucks	413	453	477	488	512
Total Mexican production	1,617	1,827	1,949	2,065	2,213
Automobiles	1,078	1,212	1,283	1,355	1,443

SOURCE: Levin (1999, pp. 38-44).

Brazil Automobile Production (In Thousands)

	2000	2005	% Change
Light vehicles	12,900	14,300	10.9
Vehicle sales	1,198	2,338	95.1
Light-vehicle production	1,506	2,665	77.0
Manufacturers	Daimler Chrysler, Fiat, Ford, General Motors, Honda, Renault, Toyota, Volkswagen		

SOURCE: Business Mexico, 1999.

Negotiation With Latin American Emerging Markets

Cultural expectations in Latin America can be quite diverse in both outlook and behavior. The wise executive should be cautious to never consider these markets monocultural: Brazil is very different from Mexico. However, some similarities and generalities can be drawn between many Latin American cultures. General attitudes toward time, the pace of negotiation, decision making, and emotional aspects of business relationships are often held in common (see Exhibit 10.3).

Selected Country Analyses

Argentina, Brazil, and Mexico have emerged as the most promising markets of this region. Population, growth, liberalization, and investment opportunities have shown these countries to be the most attractive to Western businesses.

Exhibit 10.3 Nature of Negotiations in Latin American Emerging Markets

Negotiation Factors	Comments
1. Pace of negotiation	Very slow
- Value of time	Time is not money
2. Negotiation strategy	
- Offer vs. agreement	Initial offer relatively high
- Presentation of issues	Priorities not important
- Presentations	Rather informal
- Discussions	Informative to persuasive
- Communication	Indirect, ambiguous
- Interpreters	Necessary depending on country
3. Emphasis on personal relationships	High
4. Influence of third parties	Very high
5. Distance	Rather large
6. Decision making	
- Overall	Not very rational
- Hierarchy	Strong hierarchy
- Collective vs. individual	Rather collectivistic
- Degree of details	Not necessary
- Degree of bureaucracy	High
- Need for agenda	High
7. Administrative factors	
- Need for agent or local partner	Very high
8. Emotional factors	
- Degree of rationality	Not very high
- Sensitivity	High

SOURCE: Format based on Acuff (1993).

Argentina

According to the U.S. Department of Commerce (2000a), Argentina's rich natural resources, educated population, export-oriented agricultural sector, and diversified industrial base has made it the richest country in South America. Despite a long history of troubles, economic reforms in Argentina have been extremely successful, and Argentina's economy is now stabilizing. In the 1980s, Argentina went through a long period of decline and stagnation, with chronic public-sector deficit and endemic inflation. A number of stabilization plans failed to remedy these problems. Public expenditure as a share of GDP increased to 35% in the 1980s. Labor was highly unionized, industries were heavily protected from foreign competition, and public enterprises were paid high prices for their products.

In 1989, when Argentina went to the polls to elect Carlos Menem as its first democratically elected president, expert observers labeled it as further proof of Argentina's talent for self-destruction. In the first years of his presidency, Menem was the mass media's favorite figure but was viewed with some skepticism. The headlines ranged from the leader being locked out of the presidential house by his wife, to affairs with supermodels, and tales of his extravagant expenditures. Paradoxically, however, by the end of his first term as president, he brought Argentina from almost nowhere to the third-fastest-growing country in the world, after China and Thailand. From 1990 to 1999, Argentina's economy grew by 5%. In 1999, it had a GDP of $281 billion ($7,620 per capita) and an inflation rate lower than many European Union (EU) countries ("Getting From Here," 2000; "Turning Red," 2000). These achievements and certain government policies helped Menem to be reelected in May 1995.

The government took bold steps to reduce the federal bureaucracy. It decreased federal employment from 671,000 workers to 284,000. The majority of these people were relocated to regions and provinces, and others were laid off. The central bank was separated from the nonfinancial public sector and was established as an effective monetary authority. A number of national development banks and national housing banks, largely subsisting on government support, were shut down, and their staffs were reduced by 75%. As a result, GDP has been steadily growing. Lower interest rates and falling inflation (from 84.7% in 1991 to 0.9% in 1998) has stimulated many investments ("Back on the Pitch," 1997). Throughout the 1990s, Argentina was Latin America's star performer, but in early 2002, Argentina defaulted on its $155-billion public debt, the largest default by any country. After a decade of stability with the peso fixed at parity with the dollar, it had to devalue the peso, which was trading under two per dollar in March 2002. The economy is standing still, income per person has shrunk from $7,000 to less than $3,500, and unemployment has risen to 25%. Despite this, some economists believe Argentinean companies are slim and strong. If and when the exchange rate is stabilized, Argentines will bring their money back, around $100 billion, and exports and investment will take off ("A Decline Without Parallel," 2002).

Learning from the Mexico and Asian-crisis experiences, life in Argentina will also come back to normal; as long as there are well-functioning institutions, these problems can be solved. The Ministry of Economics includes secretariats such as finance, trade and investments, economic programming, and public receipts. It also includes agriculture, mining, industry, energy, transportation, and public works. Thus, it appears that the Ministry of Economics has a powerful base with which to efficiently administer its reforms. At present, Argentina is discussing a bilateral trade agreement with the United States, with congruent discussions occurring at the Mercosur level.

Despite the crisis, Argentina is considered a model example of privatization in Latin America. Other than the airport and a few energy projects, all public-sector firms have been privatized. The telecommunication companies, the two television stations, and the national airline were already sold by 1991. In 1997, Argentina had the world's first fully privatized national postal system.

U.S. companies have played a major role as partners or operators of these privatized companies. Trade between these companies and their U.S. partners or operators has increased tremendously over the years. Great opportunities for Western firms exist in sectors such as hospital management, prefabricated housing, and financial services. Other promising sectors include food processing, computers, telecommunication, power generation and transmission equipment, heavy machinery, medical equipment, motor vehicles, construction and building material, agricultural machinery, and plastic-processing machinery.

The Convertibility Law (1991), which fixed the exchange rate, prohibited the central banks from financing the federal government deficit, eliminated indexation, and legalized contracts in dollars, was a major driver for many of Argentina's economic achievements. By eliminating some uncertainty in business planning and execution, Argentina has bolstered investors' confidence in its entire political system. Argentina's investment growth of 30% per year since 1991 and consumer demand growth of 10% per year are proof of this confidence and have provided fuel for new investments (U.S. Department of Commerce, 1995a).

The improved fiscal framework has attracted substantial capital inflows. Tight fiscal policies, deregulation measures, investments in human capital, and tax policy measures have all helped to improve Argentina's trade balance. The World Bank, Inter-American Development Bank (IDB), and International Bank for Reconstruction and Development (IBRD) are very active in Argentina and are financing a number of public-sector projects with long-term loans.

Foreign investment is very welcome in Argentina, and several foreign firms operate in almost every sector of the economy. Investors are free to enter using whatever method they choose. There is no restriction on mergers, takeovers, or joint ventures. Foreign firms have also widely participated in the government's privatization program. Foreign firms pay the same taxes as local firms. There is no tax on dividends, and foreign firms are allowed to participate in government export promotion and lower import duty schemes on equal grounds with local firms. Uranium mining, the nuclear industry, and broadcasting have been the only sectors denied to the foreign investors. There are no restrictions on inward or outward flow of foreign exchange. Furthermore, the mineral sector is now open for foreign investors and has received its first infusion of foreign capital. These investments in the country's massive gas and oil reserves have already resulted in production and exports. Privatization of the energy sector has been a key part of the government's goal to become a net energy exporter to the surrounding area (see Exhibit 10.4).

Multinational companies are invited to help Argentina explore its natural resources. The agricultural sector is still lagging behind, and Argentina wants to have an agreement with the United States to lift some tariffs and other restrictions on its agricultural imports. Traditionally, this sector is the main contributor of foreign exchange earnings. Up to 1999, it accounted for more than 60% of Argentina's total exports. We can see that capital goods, parts, and intermediate goods that induce investments in the manufacturing sector are the major imports. The total imports have increased from $7 billion in 1990 to $38 billion in 1998, which is a direct effect of liberalizing the economy (U.S. Department of Commerce, 2000a).

The growing ties between Argentina and Brazil are strengthening Mercosur as a bloc. Brazil has become an important market for Argentinean firms, with even small and medium-sized firms being very active in Brazilian markets. Argentinean companies such as SanCor, which had annual revenues of $1,100 million in 2000, consider Brazil its largest market (U.S. Department of Commerce, 2001a).

A number of foreign companies have also benefited from Argentinean-Brazilian trade increases. The German company Grunding and the American company Greenwood Mills, Inc., are two good examples of companies prospering from increased trade linkages with Brazil. The rising exports to Brazil account for 0.5% of Argentina's total growth (U.S. Department of Commerce, 2001a).

The United States is Argentina's primary source for FDI, dominating almost every sector except electrical power systems, in which Japan leads. Other important investors are Germany, Italy, Switzerland, Spain, and France. Some investments are also coming from Israel, South Korea, China, and Brazil. The best sectors in which to invest in Argentina are given in Exhibit 10.5.

Exhibit 10.4 Privatization in Argentina

Since 1990, Argentina has experienced an unprecedented process of transfer of services and publicly owned firms to the private sector, both by selling assets and by contractual agreements (concessions) with or without exclusivity. In general, but not always, the sectors involved have been characterized to some degree by economies of scale and scope, which in turn required the direct regulation of the private firms. Natural gas, electricity, and telecommunications are the three main areas of privatization in Argentina.

In 1993, *Gas del Estado S.A.* was privatized. Following this privatization, natural gas in Argentina was provided through eight private distribution companies, all of which are supplied from the three main production areas in the country (Norte, Neuquina, and Austral) by two different pipelines (North and South).

In 1992, privatization initiatives focused on the electricity sector. To take advantage of the potential competition in generation, privatization of Argentina's electrical sector included a ban on vertical integration. Distribution in the greater Buenos Aires metropolitan area (which includes the city of Buenos Aires and 14 municipalities of the province of Buenos Aires), previously in the hands of the federal government, was awarded to two private concessionaires in 1992. Many provincial governments followed the same strategy when privatizing local distribution companies. Transmission of the interconnected grid was given in concession to a private firm (Transener), also in 1992, under an open-access rule.

Telecommunications were one of the earliest privatizations and were perhaps affected by many "imperfections" of institutional design. However, one of the major or more visible differences between this and later privatizations (such as natural gas and electricity) was that the tariff structure (based on pervasive cross-subsidization with a clear distributional purpose) was transferred to the new setting. In fact, at the time of the privatization, cross-subsidies were even more severe than what had been customary in Argentina. This in turn transferred all the tensions associated with a heavy cross-subsidized price structure into the future institutional setting. Therefore, it is not surprising that the undoing of this price structure and the administration or governance of the tariff rebalancing process became the central telecommunication regulatory issue in Argentina.

SOURCE: Inter-American Development Bank

According to the U.S. Department of Commerce (2000a), General Motors, which left Argentina in 1978, returned in 1995 to open a new $100-million factory to produce 25,000 pick-up trucks per year. General Motors will manufacture these trucks for domestic sales and duty-free

---

Exhibit 10.5 Best Prospects in Argentina for Western Firms

- Computers (PCs for banking, public utilities, etc.)
- Telecommunications (cellular services, voicemail, etc.)
- Travel and tourism
- Electric power generation and transmission equipment
- Oil and gas field machinery
- Motor vehicles
- Apparel
- Computer software (database and general business applications)
- Construction and building materials
- Agricultural machinery and equipment

SOURCE: U.S. Department of Commerce, 1995.

---

exports to Mercosur. Argentina sold around 70,000 automobiles to Brazil in 1995. Other projects with foreign assistance include telecommunications, oil production, steel mills, petroleum chemicals, highways (34 routes), railroads (5 lines), electrical utilities (9 power stations), natural gas, and a subway for Buenos Aires.

Preferred *entry strategies* for most U.S. companies involve operating through agents and distributors. The agency/distributor contracts are regulated by local law and must include a termination clause. A foreign firm can terminate such a contract at any time, but in case of wrongful termination, the firm may have to pay damages to the local party.

Franchising is also widely used by foreign firms, but the rights and obligations of franchisees and franchisers must be clearly stated in the contract. Argentinean law is not very clear on these disputes or in cases of bankruptcy and other commercial failures. This is also true for licensing agreements. Prior approval by the government may be beneficial for taxation purposes for know-how transfers. Joint-venture contracts have to be registered with the Commercial Registry, and the contract must contain a number of specific issues. It is thus advisable to involve a local lawyer in such transactions.

Investors are also free to enter the market without any joint venture, through a takeover or a greenfield investment, for instance. Privatization plans are also an option. There is no discrimination against overseas firms. Rules for taxes and liabilities apply equally to local and foreign investors and firms. Foreign firms are also eligible for government subsidies such as export promotion schemes.

Argentina adheres to most international agreements on intellectual property. This provides protection of copyrights even for computer software, but copyright piracy is still quite prevalent. There have been some cases of dispute settlement among Argentinean and American firms. These disputes are generally handled by local courts or administrative systems.

Foreign investors may do business in Argentina as individuals, corporations, branch offices, partnerships, or limited liability companies. The most common method for foreign companies is to open a separately incorporated foreign subsidiary to minimize their potential liability. There are no approvals or procedures required to effect foreign investments. Regardless of the amount or the area of economic activity in which they are made, foreign investments may be made without any kind of prior approval. This principle applies even if a foreign investment results in full foreign ownership of a domestic company. In banking and insurance, areas in which special statutes require all operators to apply for licenses, foreign and domestic investors are guaranteed access to them on an equal footing (Argentina Ministry of Economy, 2001). The domestic sourcing mandate was withdrawn in 1989, and currently there is no "Buy Argentina" program.

For *negotiations,* a rather conservative approach is recommended. A prior appointment is often considered important, and a rather formal dress code is used in business. Most Argentinean executives understand English, but almost all business transactions are conducted in Spanish. All documents and specifications should be presented in Spanish.

As in most of Latin America, personality and personal relationships play an important role in negotiations with Argentinean counterparts. Most Argentineans take holidays in January and February. Infrastructure with regard to telecommunication and so forth is quite adequate. Mobile telephones are becoming increasingly popular. AT&T, MCI, and Sprint have local numbers and are cheaper than official rates.

Mexico

Mexico has been working diligently to open its political system, expand its economic base, and control the trafficking of narcotics. Although Mexico's progress has been hampered by several financial, political, and economic crises, it remains a promising market to watch. Ensuring stability and gaining the confidence of new investors will be the two key factors for Mexico's future success. Its membership in NAFTA has brought a lot of stability to Mexico and as a result, a lot of foreign investment.

Mexico's economy consists primarily of private manufacturing and services, although it has several large and traditional agricultural-based enterprises. During the 1980s, the accumulation of large external debts, falling world oil prices, rapid population growth, and high rates of inflation and unemployment temporarily paralyzed Mexico's economy. But in the 1990s, the government implemented wide-ranging economic reforms, adopted a stricter fiscal policy, reduced the external debt, and brought inflation under control. As a result, Mexico was able to produce budgetary surpluses in 1992 and 1993.

Beginning in 1994, however, Mexico began to stumble. In January, peasants in the state of Chiapas briefly took up arms against the government, claiming governmental indifference to poverty and oppression. In March, Institutional Revolutionary Party (PRI) presidential candidate Luis Donaldo Colosio was assassinated, followed by the September assassination of PRI Secretary General Jose Francisco Ruiz. The brother of former president Carlos Salinas was suspected to be the mastermind of the second crime, and charges were filed for obstructing investigations into the murder, causing many eyebrows to be raised. International confidence was further weakened when additional charges involving multimillion-dollar fortunes in overseas banks were charged against him (U.S. Department of State, 1999).

In December 1994, strong devaluation of the peso spawned a serious financial crisis in early 1995. Mexico's economic activity contracted 7% in 1995. However, an international bailout effort led by the United States has helped stabilize the Mexican economy and has allowed Mexico to repay loans to the United States more than 3 years ahead of schedule. Recovering much more quickly than anticipated, Mexico's economy grew more than 5% in 1996, and by 2000, it was fully recovered. Inflation and unemployment are down, and experts predict that Mexican real GDP will continue to grow (U.S. Department of State, 2001).

NAFTA has played a strong role in strengthening ties between Mexico and the United States. Both countries continue to benefit from the free trade agreement, which hopes to eliminate all trade restrictions in the next decade. The peso crisis, however, revived doubts as to whether knitting together the three economies would ever work effectively. Still, most experts believe that basic economic conditions in Mexico remain very sound, and the devaluation of the peso has in fact made foreign investments even more attractive. Mexico has cleaned up its economy in recent years, and the budget deficit of 1% of Mexico's GNP is now relatively very small (U.S. Department of State, 2001).

Mexico continues to liberalize its foreign investment regime. The present government is trying to restore investor confidence through budgetary measures aimed at slashing the current-account deficit in half (to $14 billion). In 1993, Mexico passed a new foreign investment law that replaced a

---

Exhibit 10.6 Best Prospects in Mexico for Western Firms

- Automotive parts and service equipment
- Franchising services
- Pollution control equipment
- Chemical production machinery
- Telecommunications equipment
- Computers and peripherals
- Building materials
- Management consulting services
- Apparel
- Air-conditioning and refrigeration equipment

SOURCE: Department of Commerce, 1995.

---

restrictive 1973 statute. The new law provides national treatment for most foreign investments, eliminates many performance requirements for foreign investment projects, and liberalizes criteria for the automatic approval of foreign investment projects. Investors are invited to participate in building ports, railroads, local phone services, and satellite communication—sectors that were not previously open to foreign investors (U.S. Department of Commerce, 2000e). (See Exhibit 10.6.)

The Mexican government is facing economic pressure from all sides. Foreign investors and local businessmen are pressing for price increases to counteract the peso devaluation, and workers are demanding wage increases for the same reasons. As a whole, however, foreign investors with long-term perspectives are positive about these developments because they will trigger further economic reforms. Companies such as Chrysler Corporation, which exports minivan engines, Neon subcompacts, and Dodge pick-up trucks from Mexico consider these developments of little negative consequence to their long-term business prospects. On the contrary, the devaluation of the peso has made Mexico an attractive place for investments. A number of companies, such as American R.R. Donnelley & Sons (a commercial printer) and Dean Foods Company, have expanded their operations in Mexico. WalMart has approximately 500 stores in Mexico (WalMart Stores, 2001).

Facing a public credibility problem, the government has also launched a campaign to enhance the image of the government and gain the confidence of the people. The rescue plan includes measures such as the following (Smith & Malkin, 1995):

1. A proposal to raise the value-added tax from 10% to 15%

2. Tightening credit and boosting fuel prices

3. Offering assistance worth $9.4 billion to banks to help restructure bad loans, with another $3 billion to boost bank capital

4. Spending $245 million to create 550,000 new jobs

5. Raising $12 to $14 billion through selling ports, railroads, petrochemical plants, and telecommunications licensing

So far, the plan seems to be working. The speeded-up privatization program has raised billions of dollars needed to introduce anti-inflationary measures. It has helped companies become more competitive and export oriented. In February 1999, Mexico showed a trade deficit of $5 billion.

According to the U.S. Department of Commerce (2000e), Mexico is the third-largest market for U.S. exports, after Canada and Japan. In 1999, Mexico accounted for 11% of all U.S. trade. The United States exported $105.2 billion worth of goods to Mexico—almost equal to U.S. exports to Japan, even though the Mexican economy is just one seventh the size of Japan's. In turn, bolstered by NAFTA, 88% of Mexico's exports went to the United States. Trade with the U.S. has doubled since NAFTA was implemented in 1994. Mexico is signing trade agreements with most countries in Latin America and has signed a free trade deal with the EU to lessen its dependence on the United States. In 2000, Mexico had a 4.5% growth rate and expects to keep that rate for the next couple of years, due to high oil prices.

Since the NAFTA agreement went into effect in January 1994, most U.S. exports to Mexico have been exempted from Mexican tariffs. Due to the ease of communications, better-quality perception, familiarity with U.S. products, and now low or no tariffs, there is a great preference for U.S. products. NAFTA provisions to improve safeguards for intellectual property rights is helping to make Mexico increasingly attractive to more investors (U.S. Department of Commerce, National Trade Data Bank [NTDB], 2000).

The Secretariat of Social Development (SEDESOL) in Mexico has provided incentives to U.S. firms to enter a number of markets in Mexico. The North American Bank (NAD-Bank) provides finances for border environmental projects. The bank, established jointly by the United States and Mexico, finances projects in areas such as wastewater treatment, water pollution, and municipal waste problems. It can make loans and guarantees up to $3 billion. In the last decade, Mexico has also become a member of the Asia Pacific Economic Community (APEC) and the Organization for

Economic Cooperation and Development (OECD), demonstrating Mexico's desire to have trade relationships beyond the Americas and play a role in the world economy.

Regarding *entry strategies,* the time is right for Western firms to enter Mexico. Infrastructure has been drastically improved. A 4,000-kilometer, modern four-lane highway has been built by the private sector. A number of private companies have invested in the project and plan to get returns through tolls charged over the next 10 years. An additional 6,000 km of highways are planned to be built by the end of the decade. Although the Federal Electricity Commission (CFE) possesses a monopoly in the public supply of electricity, private companies are allowed to generate electricity for their own use. The national telephone company (Telefonos de Mexico) has been privatized, and this has opened up a huge market for Western firms. The privatized company Telemex plans to buy equipment worth $2 billion per year from foreign sources to improve its services and to offer new lines. There are no restrictions on inward or outward flow of foreign exchange.

Most foreign firms sell into Mexico through agents and distributors. A number of retailers, such as WalMart, Kmart, and Price Club, have opened their own stores. Quite a few U.S. firms also have their own manufacturing facilities in Mexico, so-called maquiladoras. These are mostly assembly plants in which parts and raw material are primarily sourced from the United States. The 1992 NAFTA agreement has transformed Mexico's economy. U.S. manufacturers have opened several plants, which has created an enormous number of jobs. As a result, a new middle class has emerged. There is a stable political atmosphere, inflation is down, and the country's debt rating has been upgraded. WalMart of Mexico (Walmex) has achieved the status of the largest retailer in the country, with 1999 sales of $6 billion (WalMart Stores, 2001).

For businesses planning to do business in Mexico, personal visits are extremely beneficial toward building good relations and establishing a network. It is not always easy to find the right agent or distributor. The best way is to find companies that are already established in the same field and use them as agents/distributors. It is also important to determine whether these firms have branches or are able to cover smaller cities. Access to a network of distributors will be necessary for success in Mexico. One way to find agents/distributors is to participate in trade shows and exhibitions. There are a number of such exhibitions every year in most regions.

Several foreign services companies have found entry into Mexico through franchising arrangements with Mexican counterparts. In fact, this method of entering the market has been increasing by around 30% per year since 1991

(U.S. Department of Commerce, 1999a). Restaurants, communication services, hotels, car rentals, video sales, and rental/real estate companies are some examples of franchising sectors. There are no restrictions on foreign franchises that employ 24,000 workers.

Mexico is a typical technology transfer, joint-venture country in which the foreign partner provides the technology and the local partner contributes with its hard-won market knowledge. Due to the size of the market and cheaper manufacturing conditions, joint ventures and other FDI are increasing. During the period 1994 to March 2000, Mexico received $74.1 billion in FDI (U.S. Department of Commerce, 2001c). In most sectors, there are no limits on foreign ownership.

A large number of attorneys and consultants are available to help foreign companies registering with different institutions, such as tax authorities, chambers of commerce, and social security organizations. Advertising and marketing are also quite developed. Mexico City alone has 15 newspapers. There are 25 FM and 35 AM Spanish-language radio stations with commercials and 7 television stations in Mexico City. Advertising requires local adaptation, and foreign firms should consider using a local agency. Most international advertising agencies also have their offices in Mexico.

For *negotiations,* Mexico is a rather typical Latin American country, but it is a member of all major international organizations for international property rights. To obtain copyright or patent protection, a firm must apply to the Director General of Copyrights. Despite these safeguards, piracy is prevalent, and foreign firms should be very specific on rights and obligations while negotiating with Mexican counterparts.

The law regarding FDI is consistent with the foreign investment chapter of NAFTA. Foreign companies should therefore have proper knowledge of NAFTA rules and regulations while negotiating with Mexican firms. A dispute between governments can also be solved under NAFTA rules. In case of disputes, a mutually acceptable 5-member panel is appointed to resolve the conflict in accordance with NAFTA rules.

Mexican businessmen are shrewd and often well educated. In the countryside and regional areas, however, English is not very common. A Spanish-speaking translator or assistant is recommended. In the cities, businessmen are becoming increasingly Americanized and often try to behave accordingly. Attitudes toward time and personal space, however, are still very much Latin American and so is the importance given to contract details. There may also be a tendency to promise too much. It is therefore important for foreign firms to check the credentials and track records of Mexican counterparts, potential agents, or distributors.

Exhibit 10.7 How Brazil Stacks Up Against Other
Emerging Markets

	Population (Millions)	GDP ($ Billions)	GNP/Capita ($ at PPP)	Exports ($ Billions)	Exports (as % of GDP)
Brazil	**168**	**760**	**6,317**	**58.7**	**10**
China	1,250	991	3,291	207.5	22
India	998	459	2,149	47.4	11
Indonesia	207	140	2,439	54.8	54
Mexico	97	474	7,719	129.5	31
Russia	47	375	6,339	87.7	48

SOURCE: WDI, 2001.

Brazil

For much of this century, Brazil has been one of the fastest-growing economies in the world. With a GDP of $1.13 trillion, Brazil is South America's largest economy and is one of the 10 largest economies in the world (Central Intelligence Agency, 2001). More than 81% of its 168 million people reside in urban areas, and its industry and service sectors continue to grow. Brazil has huge reserves of valuable resources, such as gold, gems, metals, forests, and rivers, but these have traditionally remained underused. If Brazil can maintain control of its economic situation, its abundant natural resources will give it a long-term economic advantage. In reforms undertaken in 1999 as a result of a "Plano Real," the banks were restructured, and several state-owned businesses were privatized. As a result, there is a huge middle class with increased buying power and demands. A comparison of Brazil with other major emerging markets is given in Exhibit 10.7.

Brazil has large and well-developed agricultural, mining, manufacturing, and service sectors, but rampant inflation has been the primary obstacle toward further development and investment. Prior to instituting a stabilization plan in 1994, skyrocketing inflation ravaged the economy. Inflation was reduced in from more than 1,000% in 1994 to about 5% (consumer prices) in 1999. During 1990 to 1999, annual GDP growth averaged 2.9% as credit was tightened and the appreciating *real* (Brazilian currency unit) encouraged imports while depressing export growth (U.S. Department of Commerce, 2000b). Brazil is often grouped with China and India to form the three biggest emerging markets (Prahalad & Lieberthal, 1998). A comparison of these three markets is presented in Exhibit 10.8.

Exhibit 10.8 Market Size: Brazil Versus China, India, and the United States

Product	China	India	Brazil	United States
Televisions (millions of units)	13.6	5.2	7.8	23.0
Detergent (kilograms per person;	2.5	2.7	7.3	14.4
millions of tons)	3.5	2.3	11	3.9
Shampoo ($ billions)	1.0	0.8	1.0	1.5
Pharmaceuticals ($ billions)	5.0	2.8	8.0	60.6
Automotive (millions of units)	1.6	0.7	2.1	15.5
Power (megawatt capacity)	236,542	81,736	59,950	810,964

SOURCE: Prahalad & Lieberthal (1998).

In previous administrations, the federal government has played a large role in providing the shape and incentive for economic growth. This influence was felt not only in the day-to-day activities of governmental organizations but also in wage, price, and credit policies. However, more recently, the Brazilian government has tried to reduce its role in guiding the economy. As a result, many new opportunities in the private sector have opened up, and the government is refocusing its attention on improving public health, safety, and education.

According to most estimates, Brazil has an overall growth potential of around 19%, and in sectors such as software and information technology, the expected growth rate is 15% annually or more. Telecommunications are expected to grow by more than 200% by the end of this decade. Sectors such as power generation and energy technologies have similar growth potential. The most attractive sectors for foreign firms are listed in Exhibit 10.9.

Local content requirements are a major restraint to doing business in Brazil. Domestic law also gives considerable preference to local producers when sourcing for public-sector projects. Foreign investors are allowed in government projects only when local services are not available. However, Brazil's industrial sectors are dominated by subsidiaries of multinational companies. Many multinationals and local companies produce in Brazil for the global market.

For the domestic market, the taxation system for imported goods provides a competitive edge to locally produced products. Tariffs are the primary instrument to regulate imports. The trade-weighted average is around 12.5%, and the maximum is 35—down from 105% in 1990 (U.S. Department of Commerce, 2000b). The U.S. government is continually

---

Exhibit 10.9 Best Prospects in Brazil for Western Firms

- Computer software (PC, LAN, and graphics software)
- Computers and peripherals (notebooks, palmtop devices, high-end microcomputers)
- Plastic materials and resin
- Security and safety equipment
- Sporting goods and recreational equipment
- Electrical power systems
- Aircraft and parts
- Telecommunications
- Pollution control equipment
- Food-processing equipment

SOURCE: U.S. Department of Commerce (1995).

---

negotiating with the Brazilian government for bilateral tariff reductions for U.S. products.

Capitalizing on the expanding opportunities in Brazil can be very difficult but profitable. Telecommunications, computer software, and oil and petroleum are the three most promising industries in Brazil. Brazil boasts the largest telecommunications sector in Latin America with an estimated market of $8.5 billion for equipment and services. Unmet demand in basic wireline and cellular services makes Brazil an attractive market for investment and export opportunities. However, under Brazil's constitution, telecommunications and petroleum industries are government-run monopolies. Legislation to allow private-sector participation in these areas is currently under consideration.

The computer software market in Brazil has shown strong growth in recent years. The total market was worth more than $2 billion in 2000, with more than 40% of that consisting of U.S. imports. The information technology (IT) sector has grown 15.3% more than in the previous year. For every 100 software packages, there is only one distributor in Brazil. The United States also enjoys a 70% share of the market (U.S. Department of Commerce, 2001b). Piracy, however, continues to be an issue in expanding the market. However, the Brazilian Association of Software Companies has successfully raised awareness of the issue among the business community, and intellectual property considerations continue to improve.

Many opportunities also exist in the petroleum and oil industry. However, it could take several years before investment opportunities can be fully realized. The government-run monopoly in oil is currently being phased out, but a regulatory framework necessary for attracting investments has not yet been implemented. Private investments will coexist with the government-run supplier, Petrobas, and interested investors should continue to monitor Brazilian legislative changes that might allow further market access. The total market size of the petroleum industry is $3.6 billion, with about $960 million in imports, half of which come from the United States (U.S. Department of Commerce, 2000b).

For many kinds of product groups, patent or property rights protection in Brazil is not available. These products include chemical compounds, foodstuff, pharmaceutical products, metal alloys, and biotechnology products. The government eventually intends to revise its policy on these issues, especially for products such as pharmaceuticals. A number of such amendments have already been made in the government rules and regulations in 1990, 1992, and even further in 1994, as a requirement of the General Agreement on Tariffs and Trade (GATT) Uruguay Round results. According to the 1992 amendments, Brazil implemented the Paris Convention rules for property rights and provides protection to trademarks.

Clearly, there are many reforms the Brazilian government must implement to increase the FDI it receives. However, it has made slow but steady progress toward getting these things in order. With its relatively large market and many natural resources, the potential for doing business in Brazil is very promising. For entry strategies, a number of foreign companies have successfully used the traditional export channels of agents and distributors. The typical import transaction, however, involves the importation of capital goods or raw material by an individual firm for its own use or production process. Due to a shortage of foreign currency, Brazilian importers do not generally keep large stocks of imported goods.

Selecting an agent or distributor in Brazil deserves extra care and caution because Brazil is a huge country and most agents/distributors do not cover the whole market. In general, it is better for a foreign firm to select different agents for different regions than to have one agent cover the whole market. Be aware that different types of contracts with these agents may also have different tax implications. In some cases, the foreign firm may end up paying income tax for transactions concluded by its agent. It is thus advisable to consult a tax lawyer before signing an agency contract. Once an agency contract is signed, the foreign participant cannot unilaterally terminate the contract without "just cause."

Joint ventures are a very common way of doing business in Brazil. Foreign firms used to look for local joint-venture partners to be able to compete for public-sector projects. At present, however, joint ventures are a recommended mode of entry into a market that can be rather difficult to handle by a foreign firm on its own. No formal legislation regulates franchising in Brazil, but such agreements must be registered with INPI (federal trademark and patent office) to obtain the authorization of the Brazilian Central Bank for remittance of royalties, and so forth, to a foreign franchiser. For trademarks, foreign franchisers should register with INPI before entering into negotiations with the local franchisee.

For *negotiations,* Brazil is typically a price-driven market. The negotiators consider price and price discounts to be very important, although awareness of quality and after-sales service is increasing. Marketers should reserve some price-reduction possibilities at the final stage of the negotiation process. For consumer products, advertising will be extremely important. Even for industrial products, there are a number of professionals available. Foreign firms are thus advised to establish their corporate identities in the market before coming to the negotiation table. Trade fairs are one way of building corporate image.

Doing Business in Africa

Africa is perhaps the only continent in the emerging world whose condition keeps worsening. The combined GDP of African countries south of the Sahara, excluding South Africa, is less than that of Belgium. It has no shining examples like the "Asian tigers" or the Latin American emerging markets. African countries routinely ignore the advice of the World Bank and the International Monetary Fund (IMF), and thus have been considered unsuitable for investment. As long as these countries do not get approval for good housekeeping from these two organizations, they are unable to borrow money from outside or attract any foreign investments.

Moreover, structural reforms involving reduction of budget deficits, currency devaluation, removal of state subsidies, free pricing, liberalization of trade, and elimination of state subsidies have not stimulated growth, decreased poverty, or attracted foreign investments ("South Africa," 2000). Although the World Bank and IMF and many experts accept that structural reforms might not have been able to help African countries, it is generally believed that such reforms are not properly implemented. For example, during 1980 to 1990, Kenya sold only one state enterprise. Zimbabwe did not even start the reforms it promised. Nigeria refused to lift its petrol subsidies and annoyed Western countries on human rights issues to the extent that it was expelled from the commonwealth. However, there is one country that has reinvented itself. The only country in Africa that can be treated as an emerging market is South Africa.

South Africa

The collapse of apartheid in South Africa had the same impact as the fall of the Berlin Wall in Eastern Europe. The dramatic changes that have taken place after the apartheid policies and handing over power to the African National Congress (ANC) in 1994 have brought South Africa back into the world scene. The Western world has already embraced South Africa as a lost child coming home. The way back to prosperity is, however, not very easy. Accustomed to state protection, its industry is generally not very competitive. The country also suffers from a serious unemployment problem. The main job ahead is therefore to increase the competitiveness of its industries and reduce the disparities between blacks and whites in the population.

It is said that South Africa has two parallel First and Third World economies existing side by side. To succeed, it must bring these economies together into a middle-income, emerging-level country. This being said, South Africa has many advantages as an emerging market. Its infrastructure is comparable to most countries of the developed world, and it offers enormous opportunities in a number of sectors, such as financial services, construction, mining, and project management. The rapidly growing black middle class is giving a boost to consumer spending, fueling unprecedented growth in this sector. Other than consumer products, the market has opened up for strong demand in industries such as aerospace and aircraft parts, chemicals, machinery, computers, electronics, and pharmaceutical equipment.

According to the U.S. Department of Commerce (2000f), South Africa is the largest and most advanced economy in Africa. With a population of more than 40 million and GDP of $131.1 billion, it has a rather diversified economy. Manufacturing is the largest sector, representing 26% of GDP. Other than petroleum and bauxite, it has an abundance of the most valuable mineral resources, ranging from gold and diamonds to coal and iron ore. It also has a considerable agricultural sector. South Africa has recovered strongly in terms of economic growth in recent years, with an increase in the growth rate from 1.1% in 1993 to around 4% in 1995 (U.S. Department of Commerce, NTDB, 1995). However, in 1999, the growth rate declined to 1.2%.

The constraints on growth include an unskilled labor force, inefficient trade policies, concentration of economic power among conglomerates, and the taxation system. Moreover, rapid growth of the population and slow growth in the industrial sector is causing a decline in per capita GDP. During the early 1990s, South Africa had double-digit inflation, which was subsequently restrained to the current rate of around 6% ("Jobless and Joyless," 2001). These positive developments, together with the government's proactive attitude to problem solving, could lead South Africa to an economic boom in the next few decades.

According to the U.S. Department of Commerce (2000f), South Africa is the largest market in sub-Saharan Africa. U.S. exports have doubled during the period 1990 to 1999 and account for around 13% of South Africa's total imports. The $24-billion import market is increasing every year, and almost all Western (European as well as U.S.) companies are coming back to South Africa with fresh investments. Since the end of apartheid, more than 60 American companies have returned to or have entered South Africa.

Companies are investing not only to cover the domestic market but also to access other African markets from South Africa. Germany tops the list of the top 10 exporters to South Africa, followed by the United States, Japan, the United Kingdom, and France. Switzerland is the leading importer from South Africa, followed by the United States, the United Kingdom, Japan, and Germany.

South Africa's infrastructure, though largely controlled by the government-owned Transnet, is quite efficient and comparable with Western standards. The divisions under Transnet include Spoornet (railways), Portnet (ports), Autonet (roads), Petronet (pipelines), and South African Airways. These divisions operate as separate companies and use a number of private companies as subcontractors. Recently, these divisions have been facing some competition from private companies, especially in the transport and airways sectors. The population in South Africa is quite urbanized, and almost 90% of its population lives around five major cities: Johannesburg, Cape Town, Durban, Pretoria, and Port Elizabeth.

The area around Johannesburg and Witwatersrand, including Pretoria, specializes in minerals and raw material. The area around Durban (Natal) is home to South Africa's most important port and specializes in manufacturing industries such as textiles, footwear, chemicals, sugar, petroleum products, and processed food. The area around Cape Town has moved toward agriculture and commerce. It has rich farmlands and vineyards and is also a center for service sectors such as insurance and banking. Finally, Port Elizabeth has the biggest seaport in the country and has large fruit and vegetable plantations. Port Elizabeth also has the country's largest motor vehicle assembly plants, providing a major source of employment to its residents.

Although government involvement in the economy has been quite high, South Africa remains a relatively open economy from an emerging-market perspective. Protectionist policies shielding infant industries and promoting import substitution are now undergoing change, and the government is encouraging the private sector and competition. Tax rates have been lowered, and a reform program of trade liberalization and privatization has begun. South Africa is catching up with emerging markets from other regions.

There are reasons to believe that confidence in South Africa is increasing. During 1990 to 1999, domestic investments increased by an average of 3% annually. The main problem stems from the ill effects of state protection of companies. State protection of industries had engendered complacency and stagnation in corporate circles. For example, two companies together enjoy 75% of the sugar market, three companies jointly control 75% of the fertilizer market, and three companies together control 90% of the chemical fabric market that supplies the textile industry. The oligopolistic structure of most industries makes it difficult to attract newcomers from abroad. Despite this, FDI rose to more than $1.4 billion in 1999 from around $800 million in 1992. Companies such as Pepsi-Cola are spending hundreds of millions of dollars. South Korea's Samsung, British and American telecommunication companies, and McDonald's are investors in South Africa (U.S. Department of Commerce, NTDB, 2000).

The government is encouraging foreign investment and provides the same rights and rules to foreign investors as it does to domestic investors. Some sectors considered important to national security are reserved as domestic sectors. All other sectors are open for foreign firms that can own up to 100% of the subsidiaries. There is no special screening or permission required for foreign investments. The only difference is the two-tier exchange rate. There is a special exchange rate for investments coming from abroad. Other than the incentives offered by the government, the main attraction of South Africa is its excellent infrastructure and that it provides convenient access to other markets in Africa. There are no restrictions on repatriation of profits and other earnings. Foreign firms can avail equal opportunities for export incentives and tariff protection provided by the government. The new regional industrial-development program provides an incentive for new or relocating businesses anywhere outside the Johannesburg, Pretoria, and Durban areas. The incentive includes an establishment grant of 10.5% of total operating assets, plus a 3-year, profit-based tax break. The Income Tax Act provides capital allowances for new factory buildings and improvements and also for new manufacturing plants, equipment, and scientific research expenditure. Moreover, a number of export incentives are available for exporting firms. The export incentives include income tax allowance for expenses incurred in promoting or maintaining the export market, assistance for export market research, and additional export incentives for specific industries such as motor vehicles and textiles. South Africa has a number of bilateral investment agreements with several African countries that facilitate investment flows between these countries and allow free flow of trade. At present, there are no special trade zones or free ports in South Africa, although the government is considering these options.

Exhibit 10.10	Foreign Companies in South Africa, by Country

Country	Number
United States	636
Germany	467
United Kingdom	271
Belgium	150
Netherlands	136
France	135
Italy	69
Switzerland	61
Japan	58
Denmark	49

SOURCE: National Trade and Investment Promotion Agency, South Africa (2001).

A total of $1.2 billion of FDI came to South Africa in 1999, 40% of which came from EU countries (U.S. Department of Commerce, NTDB, 2000). Most of these investments were concentrated in the manufacturing, financial services, and trade sectors. After the 1994 elections, FDI and the presence of foreign companies in South Africa has increased considerably (see Exhibit 10.10).

Entry and Negotiation Strategies for South Africa

After the 1994 elections and the installation of the new government, all international restrictions for exports to South Africa were lifted. The local government is offering a number of incentives to foreign firms. For goods exported from South Africa, export licenses are required for some goods, such as agricultural products, metal waste, and diamonds. For export to South Africa, there are no restrictions. Beyond normal trade documentation, such as invoices, bills of lading, and certificates of origin, no extra licenses or documents are required. There is no law regulating barter or countertrade. Some restrictions exist, such as requiring prior permission on import of used goods into the country.

All possible methods of distribution and sales are available. There are well-established distributors and wholesalers in almost all sectors. As a result, a number of producers, domestic as well as foreign, sell directly to these retailers. Foreign firms may also appoint an agent or sell directly to retailers or department stores. While choosing a distributor, foreign firms should check the existing portfolio of the distributor for directly competing products or brands. A distributor is particularly recommended for capital goods because these distributors buy from producers and sell with guarantees. They also sell spare parts and provide maintenance services. For such goods, the foreign firm should provide training to the distributor for equipment handling and maintenance. It is possible to find a single agent/distributor for the whole country. These agents and distributors normally take care of all local formalities and custom clearances.

Licensing and franchising are the most prevalent methods of doing business in South Africa. There are a large number of franchisers in South Africa. There is also a Franchisee Association of South Africa (FASA), with membership extending to 2,700 franchise outlets and sales of more than $2 billion. In case of licensing and franchising, payment of royalties must be approved by the South African Reserve Bank (SARB). Royalty fees are based on a percentage of total factory sales, with maximums of 4% for consumer goods and 6% for intermediate and final capital goods. Exchange approvals are normally granted for an initial period of 5 years. Foreign investors and firms are allowed to open their own offices and wholly owned subsidiaries. The same rules apply as for domestic firms. Private firms may have up to 50 shareholders, who need not be South African nationals. Foreign firms may also open a local branch office by registering the branch with the registrar of companies as an "external company." Branch profits remitted to the foreign head office are not subject to withholding tax.

South Africa offers a full range of infrastructural facilities, from modern ports to advertising companies and agencies. The media, newspapers, magazines (7 daily and 12 weekly national papers), and radio and television advertising are well developed and available. Of late, direct marketing has also become quite popular.

While negotiating with South African counterparts, the Western firms should feel quite comfortable. The infrastructure and business environments are quite compatible with the Western world. The white population speaks Afrikaans and English, and the black and Asian populations speak a variety of languages and many of them also speak English and/or Afrikaans. Printed material aimed at the nonwhite population is mostly in the English language. As a result, South Africa is not the typical African country. A well-developed industrial and trade infrastructure has influenced the mentality of people. The managers and executives with whom Western firms transact are often well-educated and experienced negotiators. The important negotiation factors are dealt with in Exhibit 10.11.

The public sector is a significant buyer in South Africa, and government purchasing is often conducted through competitive bidding on invitation

Exhibit 10.11   Nature of Negotiations in South Africa

Negotiation Factors	Comments
1. Pace of negotiation	Very slow
- Value of time	Time is not money
2. Negotiation strategy	
- Offer vs. agreement	Initial offer relatively high
- Presentation of issues	Priorities not important
- Presentations	Rather informal
- Discussions	Informative to persuasive
- Communication	Indirect, ambiguous
- Interpreters	Necessary depending on country
3. Emphasis on personal relationships	High
4. Influence of third parties	Very high (government)
5. Distance	Rather short
6. Decision making	
- Overall	Not very rational
- Hierarchy	Strong hierarchy
- Collective vs. individual	Rather individual
- Degree of details	Not necessary
- Degree of bureaucracy	High
- Need for agenda	High
7. Administrative factors	
- Need for agent or local partner	Very high
8. Emotional factors	
- Degree of rationality	Not very high
- Sensitivity	High

SOURCE: Format based on Acuff (1993).

for tenders, published in official state publications. Purchasing in central government is highly centralized, the State Tender Board being responsible for procurement for more than 40 government departments. Foreign firms can bid for public purchasing, but through a local agent.

Doing Business in Turkey

Successful business operations in Turkey will require a careful balance of strategic planning and risk assessment. Many economic and demographic factors indicate Turkey's tremendous promise as an emerging market. However, these optimistic figures are often offset by an unstable economic and political environment.

Located at the nexus of Europe, the Middle East, and Central Asia, Turkey occupies a land area slightly larger than that of Texas or Germany. Inhabited by about 65 million people, the U.S. Department of Commerce recently designated Turkey as one the largest emerging markets and seventh-largest emerging economy in the world ("Economic and Financial Statistics," 1999). Over the last several decades, Turkey's population has increasingly become urbanized. Fifty-six percent of the people now reside in cities (primarily Istanbul, Ankara, and Izmir), and this figure continues to climb. Although Turkey is a secular society, the population is overwhelmingly Muslim, with a dominant share of its population identifying itself as ethnically Turkish.

Turkey's history as a nation-state began after World War I, when the Treaty of Sèvres dismantled the Ottoman Empire in 1920. In 1923, the present boundaries of Turkey (with the exception of Alexandretta, acquired in 1939) were established, and Turkey was formally proclaimed a republic. Despite its Islamic background, Turkey is becoming an increasingly Westernized state. As a member of NATO since 1952, Turkey has allowed the establishment of several U.S. military bases. Despite its official standing as a parliamentary democracy, Turkey's political history has been plagued by numerous military interventions.

Although liberalization efforts have been taking place since the early 1950s, Turkey's efforts to shift from a state-run economy to a market-driven system began in earnest during the 1980s. In 1986, the Privatization Law was enacted, and the first state-run enterprise passed into private ownership in 1988. Freed from the burdens of state-owned enterprises, the government has now shifted its investments toward improving the country's infrastructure.

Turkey has experienced some remarkable periods of growth over the last several years. In 1980, total trade volume amounted to $11 billion. By 1999, Turkey's trade volume had swollen to more than $71 billion per year. Exports increased more than sevenfold during this period, growing from $2.9 billion to $26.5 billion. Once consisting primarily of agricultural products, 40% of Turkey's exports are now textiles, and 9% are iron and steel products. As a result of the tremendous transformations occurring in Turkey, its GNP grew an average of 5% per year during the 1990s, hitting an impressive high of 7.6% in 1993 (U.S. Department of Commerce, 2000g).

According to the U.S. Department of Commerce (NTDB, 2000), despite a very promising record of growth in the 1980s and early 1990s, Turkey's progress is still rather inconsistent. In 1994, Turkey's inflation hit a record annual rate of 126%, and GDP dropped to a *negative* 5% for 1994, down

Exhibit 10.12 The Big Emerging Sectors in Turkey	
Major infrastructure projects	Exceeding $18 billion
Industrial chemicals	Exceeding $8.8 billion
Tourism	Exceeding $6 billion
Telecommunications services and equipment	Exceeding $4 billion
Electrical power systems	Exceeding $2.1 billion
Aerospace	Exceeding $1.5 billion
Computers and peripherals	Exceeding $650 million
Environmental technology	Exceeding $500 million
Medical equipment	Exceeding $350 million

SOURCE: U.S. Department of Commerce (2001d).

from 7.6% in 1993. In 1999, the inflation rate decreased to 65%. During the period 1990 to 1999, GDP growth rate averaged around 4% annually. In 1999, a global economic crisis and two serious earthquakes adversely affected Turkey. The public-sector fiscal deficit increased in 1999 to nearly 14% of GDP (interest payment burden amounting to 42%). Direct investment remained low, less than $1 billion annually, because of investors' concerns about economic and political stability. Prospects for the future, however, are brighter. Current political will favors fundamental transformation, including a major economic reform, tighter budget, social security reform, reorganization of national banks, and accelerated privatization.

Despite problems with an unstable political scene causing frequent changes in parliamentary leadership, internal unrest, and friction with bordering countries, Turkey is emerging as a promising market for investment. Indeed, the Turkish government has made a clear effort to create a friendly environment for international investors. For example, in 1980, the Foreign Capital Board was established to ease bureaucratic transactions on the flow of capital. Turkey also permits and welcomes foreign management. Currently, complete foreign ownership is allowed, and 100% of profits may be repatriated. With privatization of state-owned enterprises continuing, many opportunities will continue to open up. The U.S. Department of Commerce (NTDB, 2001) has identified infrastructure, energy, aerospace, information technology, transportation, and environmental technology as the biggest emerging sectors in Turkey (see Exhibit 10.12).

Recently, Turkey simplified its investment procedures by establishing the General Directorate of Foreign Investment (GDFI). This office centralizes investment procedures in one office. Turkey, however, continues to screen investment. The screening mechanism is routine and nondiscriminatory but could be an impediment to the free flow of capital. Furthermore, criteria for rejecting an investment is not limited to national security concerns, and Turkey may impose performance requirements for completing an investment if the investor will benefit from tax or investment incentives.

As Turkey attempts to establish and support rapid economic and industrial growth, projects developing Turkey's infrastructure are numerous. U.S. firms are currently undertaking many projects, ranging from building highways to providing satellite data transmission services. Power plants, water and sewage systems, seaports, and airports continue to be government-emphasized "megaprojects."

The Turkish government employs the build-operate-transfer (BOT) model to carry out these projects. According to this model, the government grants certain concessions to investors for a period of time to develop a particular project. The investors then build, operate, and manage the project for a number of years after its completion to recoup its investment costs and make an additional profit. At the end of the concessionary period, the project is then transferred over to the government. Current BOT projects in Turkey include hydraulic dams, power plants, free trade zones, and various transportation projects.

Turkey's energy sector is also expected to expand. According to the U.S. Department of Commerce (2000g), Turkey will require an average of 2,500 megawatts of additional power capacity each year through 2010 to meet increased demand. U.S. technology in this sector is well-known for its quality and increasingly competitive price. Nuclear reactors, boilers and heat exchangers, turbines, transformers, switch and switch-gear apparatus, and insulated electric conductors will be good sales prospects for American exporters.

Aerospace needs in Turkey continue to expand as well. In 1993, $1.4 billion worth of aircraft and aircraft parts were imported by Turkey. Local production in Turkey is nonexistent, and imports are expected to grow steadily in the future. Although U.S. suppliers will be competing with Western Europe, the United States currently enjoys an 80% market share (U.S. Department of Commerce, NTDB, 2001).

As Turkey continues its urbanization and industrialization process, telecommunications and information technology will be in demand. U.S. imports in this area are expected to grow at an average rate of almost 12% annually over the next few years (U.S. Department of Commerce, NTDB, 2001). Good sales prospects for U.S. exporters include fiber-optic cable, satellite systems, GSM-type pocket phones, data transmission equipment, cable television equipment, and various other electronics.

Exhibit 10.13   Foreign Companies in Turkey

Turkey is considered an attractive market and investment location by many foreign investors. The experience of more than 4,000 foreign capital establishments, including 105 of the *Fortune 500* companies, confirms Turkey as an attractive investment destination.

Coca-Cola's 10th Turkish plant came on-line in June 1997 with an investment of $35 million. It employs 3,000 people and is Coke's biggest plant in Eastern Europe, covering some 40,000 square meters. Coca-Cola has invested $247 million in Turkey since 1991. It plans a further $400-million expansion over the next 3 years. Not all investors are as confident.

Mercedes Benz' only bus-manufacturing plant outside Germany is in Istanbul; Turkey is Marks & Spencer's largest non-U.K. franchise, with the company planning to have 12 stores there by the year 2002; and the French supermarket company Carrefour is to invest $1 billion building 10 supermarkets by 2003 in a joint venture with Turkey's largest holding company, the Sabanci Group.

SOURCE: "Turkey: Infrastructure and Investment" (2002, pp. 13-15).

The demand for cars in Turkey is also rising, necessitating better roads as well as boosting automotive sales. Although Europeans dominate the market with imported parts, joint-venture partnerships, and licensed production, certain parts, such as catalytic converters, engine bearings, radiators, and mufflers, are still viable investment areas. Expanded automobile service facilities will provide an additional market for service equipment totaling $60 to $70 million.

Environmental issues are gradually gaining importance in Turkey and are expected to create many opportunities. Turkey established a Ministry of Environment in 1991 and is now requiring industrial investors to prepare environmental-impact assessments. New regulations regarding waste management and pollution will increase the demand for environmental-engineering products. Although European engineering and contract firms are more active in Turkey than their American counterparts, the opportunities for American firms to exert themselves remain promising.

As a result of these industrial sectors growing at a rapid rate in Turkey, the overall investment potential is excellent as long as the risks due to instability are managed. Although the short-term outlook in Turkey is unstable, the long-term forecast is full of growth. Furthermore, as urbanization continues and standards of living rise, Turkey is expected to develop a promising consumer market. With a relatively young and growing population, demand for American consumer products will soon be quite high. Some of the companies that are very active in Turkey are presented in Exhibit 10.13.

Finally, Turkey's ideal location merits some discussion. Sitting on the edge of Central Asia, the Middle East, and Europe, Turkey might be an excellent base for launching other economic activities throughout the region. As these other markets develop, investors in Turkey will already have an established presence in the region, and perhaps they will be able to parlay this influence and knowledge into successful ventures in other areas.

Doing business in Turkey is not for the fainthearted. Rapidly changing conditions make forecasting problematic, and frequent political problems may cause frustrating delays. (See Exhibit 10.14.) However, although current events in Turkey are erratic and unpredictable, its long-term promise for growth is overwhelmingly positive.

Exhibit 10.14   Nature of Negotiations in Turkey

Negotiation Factors	Comments
1. Pace of negotiation	Slow
- Value of time	Low
2. Negotiation strategy	
- Offer vs. agreement	High initial offer
- Presentation of issues	Personal issues presented
- Presentations	Informal
- Discussions	Seeking agreement
- Communication	Moderately indirect
- Interpreters	Recommended
3. Emphasis on personal relationships	Moderately high
4. Influence of third parties	Moderate
5. Distance	Personal space shorter
6. Decision making	
- Overall	Emotional
- Emphasis	Personalized manners
- Hierarchy	Strong hierarchical
- Collective vs. individual	Collective
- Degree of details	More than average
- Degree of bureaucracy	Moderately high
- Need for agenda	High
7. Administrative factors	
- Need for agent or local partner	Average
8. Emotional factors	
- Degree of rationality	Average
- Sensitivity	High

SOURCE: Format based on Acuff (1993).

11

Conclusions

Some Guidelines for Doing Business in Emerging Markets

After the Asian crisis and more recently, the 11th of September 2001, there has been some discussion about the future of globalization and global trade. Globalization is considered to be in danger because countries may close their borders. The September 11th attack has been referred to by some as "globalization's Chernobyl." However, at the same time there is a strong opinion that the event may have achieved the exact opposite: brought forward an era of globalized government, the cross-border (global) invention of politics and alliances through networking and cooperation. It may just turn out to have accelerated globalization's development (Beck, 2001).

This is particularly true for emerging markets as they realize that they must open up and join the world economy. Whereas the United States and some of the Western countries are afraid of entering a deep recession, there are still enormous opportunities for growth in emerging markets. Foreign direct investment (FDI) flows to these markets, and they continue to grow, as shown by Exhibit 11.1 ("FDI Inflows to Asia," 2001).

Emerging markets indeed provide enormous opportunities for Western firms, but like all opportunities, they also entail some risks. If these markets are not handled properly, firms can lose considerable amounts of money and their reputations. There are at least as many examples of failure as of success. The biggest problems lie in the countries that have not yet achieved political stability, such as Russia after the downfall of the Soviet Union and Indonesia after the Asian crisis and the departure of Suharto. In this respect,

Exhibit 11.1 FDI Inflows to Asia, $ Billions

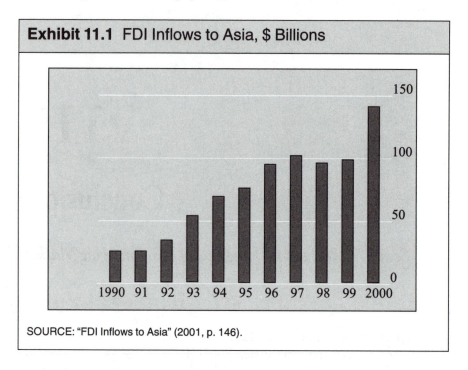

SOURCE: "FDI Inflows to Asia" (2001, p. 146).

some responsibility lies also with the developed world and its organizations, such as the International Monetary Fund (IMF), World Bank, and the European Bank for Reconstruction and Development (EBRD).

Multinational companies (MNCs) cannot, however, wait for politicians and bureaucrats to stabilize markets for them. They have to develop capabilities that allow them to anticipate and respond to upcoming opportunities as well as disruptions and risk in emerging markets. They must find ways of cooperation between private and public sectors and other ways of handling the risks of doing business in emerging markets (Garten, 1997). MNCs also have to balance their acts: Although their arrival in these markets creates several consumer benefits, it also brings a death sentence to a number of local firms (Dawar & Frost, 1999). At the same time, foreign firms face tough competition from local firms. Companies such as Kellogg, Coca Cola, and WalMart have experienced these competitive hurdles in countries such as India and South Korea. As a result, on one hand, MNCs have no choice but to compete in big emerging markets, but on the other hand, they cannot just sell standardized products with standardized marketing strategies. A ranking of emerging markets according to the market size, market growth, and other market opportunities is provided in Exhibit 11.2.

Exhibit 11.2 Ranking of Emerging Markets

Country	Market Size Rank	Market Size Index	Market Growth Rate Rank	Market Growth Rate Index	Market Intensity Rank	Market Intensity Index	Market Consumption Rank	Market Consumption Index	Commercial Infrastructure Rank	Commercial Infrastructure Index	Economic Freedom Rank	Economic Freedom Index	Market Receptivity Rank	Market Receptivity Index	Overall Market Opportunity Rank	Overall Market Opportunity Index
China	1	100	1	100	22	4	4	88	20	13	23	1	5	42	2	83
Hong Kong	21	1	16	51	1	100	9	71	6	50	1	100	10	25	3	66
India	2	76	16	51	23	1	6	80	22	4	22	5	18	11	12	31
Indonesia	3	17	2	81	21	7	7	77	21	9	20	18	15	18	20	13
Malaysia	15	2	15	51	10	28	14	46	14	32	4	65	13	20	8	37
Singapore	23	1			2	89	10	64	3	54	1	100	1	100	1	100
South Korea	10	4	10	59	6	44	5	82	5	52	4	65	4	44	4	58
Thailand	9	6	6	70	16	19	13	53	17	26	6	59	2	56	6	48
Argentina	13	4	3	72	9	28	18	1	4	53	11	38	17	11	10	32
Brazil	4	14	4	71	15	22	16	25	19	16	18	20	6	38	15	23
Chile	16	2	5	71	7	29	15	39	18	24	7	51	8	34	13	31
Mexico	6	8	13	53	14	26	17	12	16	26	15	30	3	50	11	32
South Africa	11	4	14	52	13	26			12	32	12	32	9	27	19	15
Turkey	8	6	11	57	19	15			13	32	12	32	20	6	21	11
Czech Rep.	18	2	20	30	12	27			15	31	3	67	12	22	18	17
Hungary	19	2	12	56	11	27	1	100	9	43	8	40	23	1	14	24
Poland	12	4	7	64	18	16	2	100	10	40	17	22	21	4	16	22
Russia	5	13	21	1	17	18	8	72	11	32	21	17	7	35	22	7

SOURCE: Cavusgil (1997).

As suggested by Prahalad and Lieberthal (1998), MNCs themselves will be transformed as of result of their experiences in the emerging markets. They will have to rethink their cost structures and business models and redesign their product-development processes for success. Prahalad and Lieberthal also suggest that MNCs must answer five basic questions to compete in the big emerging markets (pp. 69-70):

1. Who is the middle class in these markets, and what kind of business model will serve their needs?

2. What are the characteristics of the distribution in these markets, and how are the networks evolving?

3. What mix of local and global leadership is required to avail the opportunities?

4. Should the MNC adopt a consistent strategy for all its business units within one country?

5. Will local partners accelerate the multinational's ability to learn about the local market?

Throughout this book, our message has been that MNCs as well as smaller companies that are planning to reap the benefits of emerging markets must rethink and adapt their strategies to these markets. We have tackled two of the most difficult aspects of doing business in these markets: entry and negotiation strategies. As we can see, while planning to enter and negotiate, in addition to the above questions, you also need to address the following areas:

1. Be able to evaluate the potential of the particular market (Chapter 2).

2. Have some knowledge of the infrastructure and distribution channels (Chapter 2).

3. Decide about the people to negotiate and to run the business in these markets (Chapter 7).

4. Formulate your strategy on a country-by-country basis and not on a regional basis (Chapters 3 and 5) and decide which entry strategy—export, joint venture, licensing, direct investment—will help you to reap the maximum benefits from a particular market.

Evaluating the Potential of Emerging Markets

The economic potential of emerging markets is by now well established. As a group, they comprise more than half of the world population and account for a large share of the world output. These markets pose special challenges

---

Exhibit 11.3 Issues to Be Handled While Entering
Emerging Markets

PHASE ONE: MARKET POTENTIAL ASSESSMENT AND ACCESS
- Engage in formal market potential analysis
- Gather market intelligence
- Employ early monitoring and be a "first mover"
- Tie into informal networks of influence
- Offer financing as well as technical expertise and solutions
- Explore government incentives and procurement

PHASE TWO: MARKET ENTRY
- Choose qualified partners carefully; build their capabilities
- Invest in long-term relationships
- Be culturally sensitive
- Consider adapting product features, selling approach, etc.
- Be prepared to deal with inadequate commercial infrastructure

PHASE THREE: MARKET ESTABLISHMENT
- Adjust to operate in a high inflation/debt environment, leading to commercial and currency risk
- Learn to deal with labor force productivity and motivation issues
- Be prepared to deal with government bureaucracy and regulations
- Look for opportunities in sourcing
- Expand networks and alliances

SOURCE: Cavusgil (1997).

---

for Western firms because Western firms often have difficulty identifying qualified competent intermediaries. The government sector is often involved with issues, such as slow decision-making processes, national debt, and balance of payment, with which many Western managers are not familiar. Moreover, environmental issues, social responsibility of companies, and ethical issues are increasing in emerging markets.

Despite these challenges, no growth-minded company can overlook the potential of emerging markets. For developing strategies to enter these markets, these issues must be handled, as explained in Exhibit 11.3.

1. Market potential estimation and access

2. Market entry

3. Market establishment

Although each of the above steps is critical, the initial assessment of opportunities is especially important. Various techniques can be used, such as gathering background information (desk research), evaluating unsolicited inquiries from foreign customers, and monitoring competitor activity (Cavusgil, 1997).

A formal and systematic analysis of aggregate can be particularly fruitful. One way of assessing the market is as done by *The Economist,* in which an index is developed to measure market potential in emerging markets. First, seven economic, political, and social variables are selected to characterize a market's attractiveness. Next, an index is created to obtain raw values of these variables by standardizing the items and putting them into a scale of 1 to 100 by a formula (*standardization* is a statistical procedure enabling us to directly compare variables with very different distributions). Third, the relative importance of each dimension is determined by interviewing a small number of international business professionals and educators (a *delphi* process). The results are the *relative weight* shown in Exhibit 11.4.

The Seven Dimensions of Market Opportunity

Each of the dimensions that constitute the Market Opportunity Index (MOI) is described briefly as follows:

Market Size. Measured by a country's total population, market size serves as a rough estimate of market potential. Although the entire country may not be targeted by any one company, total population indicates the relative importance of that country's market. The relative weight for this variable is 4/20.

Market Growth Rate. Also measured by a single variable, average annual growth rate of industry, this important dimension was given a weight of 3/20. Industrialization triggers expenditures on a wide variety of goods and services.

Market Intensity. Two variables were used to measure market intensity: (a) purchasing-power parity (PPP) estimates of gross national product (GNP) per capita and (b) personal consumption expenditure per capita, in U.S. dollars. PPP is measured by wages, salaries, employee benefits, corporate earnings, income from business operations, net interest, and royalties, using the United States as a benchmark (*Value* = 100 for the United States, with other countries estimated proportionately). Personal-consumption

Exhibit 11.4   Dimensions and Measures of Market Potential

DIMENSION	WEIGHT	MEASURES USED
Market Size	4/20	• Total population
Market Growth Rate	3/20	• Average annual growth rate of industry
Market Intensity	3/20	• Purchasing Power Parity estimates of GNP per capita (50% weight) • Private consumption expenditure per capita (50% weight)
Market Consumption Capacity	2/20	• Size of the middle class
Commercial Infrastructure	2/20	• Telephone mainlines per capita (20% weight) • Paved road density (20% weight) • Trucks and buses per capita (20% weight) • Population per retail outlet (20% weight) • Percentage of homes with color TV (20% weight)
Economic Freedom	2/20	• The Economic Freedom Index (Johnson & Sheehy, 1995), which measures trade policy, taxation policy, government consumption of economic output, monetary and banking policy, capital flows and foreign investment, banking policy, wage and price controls, property rights, regulatory climate, and black-market activity.
Market Receptivity	4/20	• Average annual growth rate of imports from USA over the past five years (60% weight) • Per capita imports from USA (40% weight)

SOURCE: Cavusgil (1997).

expenditure per capita represents the value of purchases by households and private nonprofit institutions on current goods and services less the sale of similar goods, divided by the total population. Unlike GNP per capita, this variable is oriented more toward private expenditures and excludes business transactions. To produce a single index of market intensity, each measure was converted to a Z-score and averaged for each country, with the mean values expressed by a 1 to 100 scale. The weight of this dimension is 3/20.

Market Consumption Capacity. The size of the middle class was used as a measure of market consumption capacity. The proportion of the population earning 20% to 30% of a nation's income indicates the spread of the consumption base. Neither poor nor rich, middle-class consumers have a reasonable degree of spending capacity. For most marketers of consumer goods, this is the target segment. The dimension was given a weight of 2/20.

Commercial Infrastructure. The ease of access to distribution and communication channels indicates the attractiveness of a market from the standpoint of commercial infrastructure. Five variables measure this dimension: telephone mainlines per capita, density of paved roads, trucks and buses per capita, population per retail outlet, and percentage of homes with color television sets. All five were standardized and given equal weight within the dimension. Then, converted into a 1 to 100 scale, the dimension was weighted 2/20.

Economic Freedom. The measure of economic freedom is an index developed for the Heritage Foundation by Johnson and Sheehy (1995). It incorporates trade and taxation policy, government consumption of economic output, monetary and banking policy, capital flows and foreign investment, wage and price controls, property rights, regulatory policy, and black-market activity. The index ranges from 10 to 5 (*most free* to *least free*), but for the purposes of this study, it was reversed (so that higher values represent freer markets) and reconverted into a 1 to 100 scale. The dimension was weighted as 2/20.

Market Receptivity. The extent to which a foreign market is open to U.S. imports is represented by two variables: per capita imports from the United States and the average annual growth in U.S. imports over the past 5 years. The dimension has a weight of 4/20.

Limitations of the Index

Managers need to use some care in applying the index presented in Exhibit 11.4. First, the MOI is an aggregate measure of an emerging market's (EM) attractiveness and is useful only in the initial stage of qualifying and ranking countries. For the market entry and market establishment stages, much more detailed and in-depth analysis is required, such as that provided in Cavusgil (1986). Second, although the seven dimensions provide a comprehensive characterization, additional aspects and alternative measures can be considered. For example, a more explicit representation of risk (commercial, monetary, and political) can be accommodated. In the MOI, risk is embedded in the market receptivity dimension, because it reflects the openness of a country's U.S. imports. Third, the index is designed primarily for exporting companies. Businesses considering other forms of entry, such as direct investments and equity ventures, need to examine additional variables. A final caveat about the reliability of the statistics used: The most credible sources and most recent available data were used, but as with any data set, there is always room for improvement.

Measuring Market Attractiveness Using the MOI

With the state limitations in mind, the MOI can provide managers with valuable insights into the nature of EMs. Although the EMs do share certain features, the index shows that considerable diversity remains. The rankings for each dimension (shown in Exhibit 11.2) reveal significant variation. China, for example, is first in market size, but next to last in market intensity, low in commercial infrastructure, and last in economic freedom. Nevertheless, because of weighting, China's MOI is high.

EMs near the top in overall market opportunity are Singapore, China, Hong Kong, South Korea, Israel, Thailand, Greece, and Malaysia. It is noteworthy that six of these are in Asia. This is further evidence that Western companies eager to tap high-growth markets should concentrate on the Far East and develop their capabilities and resources accordingly. Progressive managers should be building relationships with potential business partners in these markets. Other considerations, of course, need to be examined. Singapore ranks first among EMs but is limited in resources and population. Companies should also be developing a regional strategy to maximize potential synergies among Asian countries.

It is important for managers to focus especially on the dimensions and measures most relevant to their own products or services, such as the target market, distribution channels, and intensity of competition. For example, marketers of soft drinks will concentrate on surrogate indicators of product demand that are very different from those examined by medical-equipment marketers. It is also reasonable to expect that the weight of each dimension may have to be revised for different companies and circumstances.

The MOI rankings are perhaps most useful for gaining insight about individual markets in a comparative sense. The index helps reduce the complexity of evaluating the relative attractiveness of EMs. With this knowledge of the trade-offs involved in choosing among EMs, managers can be more objective and systematic in selecting candidate markets. Once the number to be investigated is reduced to a manageable few, managers then can proceed to in-depth analysis of the most promising EMs.

The value of an approach that ranks countries by their attractiveness as export markets can best be achieved over time. It is hoped that the rankings will be validated in time as they parallel actual exports to those countries. Thoughtful managers may wish to monitor the degree to which their exports correspond to the MOI, as well as the individual dimensions and measures. Adjustments may need to be made to the weights, dimensions, or measures if the MOI is failing to anticipate actual export activity.

Managers should also be cognizant of major macroeconomic events or country-specific developments that can cause readjustments in the rankings. For example, India—now ranked 12th overall—may fall several places if market liberalization is fundamentally reversed by a conservative political regime. Accession of Hungary and Poland into the European Union may lead to their transacting a higher proportion of external trade with Western Europe than with the United States. Rapid introduction of modern banking and legal infrastructure, on the other hand, should enable Russia to move into a position of a more attractive export market than is suggested by its current MOI ranking. And in South America, the establishment of the Mercosur Trading Area should substantially enhance the attractiveness of countries such as Argentina and Brazil.

Considering all these circumstances, companies need to seriously look into these markets. Even the poorest of these markets provide enormous opportunities. The investments in these markets do not require a lot of resources relative to Western markets. Labor, materials, and marketing are very cheap, but potential for profit is high (Prahalad, 2001). According to Prahalad, there are 4 billion new customers in existing markets: "Four billion people are joining the pre-markets of the world, and they are yearning for a way of life they see on TV and Internet. They can see how the rest of the world lives, and they are eager to become consumers" (p. 11). The education levels and health and income levels are increasing in most EMs, and according to the World Bank, the average economic growth rate of those countries was triple (2.8%) the high-income Western countries (0.9%) in 2001, the year of crisis. Next year, the growth rate in EMs will pick up to about 3.8%, whereas in developed countries it will be stagnant, if not lower than it was in 2001 (Prahalad, 2001).

There is therefore a reason to be upbeat about emerging markets, especially at a time when Western markets are slowing down. The emerging markets might well be the saviors for many countries.

References

Acuff, F. (1993). *How to negotiate anything with anyone anywhere in the world.* New York: American Management Association.

All the world's a shop. (1995, March 4). *The Economist,* pp. 15-17.

Analysts predict China will attract only $40 billion in foreign investment in 2000. (2000, January 6). Retrieved from the World Wide Web on May 5th, 2001, at http://www.chinaonline.com.

An India that still says no. (1995, August 12). *The Economist,* p. 12.

Another blow to Mercosur. (2001, March 31). *The Economist,* pp. 33-34.

Austin, J. E. (1990). *Managing in developing countries: Strategic analysis and operating techniques* (pp. 167-176). New York: Free Press.

Autopolis. (2001, October). *Global overview.* Retrieved from the World Wide Web on March 27, 2002, at http://www.autopolis.com/publications.htm.

Autopolis. (2002, March). *Asian market reports.* Retrieved from the World Wide Web on March 27, 2002, at http://www.autopolis.com/publications.htm.

Back on the pitch. (1997, December 6). *The Economist,* pp. S3-S5.

Bangko Sentralng Pilipinas. (2000). *International financial statistics: Indonesia.* Manila: Central Bank of the Philippines.

Bank of Thailand. (2000). *Manufacturing in 2000, manufacturing production index.* Retrieved from the World Wide Web on March 23, 2002, at http://www.bot.or.th/BOTHomepage/DataBank/Real_Sector/Industry/Industry_Situation/annual/6-14-2001-Eng-i/Year2000-Eng.pdf.

Bank of Thailand. (2001). *Foreign trade and balance of payments.* Retrieved from the World Wide Web on January 10, 2001, at http://www.bot.or.th/bothomepage/databank/EconData/Econ&Finance/index3e.htm.

Barnathan, J., Moshavi, S., Dawley, H., Sunita, W., & Chang, H. (1995, July 3). Passage back to India. *Business Week,* pp. 44-45.

Beck, U. (2001, November 5). The fight for a cosmopolitan future. *New Statesman,* p. 33.

Big emerging markets. (March, 1994). *Business America,* pp. 4-6.

Boland, V. (1995, April 18). Jewel in the Czech crown. *Financial Times, FT Exporter,* p. 16.

Buckley, P., & Ghauri, P. (1994). *The economics of change in East and Central Europe: Its impact on international business.* London: ITB.

Buckley, P., & Ghauri, P. (Eds.). (1999). *The internationalization of the firm: A reader.* London: ITB.

Budget constraints vs. big projects. (2000, June). *Business in Thailand Magazine.* Retrieved from the World Wide Web on April 4, 2002, at http://www.businessinthailandmag.com/archive/jun00/14.html.

Bussard, W. A. (1984). *Results of a countertrade survey* (Press release). New York: Foreign Trade Council.

Cateora, P., & Ghauri, P. (2000). *International marketing: European edition.* London: McGraw-Hill.

Cavusgil, S. T. (1986). Global dimensions of marketing. In P. E Murphy & B. M. Enis (Eds.), *Marketing.* Glenview, IL: Scott, Foresman.

Cavusgil, S. T. (1997, January/February). Measuring the potential of emerging markets: An indexing approach. *Business Horizon,* pp. 87-92.

Cavusgil, S. T., Yaprak, A., & Poh-Lin Yeoh. (1993). A decision-making framework for global sourcing. *International Business Review, 2*(2), 143-155.

Central and Eastern Europe Business Information Center. (2001). *Hungary commercial country guide 2001.* Retrieved from the World Wide Web on May 5, 2001, at http://www.mac.doc.gov/eebic/countryr/HUNGARY/ccg2001/EST.htm.

Central Bank of Malaysia. (2001). *BNM annual report 2001.* Retrieved from the World Wide Web on March 24, 2002, at http://www.bnm.gov.my/en/Publications/ar.asp?yr=2001.

Central Intelligence Agency. (2000). *CIA world factbook 2000.* Washington, DC: Brassey's.

Central Intelligence Agency. (2001). *CIA world factbook 2001.* Washington, DC: Brassey's.

Chambers, C. M., Chambers, P. E., & Whitehead, J. C. (1993). Environmental preservation and corporate involvement: Green products and debt-for-nature swaps. *Review of Business, 15*(1), 17-21.

Clarke, P. (2001, April 30). Fab contracting boosts Hungary. *Electronic Engineering Times,* p. 54.

Convertibility Law. (1991). Law 23,928, Austral Convertibility Act, March 27, 1991.

Copeland, L., & Griggs, L. (1985). *Going international: How to make friends and deal effectively in the global marketplace.* New York: Plyme.

Cronin, M. J. (1994). The desktop as global village. *Doing business on the Internet* (pp. 90-91). New York: Van Nostrand Reinhold.

Czech Agency for Foreign Investment. (2000). *News.* Retrieved from the World Wide Web on December 12, 2000, at http://www.czechinvest.org.

Czech National Bank. (2000). *Czech Republic: Inward foreign direct investment by industry and country, 1993–2000.* Retrieved from the World Wide Web on March 20, 2002, at http://www.cnb.cz/en/index.html.

Dalgic, T., & Heijblom, R. (1996). International marketing blunders revisited—Some lessons for managers. *Journal of International Marketing, 1,* 84-87.

Dana, P. L. (1997). A contrast of Argentina and Uruguay: The effects of government policy on entrepreneurship. *Journal of Small Business Management, 35*(2), pp. 99-104.

Daniels, J. D., & and Radebaugh, L. H. (1995). *International business: Environments and operations* (7th ed., pp. 117-190). Reading, MA: Addison-Wesley.

Davis, P. (1993, September). Investors' hunger for higher returns meets an emerging appetite for capital. *Euromoney,* pp. 2-6.

Dawar, N., & Frost, T. (1999, March-April). Competing with giants: Survival strategies for local companies in emerging markets. *Harvard Business Review,* pp. 119-129.

A decline without parallel: Argentina's collapse. (2002, March 2). *The Economist* (Special report).

Delphos, W. (1992, March). Funds for global greening. *Global Trade,* p. 29.

Dohrs, L. S. (1987, Spring). Thailand: Good times mean more bickering. *Southeast Asia Business,* pp. 20-22.

Dunbar, E., & Katcher, A. (1990, September). Preparing managers for foreign assignments. *Training and Development Journal,* pp. 45-46.

Dunham, R. (1993, November). Developing countries drawing power. *Accountancy,* pp. 54-55.

Dunning, J. H. (1994). The prospects for foreign direct investment in Central and Eastern Europe. In P. Buckley & P. Ghauri (Eds.), *The economics of change in East and Central Europe: Its impact on international business.* London: Academic Press.

The Economist. (January 13, 2001, p. 110).

Economic and financial statistics on 25 emerging economies. (1999, October 2). *The Economist,* p. 116.

Economist Intelligence Unit. (1999, April 4). Business news: Carlsberg buys the Svyturys brewery. *Country Report: Lithuania*, p. 29.

Economist Intelligence Unit. (2000). EUI business environment ratings. *Country indicators, China, Philippines, and Thailand.* Retrieved from the World Wide Web on April 20, 2001, at http://www.eiu.com/.

Economist Intelligence Unit. (2001, July 16). Russia: GM seals AvtoVAZ deal. *Country Monitor*, p. 21.

Economist Intelligence Unit and Financial Times. (1994, November 23) P. 21.

Elashmawi, F. (1991, February). Multicultural management: New skills for global success. *Tokyo Business Today*, pp. 54-56.

Emerging market indicators. (2001, January 13). *The Economist*, p. 110.

Euro-China Association for Management Development. (1986). *Chinese culture and management.* Brussels, Belgium: European Foundation for Management Development, International Association Center.

Euromonitor. (1998). *Eastern Europe: A directory and sourcebook.* London: Euromonitor Publishers.

European Bank for Reconstruction and Development. (2000). Projects approved in 2000: Poland. *Annual report 2000.* Retrieved from the World Wide Web on March 13, 2001, at http://www.ebrd.org/english/pubs/index.htm.

FDI inflows to Asia. (2001, June 23). *The Economist*, p. 146.

Fisher, R., & Ury, W. (1991). *Getting past no: Negotiating with difficult people.* New York: Bantam.

Fisher, R., Ury, W., & Patten, B. (1991). *Getting to yes: Negotiating agreement without giving in* (2nd ed., p. 40). New York: Penguin Books.

Foreign Corrupt Practices Act. (1977). United States Code 15, Commerce and Trade, Chapter 2B: Securities Exchanges, §§ 78dd-1, *et seq.*

Foreign direct investment in China. (2000, November-December). *The China Business Review*, pp. 10-11.

Franklin, D., & Moreton, E. (1994, April 20). A little late in learning the facts. *The Economist*, p. 5.

Ganguly, S. (1998, February). *India in 1997: Another year of turmoil*, pp. 126-134.

Garten, J. (1997). *The big ten: The big emerging markets and how they will change our lives.* New York: Basic Books.

Gearing, J. (1999, December 3). Aliens no longer: How a new Thai law affects foreign investors. *Asiaweek.* Retrieved from the World Wide Web on March 23, 2002, at http://www.asiaweek.com/asiaweek/magazine/99/1203/biz.thailand.reform.html.

Gesteland, R. R. (1996). *Cross-cultural business behavior.* Copenhagen, Denmark: Copenhagen Business School Press.

Getting from here to there. (2000, May 6). *The Economist*, p. 3.

Ghauri, P. N. (1986). Guidelines for international business negotiations. *International Marketing Review 3*(3), 72-82.

Ghauri, P. N. (1995). Marketing to Eastern Europe. In M. Baker (Ed.), *Marketing: Theory and practice.* London: McMillan.

Ghauri, P. N. (1999). Relationship games: Creating competitive advantage through cooperation. In S. Urban (Ed.), *Relations of complex organizational systems* (pp. 59-83). Wiesbaden, Germany: Gabler.

Ghauri, P. N. (2000). Using cooperative strategies to compete in a changing world. In C. P. Rao (Ed.), *Globalization and its managerial implications* (pp. 29-43). Westport, CT: Quoram.

Ghauri, P. N., & Fang, T. (2001). Understanding Chinese negotiation behavior: A sociocultural perspective. *Journal of World Business, 36*(3), 303-325.

Ghauri, P. N., & Holstius, K. (1996). The role of matching in the foreign market entry process in the Baltic states. *European Journal of Marketing, 30*(2), 75-88.

Ghauri, P. N., & Usunier, J. C. (1996). *International business negotiations*. Oxford, UK: Pergamon.

GM likely to source forgings from India. (1993, March 28,). *Economic Times*, p. 16.

Gomes-Casseres, B. (1994, July-August). Group versus group: How alliance networks compete. *Harvard Business Review*, pp. 62-74.

Graham, J., & Herberger, R. A., Jr. (1983, July–August). Negotiators abroad: Don't shoot from the hip. *Harvard Business Review*, pp. 160-168.

Gross, A. C., Hester, E. D., & Javalgi, R. G. (1995, October). Industry corner: Global telecommunications: The market and the industry. *Business Economics*, pp. 55-60.

G-III Apparel launches a global sourcing unit. (1993, May). *Women's Wear Daily*, p. 10.

Guy, C. M. (1998, May). Controlling new retail spaces: The impress of planning policies in Western Europe. *Urban Studies*, pp. 953-979.

Harris, P. R., & Moran, R. T. (1996). *Managing cultural differences* (4th ed., pp. 49-50). Texas: Gulf.

Harrison, R., & Hopkins, R. (1967). The design of cross-cultural training: An alternative to the university model. *Journal of Applied Behavioral Science, 3*(4), 431-460.

Havlik, P. (Ed.). (1991). *Dismantling the command economy in Eastern Europe*. Boulder, CO: Westview.

He wants your job. (1993, June 1). *The Economist*, p. 15.

Hendon, D. W., Hendon, R. A., & Herbig, P. (1996). *Cross-cultural business negotiations*. Westport, CT: Quorum Books.

Hertzfeld, J. M. (1991, January-February). Joint ventures: Saving the Soviets from perestroika. *Harvard Business Review*, pp. 80-91.

Hill, C. W. (2001). *International business: Competing in the global marketplace* (3rd ed.). Irwin: McGraw-Hill.

Ikle, F. C. (1964). *How nations negotiate*. New York: Praeger.

Indian Investment Center. (2000). *India's investment climate*. Retrieved from the World Wide Web on June 12, 2001, at http://iic.nic.in/vsiic/iic2_c.htm.

International Monetary Fund. (2000a). *Direction of trade statistics yearbook*. Washington, DC: Author.

International Monetary Fund. (2000b). *International capital markets: Developments, prospects, and key issues*. Washington, DC: Author.

International Monetary Fund. (2000c). *People's Republic of China and the IMF*. Retrieved from the World Wide Web on February 21, 2001, at http://www.imf.org/external/country/CHN/index.htm.

International Monetary Fund. (2000d, October). *World economic outlook: Focus on transition economies*. Retrieved from the World Wide Web on February 4, 2002, at http://www.imf.org/external/pubs/ft/weo/2000/02/index.htm.

International Monetary Fund. (2001). *Thailand and the IMF*. Retrieved from the World Wide Web on May 21, 2001, at http://www.imf.org/external/country/THA/index.htm.

Jain, S., & Tucker, L. R. (1994). Market opportunities in Eastern Europe: MNCs response. In P. Buckley & P. Ghauri (Eds.), *The economics of change in East and Central Europe: Its impact on international business*. London: Academic Press.

Jansson, H. (1986). Purchasing strategies of transnational corporations in import substitution countries. In S. T. Cavusgil (Ed.), *Advances in international marketing*. Greenwich, CT: JAI.

Japan External Trade Organization. (2000). *Survey 2000*. Available on the World Wide Web at http://www.jetro.go.jp.

Jayasankaran, S. (1995, January 19). Privatization pioneer. *Far Eastern Economic Review*, p. 42.

Jayasankaran, S. (2001, January 25). National burden. *Far Eastern Economic Review*, pp. 53-54.

Jobless and joyless. (2001, February 24). *The Economist*, p. 7.

Johnson, B. T., & Sheehy, T. P. (1995). *Index of economic freedom*. Washington, DC: Heritage Foundation.

Kaushik, S. (1996, September-October). India's democratic economic transformation. *Challenge*, pp. 54-61.

Kenan Institute Asia. (2000, September 1). *North Carolina governor says education and workforce training are the key factors in attracting investment*. Retrieved from the World Wide Web on February 25, 2001, at http://www.kiasia.org/press/ncgovernor.htm.

Knutsson, J. (1986). Chinese commercial negotiating behavior: Institutional and cultural determinants. In Euro-China Association for Management Development, *Chinese culture and management* (p. 20). Brussels, Belgium: European Foundation for Management Development, International Association Center.

Kohn, L. (1993, Winter/Spring). Global sourcing: Broadening your supply horizons. *Business Forum*, pp. 17-20.

Kraljic, A. P. (1990, Winter). The economic gap separating East and West. *Columbia Journal of World Business*, pp. 14-19.

Krugman, P. (1994, July-August). Does Third World growth hurt First World prosperity? *Harvard Buisiness Review*, p. 153.

Laynard, R. (1995, January 21). Four reasons for gloom. *The Economist*, p. 32.

Leahy, J. (2000, January 17). M&A activity in non-Japan Asia—to record high. *Financial Times*, p. 21.

Levin, Baron F. (1999, October). Pit stop. *Business Mexico*, pp. 38-44.

Lewicki, R. J., Letterer, J. A., Minton, J. W., & Sanders, D. M. (1994). *Negotiation* (2nd ed., pp. 110-111). Homewood, IL: Irwin.

Malaysian Industrial Development Authority. (2001). *Approved manufacturing projects*. Retrieved from the World Wide Web on March 24, 2002, at http://www.mida.gov.my/stats.html.

McCormick & Co., flavor division: Purchasing bridges the gap between suppliers and customers. (1993, August). *CPI-Purchasing*, p. 14.

McDonald, H. (1995, January 12). No more fizz: Coca-Cola falls out with India's parle foods. *Far Eastern Economic Review*, January, pp. 74-75.

Mendenhall, M., & Oddou, G. (1985). The dimensions of expatriate acculturation: A review. *Academy of Management Review, 10*, 39-47.

Ministry of Economy, Argentina. (2001). *Investment climate*. Retrieved from the World Wide Web on April 20, 2001, at http://www.mecon.gov.ar/default/htm.

Ministry of Finance, Government of India. (2001). *Economic survey 2000-2001*. Retrieved from the World Wide Web on April 4, 2002, at http://indiabudget.nic.in/es2000-01/.

Monczka, R., & Trent, R. (1991, Spring). Global sourcing: A development approach. *International Journal of Purchasing and Materials Management*, pp. 1-8.

Moshavi, S. (1995a, August 21). India's pols may be turning against foreign business. *Business Week*, p. 44.

Moshavi, S. (1995b, May 1). A passage to India for the world's carmakers. *Business Week*, p. 31.

Moshavi, S., & Engardio, P. (1995, January 30). India shakes off its shackles: Free-market reforms are stirring up the country's long-stagnant economy. *Business Week*, pp. 48-49.

Moskin, R. (1988, January). The Third World asks for a fair deal. *World Press Review*, pp. 34-36.

Nadel, J. (1987). *Cracking the global market* (pp. 89-116). New York: Amacom.

National Bank of Hungary. (2001). *Balance of payment, international investment position*. Retrieved from the World Wide Web on January 24, 2001, at http://www.mnb.hu/index-a.htm.

Newby, A. (2000a, March). Country risk rankings. *Euromoney,* pp. 106-110.

Newby, A. (2000b, March). Methodology. *Euromoney,* pp. 109-110.

Nicholson, M. (1995, June 20). The politics of Indian power. *Financial Times,* p. 23.

Number of foreign direct investment projects licensed 1999 by main counterparts. (2002). *Investment projects.* Vietnamtourism. Retrieved from the World Wide Web on March 18, 2002, at http://www.vietnamtourism.gov.vn/e_pages/duan-dautu/gtchung/sdtda_ptdoitac.html.

Organization for Economic Cooperation and Development. (2000). *OECD documentation: China.* Retrieved from the World Wide Web on May 23, 2001, at http://www.oecd.org/EN/documentation/0,,EN-documentation-0-nodirectorate-CN-no-no-0,FF.html.

Powell, A. (1995). *On restructuring, regulation and competition in utility industries.* Inter-American Development Bank. Retrieved from the World Wide Web on March 20, 2002, at http://www.iadb.org/OCE/pdf/329.pdf.

Prahalad, C. K., & Lieberthal, K. (1998, July-August). The end of corporate imperialism. *Harvard Business Review,* pp. 69-79.

Pruitt, W. G., & Rubin, J. Z. (1986). *Social conflict: Escalation, statement and resolution.* New York: Random House.

Pt. Bimantara Citra Tbk. (2001). Retrieved from the World Wide Web on April 2, 2001, at http://www.bimantara.co.id/biru/menu.asp.

Purchasing in the CPI, 1983 to 2003: A look back and a glance ahead. (1993, September). *CPI-Purchasing,* p. 24.

Rahul, J. (1992, November 16). India is opening for business. *Fortune,* pp. 128-130.

Rapoport, C. (1994, September 19). Nestlé's brand building machine. *Fortune,* pp. 147-156.

Robinson, A. (1995a, April 18). Region emerges as a supplier. *Financial Times, FT Exporter,* p. 13.

Robinson, A. (1995b, April 18). Symbol of peaceful revolution. *Financial Times, FT Exporter,* p. 14.

Ronen, S. (1990). Training the international assignee. *Training and career development.* San Francisco: Jossey-Bass.

Root, F. (1987). Chapter 1: Designing entry strategies for international markets. *Entry strategies for international markets.* Lexington, MA: Lexington Books.

Rowley, I. (2000, September). Clear skies ahead. *Institutional Investor,* pp. 181-188.

Russia's Bankruptcy Bears. (1994, March 19). *The Economist,* pp. 73-74.

Schwab, K., & Smadja, C. (1994, November-December). The new rules of the game in a world of many players. *Harvard Business Review,* pp. 40-50.

Schwarz, A. (1995a, March 2). Making the switch. *Far Eastern Economic Review,* p. 60.

Schwarz, A. (1995b, November 9). Too fast for comfort. *Far Eastern Economic Review,* pp. 67-68.

Second thoughts on going global. (1995, March 13). *Business Week,* pp. 16-30.

Sheth, J., & Parvatiyar, A. (1992). Towards a theory of business alliance formation. *Scandinavian International Business Review, 1*(3), 71-87.

Simons, R. (1994). How new top managers use control systems as levers of strategic renewal. *Strategic Management Journal, 15,* 169-189.

Smith, G., & Malkin, E. (1995, April 3). Zedillo hits the road: But so far, his austerity package is no crowd-pleaser. *Business Week,* pp. 66-67.

South Africa: A golden touch? (2000, February 21). *Business Week,* p. 48.

South Africa's National Trade and Investment Promotion Agency. (2001). *Foreign companies in South Africa, by country.* Retrieved from the World Wide Web on March 20, 2002, at http://www.tradeandinvestmentsa.org.za/_index.html.

State Committee of the Russian Federation on Statistics. (2000). Population and labour market. *Handbook of Russia 2000.* Retrieved from the World Wide Web on February 20, 2002, at http://www.gks.ru/scripts/eng/1c.exe?XXXX75R.1.

Steingraber, F. (1992, Fall). Compete globally or you don't compete at all. *NewsACTION,* pp. 14-15.

Suharto's pals get a taste of the free market. (1995, June 26). *Business Week,* pp. 23.

Sung, J. (1992, July). Rio earth summit. *Business Korea,* pp. 34-35.

A survey of retailing. (1995, March 4). *The Economist,* pp. 1-18.

Templeman, J. (1995, January 30). Germans finally hop the Orient Express. *Business Week,* p. 16.

Thailand Board of Investment. (2001). *BOI incentives.* Retrieved from the World Wide Web on March 24, 2002, at http://www.boi.go.th/english/boi/incentives_conditions.html.

Thompson Financial. (2000, January 15). Ozgorkey Coca-Cola/Coca-Cola Beverages PLC. *Thomson Financial Securities Data—M&A.*

Tietz, B. (1994). The opening up of Eastern Europe: The implications for Western businesses. In P. Buckley & P. Ghauri (Eds.), *The economics of change in East and Central Europe. Its impact on international business.* London: Academic Press.

Toannou, L. (1994, June). Cultivating the new expatriate executive. *International Business,* pp. 40-50.

Transparency International. (2000). *Corruption perception index 2000.* Retrieved from the World Wide Web on March 20, 2002, at http://www.transparency.org/cpi/2000/cpi2000.html#cpi.

Transportation Research Group. (1999). *Aviation services in Vietnam: A strategic entry report.* San Diego, CA: Icon Group International.

Turkey: Infrastructure and investment. (2002, March 26). *Financial Times,* pp. 13-15.

2002 vision. (1994, October 1). *The Economist,* p. 89.

Union Bank of Switzerland. (1999). *Prices and earnings around the globe.* Zurich: Author.

United Nations. (1999). *1998 international trade statistics yearbook* (Country tables). New York: Author.

United Nations Conference on Trade and Development. (2000). *UNCTAD world investment report 2000: Cross-border mergers and acquisitions and development.* Retrieved from the World Wide Web on October 7, 2001, at http://www.unctad.org/wir/contents/wir00content.en.htm.

United Nations Population Division, Department of Economics and Social Information and Policy Analysis. *World population—1998.* Retrieved from the World Wide Web on June 5th, 2001, at http://www.undp.org/popin/wdtrends/p98/p98.htm.

U.S. Census Bureau. (2000). *U.S. Trade balance with Poland.* Retrieved from the World Wide Web on February 24, 2001, at http://www.census.gov/foreign-trade/balance/c4550.html.

U.S. Department of Commerce. Economics and Statistics Administration. Census Bureau. National Trade Data Bank. (1995). CD-ROM.

U.S. Department of Commerce. Economics and Statistics Administration. Census Bureau. National Trade Data Bank. (1999). CD-ROM.

U.S. Department of Commerce. Economics and Statistics Administration. Census Bureau. National Trade Data Bank. (2000). CD-ROM.

U.S. Department of Commerce. (1995a). *Country commercial guide for Argentina.* Washington, DC: U.S. Commercial Service.

U.S. Department of Commerce. (1995b). *Country commercial guide for Brazil.* Washington, DC: U.S. Commercial Service.

U.S. Department of Commerce. (1995c). *Country commercial guide for Mexico.* Washington, DC: U.S. Commercial Service.

U.S. Department of Commerce. (1999a). *Country commercial guide for Mexico.* Washington, DC: U.S. Commercial Service.

U.S. Department of Commerce. (2000a). *Country commercial guide for Argentina.* Washington, DC: U.S. Commercial Service.

U.S. Department of Commerce. (2000b). *Country commercial guide for Brazil.* Washington, DC: U.S. Commercial Service.

U.S. Department of Commerce. (2000c). *Country commercial guide for Chile.* Washington, DC: U.S. Commercial Service.

U.S. Department of Commerce. (2000d). *Country commercial guide for India.* Washington, DC: U.S. Commercial Service.

U.S. Department of Commerce. (2000e). *Country commercial guide for Mexico.* Washington, DC: U.S. Commercial Service.

U.S. Department of Commerce. (2000f). *Country commercial guides for South Africa.* Washington, DC: U.S. Commercial Service.

U.S. Department of Commerce. (2000g). *Country commercial guide for Turkey.* Washington, DC: U.S. Commercial Service.

U.S. Department of Commerce. (2000h). *Country commercial guide for Indonesia.* Washington, DC: U.S. Commercial Service.

U.S. Department of Commerce. (2000i). *Country commercial guide for Malaysia.* Washington, DC: U.S. Commercial Service.

U.S. Department of Commerce. (2000j). *Country commercial guide for Vietnam.* Washington, DC: U.S. Commercial Service.

U.S. Department of Commerce. (2000k). *Country commercial guide for Russia.* Washington, DC: U.S. Commercial Service.

U.S. Department of Commerce. (2000l). *Country commercial guide for Poland.* Washington, DC: U.S. Commercial Service.

U.S. Department of Commerce. (2000m). *Country commercial guide for Hungary.* Washington, DC: U.S. Commercial Service.

U.S. Department of Commerce. (2000n). *Country commercial guide for Czech Republic.* Washington, DC: U.S. Commercial Service.

U.S. Department of Commerce. (2001a). *Country commercial guide for Argentina.* Washington, DC: U.S. Commercial Service.

U.S. Department of Commerce. (2001b). *Country commercial guide for Brazil.* Washington, DC: U.S. Commercial Service.

U.S. Department of Commerce. (2001c). *Country commercial guide for Mexico.* Washington, DC: U.S. Commercial Service.

U.S. Department of Commerce. (2001d). *Country commercial guide for Turkey.* Washington, DC: U.S. Commercial Service.

U.S. Department of Commerce. (2001e). *Country commercial guide for Thailand.* Washington, DC: U.S. Commercial Service.

U.S. Department of State. (1999). *Background notes: Mexico, August 1999.* Released by the Bureau of Western Hemisphere Affairs, U.S. Department of State.

U.S. Department of State. (2000). *Background notes: Mexico, April 2000.* Released by the Bureau of Western Hemisphere Affairs, U.S. Department of State. Washington, DC: Author.

U.S. Department of State. (2001). *Background notes: Mexico, April 2001.* Released by the Bureau of Western Hemisphere Affairs, U.S. Department of State. Washington DC: Author.

U.S. Energy Information Administration. (2000). Azerbaijan: Production sharing agreements. *Azerbaijan country analysis brief.* Retrieved from the World Wide Web on March 3, 2001, at http://www.eia.doe.gov/emeu/cabs/azerproj.html.

Van Duyen, A. (1994, March). Where in the world is Japan? *Euromoney,* pp. 177-180.

Verzariu, P. (1992, November 2). Trends and developments in international trade. *Business America,* pp. 2-6.

WalMart Stores. (2001). *Annual report.* Bentonville, AR: Author.

Walton, R. E., & McKersie, R. (1965). *A behavioral theory of labor negotiations.* New York: McGraw-Hill.

Whelan, C. (2000, December 18). Emerging markets that live up to the name after repeatedly disappointing U.S. investors. *Fortune,* pp. 92-95.

World Bank. (1993). *The East Asian miracle: Economic growth and public policy.* Oxford, UK: Oxford University Press.

World Bank. (2000). *Country briefs: China.* Washington, DC: Author.

World Bank. (2001a). *Global economic prospects 2001.* Washington, DC: Author.

World Bank. (2001b). *World development report 2000-2001.* Washington, DC: Author.

World Trade Organization. (2000). *Annual report 2000.* Geneva, Switzerland: Author.

Index

About the Authors

Professor Tamer Cavusgil's teaching, research, and administrative activities have focused on international business and marketing. His specific interests include the internationalization of the firm, global marketing strategy, and internationalization of business education. In recent years, he has focused on the research development of computerized decision-support systems for international business executives. Best known among these tools is CORE, a computer program for assessment of "Company Readiness to Export."

Cavusgil has authored more than a dozen books and more than 100 refered journal articles. His work is among the most-cited contributions in international marketing. He is the founding editor of the *Journal of International Marketing,* now published by the American Marketing Association, and *Advances in International Marketing,* published by Elsevier. He serves on the editorial review boards of a dozen professional journals, including the *Journal of Marketing* and *Journal of International Business Studies.* Professor Cavusgil has been a member of Michigan State University's business faculty since 1987.

Professor Pervez Ghauri is a Professor of International Business at Manchester School of Management, UMIST, United Kingdom. He has taught in Sweden, Norway, France, the Netherlands, Indonesia, and the United States, in regular as well as executive education programs. He has written more than 10 books and numerous articles on international marketing and international business topics. He is the founding editor of *International Business Review (IBR)* and *International Business and Management Series,* published by Elsevier. He sits on editorial boards of several academic journals.

Ghauri's main research areas are the internationalization process, entry strategies, and negotiations. His publications include *The Internationalization of the Firm* (London: Thomson Learning); *The Global Challenge for*

Multinational Enterprises (Amsterdam: Elsevier); and *International Business Negotiations* (Oxford: Pergamon).

Milind R. Agarwal, B. Engg. (Electronics & Communication), MBA (Logistics/Procurement), Michigan State University, 1994, is the founder, President, and CEO of Logisitics Corporation of India, Ltd., based in Mumbai, India. During his studies at Michigan State University, he worked as a graduate research assistant for the Center for International Business Education and Research. He is a Certified Internal Quality Auditor for ISO 9001: 2000. He is an active member of various trade bodies and associations of India. He is also a Visiting Professor at various management institutes in Mumbai. He can be reached at email: *logindia @ vsnl.com.*